"A deed for which we ⟨ ⟩
for cold blooded ferocity, even in the history
of Cortez and the Mexicans or of Pizzaro
and the Peruvians."
Sydney Monitor, **19 November 1838.**

DEMONS AT DUSK

MASSACRE AT MYALL CREEK

PETER STEWART

Foreword by Peter FitzSimons

ABOUT THE AUTHOR

P eter Stewart was born in Sydney in 1954. He is a former English and History teacher who has worked in the Sydney property and parking industry for over twenty years. Since leaving teaching, he has maintained a keen interest in Australian History, particularly in relation to indigenous issues.

Peter has researched the Myall Creek Massacre for many years, was involved in the planning for the construction of the memorial at the site and now serves on the committee of the Sydney Friends of Myall Creek. He is a founding member of the Australian Independents Coalition for Political Integrity and he currently heads up a company in Sydney. Peter lives in southern Sydney with his wife, and has three adult children.

"Demons at Dusk" is his first book..

Published in Australia by Temple House Pty Ltd,
T/A Sid Harta Publishers ACN 092 197 192
Hartwell, Victoria

Telephone: 61 9560 9920, Facsimile: 61 9545 1742
E-mail: author@sidharta.com.au

First published in Australia 2007
This edition published 2007
Copyright © Peter Stewart 2007
Cover design, typesetting: Chameleon Print Design
Cover photographs by the author with thanks to the riders
of the Darkes Forest Riding School.

Stewart, Peter
Demons at Dusk
EAN13: 978-1-921206-57-3 ISBN: 1-921206-57-8
pp368

FOREWORD

Like many Australians, I had vaguely heard of the "Myall Creek Massacre" but knew nothing of the detail.

That changed, however, in February 2005 when Peter Stewart, a regular reader of my weekend newspaper columns, sent me a manuscript he had written. Peter asked if I could have a "quick look" at it, with a view to writing a sentence or two which he could use for promotional purposes on the back cover.

A quick look, huh? Once, when I asked Gough Whitlam if he had read a particular book on Paul Keating he replied, "Comrade, I have glanced at it extensively . . ." and that is exactly what I intended to do on this book.

I wanted to be polite-ish, but had neither the time nor the interest to read the damn thing. That, however, is not how it worked out. In fact, my "quick look" turned into me being drawn in from the first page, and devouring the manuscript over the next two days and nights. I finished reading it at midnight on the second night, deeply moved, and awoke with a start four hours later. Myriad sentiments were swirling within, but the most powerful was: every Australian should read this book.

I know that sounds like the mealy–mouthed thing one often reads on the back of books, but that was genuinely what I felt in those wee hours and I have firmed in my view since.

For if we are to celebrate Australia's history in the courage and hero-ism Australian's displayed at Gallipoli, Kokoda, Tobruk and Long Tan; if we are to glory in our achievements in so many fields from sport to agriculture to literature and the arts . . . then we must also remember and acknowledge Myall Creek and other stains on our national soul as a crucial part of our past.

This, too, is a part of the Australian mosaic; this, too, was a part of our journey as a people through the good, the bad and the beyond ugly to bring us to where we are today, and we cannot pretend other-wise – as much as we might like to, and mostly have to this point.

Surely, as a nation, there can be no "reconciliation" if we do not all acknowledge just what horrors we are reconciling from?

"Demons at Dusk" is an extremely powerful account of one of the most tragic and remarkable chapters of Australia's history and makes truly gripping and valuable reading.

For me, reading it helped me to understand my own country . . .

Peter FitzSimons
Neutral Bay, Sydney

May 1, 2007.

ACKNOWLEDGEMENTS

W ithout doubt the three works which have had the greatest influence on the writing of this book are Bill Wannan's *Early Colonial Scandals*, Roger Milliss's *Waterloo Creek* and Richard Trudgen's *Why Warriors Lie Down and Die*. To these authors and their works I am greatly indebted.

To Bill Wannan, because it was in his work that in 1978, I first read a detailed account of the Myall Creek Massacre. I was immediately struck by the tragedy of the case and the remarkable, story, characters and relationships involved. It was enough to convince me that I should do what I could to bring this "skeleton in the closet" of our history to the attention of the wider Australian population. Why the delay from 1978 until now? Well that's another story and virtually another book but in short, I have been trying almost continuously.

To Roger Milliss, because his wonderfully researched and written, *Waterloo Creek* is without doubt the definitive work on the Myall Creek Massacre and the various other massacres which took place in northern NSW around that time. I have relied heavily on it to maintain historical accuracy in various parts of this book. If Milliss's version of the facts ever differed from other works, I have almost invariably accepted Milliss's version. I recommend it to anyone interested in finding out the plain facts about these tragic massacres. I am also greatly indebted to Roger for his help and support of my book. His knowledge of the characters, the period and the most minor historical details was of enormous assistance.

To Richard Trudgen because *Why Warriors Lie Down and Die* is simply an amazing work which is essential reading for anyone interested in Aboriginal issues or the history of this country. In my view, it should be compulsory reading for every politician in Australia and should be studied in schools. It provides the most remarkable insights into Aboriginal culture and why that culture and lifestyle has been so dramatically and tragically impacted upon by the arrival of white man in this country. It also provides numerous examples of the mistakes which Governments have made and continue to make in dealing with the Aboriginal issues and how those mistakes have resulted in the problems which exist in certain Aboriginal communities today.

I am particularly indebted to the late Rev Merv Blacklock, who, after reading an early draft of my manuscript, recommended that I read *Why Warriors*. My book was greatly improved by my having done so.

Other works which I have used include: William Derrincourt's *Old Convict Days;* AW Howitt's The Native Tribes of South Eastern Australia; Jennifer Isaac's *Australian Dreaming*; Prof. A P Elkin's *The Australian Aborigines*; Russ Blanch 's *Massacre, Myall Creek Revisited*; Brian Harrison's UNE thesis on the Myall Creek Massacre, Barry Brown's *John Fleming, Currency Lad.* I am also indebted to Russ Blanch for the title *Demons at Dusk*.

I have also used various primary source material and for assistance with these, I would also like to thank the staff at the State Library of NSW.

Thank you to, Irina Dunn and the NSW Writer's Centre for the ceaseless encouragement and support they provide aspiring writers and to Catherine Hammond for her advice and support. Thanks also to John Marsen for his wonderful writers' conference at his beautiful

Tye Estate and to Sue Abbey for her invaluable assistance at that conference.

Thank you to Kerry Collison at Sid Harta Publishers for this wonderful opportunity and to editor, Mark Cleary, designer, Luke Harris and assessor, Clare Allen-Kamil for her extremely generous comments.

Thank you to my parents, Jack and Mary for the support they have given me with this book, as with everything. Unfortunately my mother died last year and didn't get to see it published but she believed the achievement was in the writing rather than in the recognition.

Particular thanks to; my daughter, Melanie, for her support and for assistance with research on the Old Bailey records, to my son Jacob for being such an interesting character model and for his assistance with countless computer problems over the years and to my son Damian for being "a good bloke".

I also wish to thank the members of the Myall Creek Memorial Committee for their patience in the early meetings with a stranger from Sydney and for the wonderful memorial which provides us all with a focal point for ReconciliationThank you especially to Graeme Cordiner, Des and Jenny Blake and Roger Knox for their friendship and support of this work.

Finally, a special thanks to, a man of integrity and passion, Peter FitzSimons, for his amazing support and assistance to a total stranger and to my darling wife, Jan, for her unending patience and support through the many years of night after night, writing and re-writing this book.

* * * * *

Twenty percent of the author's royalties from this book go to the Myall Creek Memorial Fund.

DEDICATION

For Jan, Melanie, Damian, Jacob and Australia's Indigenous People.

MYALL CREEK AND DISTRICT

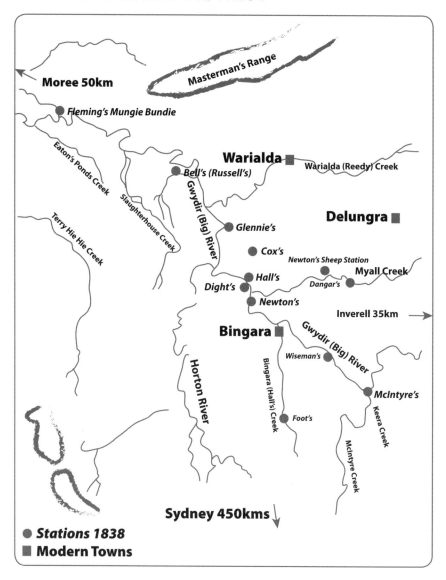

Moree 50km

Masterman's Range

Fleming's Mungie Bundie

Eaton's Ponds Creek

Slaughterhouse Creek

Terry Hie Hie Creek

Warialda ■   Warialda (Reedy) Creek

Bell's (Russell's)

Gwydir (Big) River

Delungra ■

Glennie's

Cox's

Newton's Sheep Station

Hall's   Dangar's   **Myall Creek**

Dight's

Newton's

Inverell 35km →

Bingara ■

Gwydir (Big) River

Wiseman's

Horton River

Bingara (Hall's) Creek

Foot's

McIntyre's

Keera Creek

McIntyre Creek

Sydney 450kms ↓

● *Stations 1838*
■ **Modern Towns**

LIST OF CHARACTERS

The characters and significant events in this story are true. In many cases only limited information is available about certain characters and their behaviour. What is generally known is how they behaved in the actual situations portrayed in this book, and I have at all times attempted to keep the characters' behaviour consistent with what is recorded. I apologise to any descendants of these people if they believe their ancestors' behaviour was different to that described herein.

As there were many people involved in the events surrounding the Myall Creek Massacre of 1838, for ease of reference they have been grouped.

LONDON

William Tucker – George Anderson's fellow apprentice, to John Hayford.
George Norman – Associate of George Anderson.

THE MYALL CREEK STATION

William Hobbs – Station Superintendent. A free settler.
George Anderson – Hutkeeper. Convict.
Charles Kilmeister – Stockman. Convict.
Andrew Burrowes – Stockman. Convict.
Yintatintin (Davey) – Aboriginal stockman from Peel River district.
Kamilaroi tribe.
Kuimunga (Billy) – Aboriginal stockman. Yintayintin's younger
brother.
Charles Reid – Stockman. Convict with ticket-of-leave. Occasional
worker at Myall Ck, based on another of Henry Dangar's stations.

THE SURROUNDING STATIONS

Dr Newton's Station
Thomas Foster – Station Superintendent. A free settler.
Robert Sexton – Hutkeeper. Convict.
Johnny Murphy – 14-year-old boy staying/working on the station.

McIntyre's Station.
Andrew Eaton – Hutkeeper. Convict.
John Woodward – Stockman. Convict.

Dight's Station
William Mace – Overseer. Convict with ticket-of-leave.
John Bates – Hutkeeper. Convict.

THE ABORIGINES (WERAERAI)

Old Daddy – Tribal elder.
Joey – Tribal elder.
King Sandy – Tribal elder.
Sandy – Warrior aged man.

Martha – Young woman. Sandy's wife and Charley's mother.
Ipeta – Young woman.
Charley – Six-year-old boy.
Johnny – Young boy.

THE HUNTER RIVER SQUATTERS

Henry Dangar – Landholder of various properties in the Hunter Valley and Big (Gwydir) River district, including Myall Creek Station.
Robert Scott – Magistrate, large landholder and part owner of *The Sydney Morning Herald*. Known as 'Count Bobby', and one of the most powerful men in the colony.
James Glennie – Large landholder with properties in the Hunter Valley and Big (Gwydir) River district.

AT GOVERNMENT HOUSE

Sir George Gipps – Governor of the Colony of New South Wales.
Edward Deas Thomson – Colonial Secretary.

THE INVESTIGATORS

Edward Denny Day – Police Magistrate. Head of Inquiry.
Lieutenant George Pack – Senior member of the NSW Mounted Police.
Corporal George McKnight – Second in command of the Mounted Police party.

THE LAWYERS

John Hubert Plunkett – Attorney-General.
Roger Therry – Assistant to Plunkett.
William Foster – Defence counsel.
William a'Beckett – Defence counsel.
Richard Windeyer – Defence counsel.

The Eleven

John Fleming – Squatter's son living at Mungie Bundie station.
John Russell – Head stockman at Bell's Station. Convict with ticket-of-leave.
James Lamb – Convict. Head stockman at Cobb's middle station.
James Oates – Known as 'Hall's Jemmy'. Convict stockman at Hall's station.
John 'Black' Johnstone – Stockman. Former convict based at Cox's Durra Durra run. Negro background.
George Palliser – Former convict. Stockman at Bell's Noogera Creek station.
John Blake – Convict stockman at Glennie's Gineroi station.
Edward Foley – Convict stockman at Fleming's Mungie Bundie station.
William Hawkins – Head stockman at Lethbridge's Noogera Creek station. Convict with ticket-of leave.
Charles Telluse – Convict stockman at Glennie's Gineroi station.
James Parry – Convict hutkeeper at Eaton's Biniguy station.

PROLOGUE

St Sepulchre, London – 14 November 1832.

The biting cold of this wretched London night had slithered through every crack of the large terrace house, but it did not prevent a nervous sweat from crawling down the back of the young apprentice as he crept slowly – his feet anchored by guilt – into his master's bedroom. He edged his way soundlessly to the timber dresser at the back of the room and, in the semi-darkness, inserted the pick-lock key into the lock of the dresser drawer. Nothing. No give. His tongue darted around his mouth, searching for the slightest hint of moisture, as his fingers kept urgently pushing the pick-lock this way and that. *Please, please, please just let it click.* All he wanted was to get what he had come for and be gone.

George Anderson had never done anything remotely like this before, but his colleagues had assured him it would be 'easy, George'; that the money was 'there for the taking' and there was no risk, 'if only he was man enough to do the job'. He kept jiggling the key, fighting to stop his hands from shaking, but the lock simply wouldn't move. Even in his rising panic, he couldn't stop himself from asking why on earth he was the one doing the actual job when his friend George Norman was the expert at picking locks?

Suddenly he heard a crashing noise from downstairs in the kitchen and almost fainted with fear. But then he realised it would be his fellow apprentice, William Tucker, playing his part and creating a diversion to distract his master's wife. Why was he robbing his master, anyway? He was a good man who had always been fair to him. Fool that he was, he had let Norman and Tucker persuade him. They had insisted it would be 'no bother' and that Norman had done plenty of jobs like this. And he had believed them; so now, here he was.

At last, at blessed last, the lock clicked. It was open. Anderson yanked the drawer so hard it crashed to the floor, leaving clothing strewn around his feet. But where was the money? He kicked the clothing aside. There it was! He grabbed the money sack and bolted for the door.

29 November 1832.

And now, again, George Anderson stood trembling, positively shaking, in the murky light of the privy, trying not to breathe too heavily in the foul, dank air, but failing miserably. He could hear their voices approaching as he peered down anxiously into the putrid mess at the bottom of the privy for any sign of the tell-tale pick-locks of which he had just disposed. Seeing only blackness, he turned back to the door, which he now raised his hand to push. The voices were right outside. He stood, transfixed by indecision. A moment later the door opened. The policeman briefly looked him up and down, noting he was fully attired. His brow furrowed slightly before he raised one eyebrow. 'What are you up to now then, lad? Eh? You can come along with me.'

The Old Bailey, London – 9 January 1833.

A little over a month later, nineteen-year-old George Anderson was led to the bar alongside his co-accused and fellow apprentice, William Tucker. The intervening time, experiencing the horrors of the dreaded Newgate prison, had not been kind to Anderson. Living amongst the filth and disease with the criminally insane and the morally depraved had taken its toll on him. His already small stature somehow appeared to have shrunken, withered even, while his spirit was conspicuously all but broken. He was unable to meet the eyes of his master, John Hayford, who was the first into the witness box to give evidence. As Hayford repeated the oath, his gaze shifted between Anderson and Tucker but both hung their heads, staring at the heavy chains around their wrists and avoiding the glare of the mirror reflector above their heads designed to shine light on the faces of the accused, so that their guilt could be more easily determined by the court.

'I am a lath render and live in St John Street in the parish of St Sepulchre,' Hayford began. 'On Wednesday the fourteenth of November I saw my money safe in the dresser drawer in my bedroom.'

'And how much was there, Mr Hayford?' inquired the prosecutor.

'Forty-one pound. There were twenty-eight sovereigns, four half sovereigns and two five pound bank notes.'

'And the prisoners in the dock are known to you, are they not, Mr Hayford?'

'Yes, they were both my apprentices.' Hayford went on to explain how Tucker, particularly, had appeared to have more money since the robbery, and had recently bought himself new boots and shoes.

George Anderson was unable to concentrate on the evidence though, for his mind was consumed with regret. For the next hour witnesses came and went, and although he heard all their words, knowing some were true and some were lies, they were all blurred by the knowledge of his guilt and fear of the sentence. How had he got himself into such a situation? How had he been so foolish as to let himself be led away by George Norman, his sister's ex-boyfriend, who he knew was a shady, petty criminal?

The fog in his mind was nearly as heavy as that which sat ponderously upon the wintry waters of the nearby Thames, but it cleared long enough for him to hear Norman give evidence against him. He then heard the somewhat generously proportioned defence counsel, Mr Phillips, thoroughly enjoying himself as he dragged admissions from Norman about his long list of aliases and repeated 'problems' with counterfeit money. He also had Norman admit to his hasty departure from Mrs Penhall's boarding house, without paying the rent. Finally, Phillips induced Norman to deny he even knew what a pick-lock was, before, with a rather dramatic but not entirely inappropriate flourish, he produced a pick-lock which Norman had left behind at Mrs Penhall's.

'Look at this!' Phillips declared triumphantly, holding the pick-lock up for all in the court to behold.

To a disinterested observer, it would have all been good theatre and highly amusing, but George Anderson was no disinterested observer. He wasn't even capable of gaining the slightest gratification as he watched Norman squirm under the intense questioning of Phillips. After all, Norman was not on trial here, he was, and no matter how foolish or criminal Norman was made to look, nothing could change the fact that he, even in his own eyes, was guilty.

Norman was followed into the witness box by Eliza Wood. Eliza was one of those young women whose individual facial features were not particularly pretty, but when combined with soft, youthful skin and dark blonde hair falling about her face, it was easy to understand why she was never short of male admirers. When questioned, she informed the court she lived with Norman as his wife and wasn't ashamed to admit it. Her testimony very much supported Norman's evidence, and she even stated flatly that Anderson had specifically told her of his intention to rob his master and then that 'the job was done'. She also made a scathing observation about Anderson's character, saying she believed him to be 'a very wicked youth who would do anything for money'.

The comment was enough to make Anderson look up momentarily.

Lying strumpet, he thought, before his gaze dropped back to the floor.

The case continued, with several more witnesses giving evidence, including James Newton, whose rather ghastly task it had been to search the soil from the privy. Despite a natural and very understandable inclination to want to hurry the task, Newton had been diligent in the extreme and had managed to find the pick-lock key of which Anderson had disposed. Newton had, in fact, experienced feelings of pride and triumph, as much as relief, as he held the appallingly dark key aloft for identification by the police constable.

Tucker's mother also gave evidence, explaining that she had given her son money for new shoes and that he was, in fact, 'a good lad'; while Tucker himself quite eloquently denied the crime and confirmed his mother had given him the money.

Finally the presiding judge, London Alderman Newman Knowlys, turned to Anderson and asked if he had anything to say.

George Anderson looked up and hesitated before answering in a manner which, despite the sounding board above his head designed to amplify his voice, was barely audible. 'What the witness said I told her is false.'

Knowlys strained to hear and then peered down at him. 'Is that all you have to say?'

'Yes, sir,' Anderson replied, nodding, and then fell silent.

As was customary, the jury remained in the courtroom while they deliberated on their verdict. Anderson remained standing beside his colleague, William Tucker. Neither of them could bring themselves to look the other in the eye or mutter a word of acknowledgement of their shared plight. Anderson stared at the floor in a trance-like state, the only emotion he experienced being a rising bitterness. After all, Tucker and Norman had persuaded him! Yet there was no doubt that, with his mother's help and his own gift of the gab and capacity for outright lying – something that, perversely under the circumstances, Anderson had prided himself on not doing - Tucker had been able to mount a serious defence, while Anderson felt he had little hope.

But he had to hope – hope for a miracle. The consequences of the decision the jurors were now making were extreme – either freedom or transportation for life. There was no in-between.

When the jury foreman announced they had reached a verdict, Anderson kept staring at the floor. He was unable to watch. His mouth was dry and his knees were increasingly unstable.

'How do you find the defendant, William Tucker?' Knowlys asked, his quill poised, ready to record the verdict.

'Not guilty.'

Tucker smiled across the court at his mother, who clapped briefly before Knowlys' glare from the bench rendered her silent.

'And how do you find the defendant, George Anderson?'

'Guilty.'

Patrick's Plains, New South Wales – February 1838.

The convict tensed every sinew of his body, knowing full well the excruciating pain which would soon engulf him. Fear dripped from his brow as he looked up to see a satisfied smirk on the face of his master, the affluent squatter Henry Dangar.

The drum was beaten, the whip lashed his back and the trooper shouted 'One!' The drum, the whip and the shout, 'Two!'

George Anderson bit down on the chunk of leather between his teeth as he glared at Dangar, who stood at the front of the small crowd that had gathered to watch the spectacle.

'Three!'

Still Anderson glared at the squatter, who now looked scornfully at his convict servant.

By the time the count reached twelve, however, Anderson had long since dropped his eyes, shattered not just by the pain but also by the injustice. He had been helping a fellow convict move some cattle, and Dangar had charged him with leaving his station and failing to move his sheep hurdles. Dangar had then walked him across country for eight days, down to Patrick's Plains, where the magistrate had sentenced him to two doses of fifty lashes. There was no justice to it, and he knew Dangar was simply proving he could do whatever he liked with him.

'Fifteen!'

Blood began to ooze from the welts across his back.

'Twenty-two!'

His whole back was on fire.

'Thirty-two!'

Blood now flowed freely from the lacerations.

'Forty-one!'

Strips of flesh clung to the blood-soaked lash as they were ripped from his back. Anderson forced himself to look once more in the direction of Dangar but could see nothing through the blur of blood, sweat and the darkness of unconsciousness which now began to close upon him.

Anderson did not hear the count of 'Fifty!', and his whole body had retreated into such shock that he barely felt the pain of it. He was vaguely aware of a voice ordering, 'Take him down', before he was untied and lowered to the ground.

A bucket of water splashed across his face helped clear the haze of unconsciousness. He then heard the voice of Henry Dangar above him. 'I trust you now understand, Anderson, you are to do precisely what I tell you at all times.' The crowd began to disperse as the grey-haired, finely dressed squatter remained standing over the mass of blood, filth and agony that was George Anderson. Dangar leant forward. 'And remember, Anderson, you still have another fifty to come.'

Henry Dangar knew full well he was making an enemy of an insignificant and pathetic little convict, but what he did not realise was that George Anderson also had a very stubbornly determined streak in him.

"The natives of this country ... may truly be said to be in the pure state of nature ... they are far happier than we Europeans, being wholly unacquainted not only with the superfluous but also of the necessary conveniences so much sought after in Europe, they are happy in not knowing the use of them. They live in a tranquillity which is not disturbed by the inequality of condition, the earth and the sea of their own accord furnishes them with all things necessary for life."
—**Captain James Cook.**

CHAPTER ONE

Big River District, Northern New South Wales – May 1838.

T he first time he saw her, he did not know she would change his life forever. He did not know the impact their love would have on the young colony, making him a hero in history but despised in his time. He only knew that here, standing naked before him, was the first desirable woman he had seen since he was thrown, in chains, into the bowels of that convict ship and transported to New South Wales for life. He only knew that what he felt inside him now was something he had never felt before, and he already yearned for the woman who made him feel this way.

It was the second of George Anderson's encounters with the native blacks since Dangar had banished him to the role of hutkeeper on the remote Myall Creek station, and it could not have been more disparate from his first. His initial encounter had taken place late one night after leaving the sanctuary of the isolated stockmen's hut to fetch some extra firewood. It was not a task he ever enjoyed, but it was a part of his role as hutkeeper which he accepted grudgingly.

As he left the hut he was consumed by the blackness of the still, moonless night. The solitary croak of a frog in the nearby creek was the only sound that disturbed the silence. As his battered boots trod slowly and soundlessly upon the soft soil beside the hut, he heard another noise, close by, which made him tense slightly, before he realised it was only one of the hobbled stock horses. Despite its proximity, he couldn't discern the animal's outline, though he could see the steam coming from its nostrils.

He continued cautiously to the wood pile at the back of the hut, where he bent over and began filling his arms with wood. As he did so, he had the chilling sensation of being watched. Frozen by fear, at first he dared not look up; but after a few moments he slowly raised his eyes to see, just a few yards away, as if floating in the darkness, the whites of the native's eyes. He dropped the wood and, screaming profanities, bolted back into the hut as the startled native fled into the night.

That encounter had taken place nearly three months ago, and now, as she stood in front of him on the creek bank, Anderson only allowed himself to look at her briefly – but it was long enough for him to take in every detail of her form. Her deep brown eyes were soft and kind, and her smile warm and gentle. Her smooth, dark skin glistened in the morning sunlight as water dripped from the curls of her thick black hair. For what seemed like an age to him but was actually only a moment, he watched as a droplet fell from her hair to her shoulder, slid over her breast to the tip of her nipple, where it paused momentarily before falling to the ground at her feet. Their eyes met briefly.

'Ipeta, Ipeta.' It was the voice of a small boy who walked up and took her by the hand. The boy looked at Anderson, smiled, said 'Hello', then led the woman, who had just become the centre of George Anderson's tiny universe, back to the creek behind them.

He stood and watched as they played in the water with another woman and several other children. The sound of children's laughter was something he had not heard for longer than he wanted to remember.

The evening before, Anderson had watched a mob of native blacks arrive at the remote cattle station and set up camp close to the station huts. He had remained in the hut, peering through a gap in the doorway, when Charles Kilmeister, one of the station's convict stockmen, went out to greet them. Kilmeister had invited the clan to the station at the suggestion of Andrew Eaton, who was from McIntyre's station, further up the river. After they had set up their camp, Kilmeister sat with them by their fire, but Anderson had not ventured from the hut.

Now, as he watched the young Aboriginal woman playing in the water with the children, Anderson was touched by a sense of nervous anticipation. Apart from his frightening late night encounter, it was the first time he had seen 'the blacks', as he had only been on the station for a few months, and his duties as hutkeeper meant he rarely left the immediate area of the huts, where he spent most of his days in total solitude. He had, however, heard many contrasting stories about them from the stockmen who regularly came across them as they rode around the various stations in the district.

After watching for a few minutes, Anderson climbed down the bank of the creek, but despite his attraction to the young woman, he stayed well away from the group. He filled the bucket with the cool creek water, glancing at the blacks as he did so. He then hurried back to the sanctuary of the top of the bank, where he again stood watching her as she played with the laughing children. He finally forced himself to look away and return to the hut, where he hesitated at the door before entering.

'Ya took yer time this mornin', Anderson,' observed Kilmeister, sitting on the end of his bunk while he pulled on his boots. 'When's breakfast gonna be ready?'

'Not long,' replied Anderson. His mind wandered for a time as he stirred the beef broth he had made the previous evening and which was now bubbling away in an iron pot suspended over the mud-lined open fireplace. 'Some of the blacks was at the creek,' he remarked after a while.

'Ah, what did you think? Some good looking gins, ain't there?'

Anderson merely shrugged a reply. The last thing he was going to do was tell Kilmeister what he had felt when he saw her.

Kilmeister continued. 'My oath there is. There's a couple I've taken quite a fancy to that'll be bloody good on these long winter nights.'

'I just think Mr 'obbs will be in a fearful state about them being here.'

'Don't ya be worryin' about Hobbs; I'll talk him round.'

'I just think it'd been best if ya'd waited till he got back and asked him first.'

'I don't bleedin' care what ya think. You'd be just afeard of them,' mocked the stockman, before adding, almost reassuringly, 'Look, I've known Hobbs a lot longer than you, and I say he won't make no bother about it. Ya know how much he trusts me. I'll talk him round afore ya know it.'

Anderson shrugged again as he put Kilmeister's breakfast down on the rough wooden table Anderson had made a few weeks before. Kilmeister sat down and ate his broth in virtual silence, before filling his mouth with damper and taking a long gulp of hot tea. Wiping droplets of tea from the stubble on his receding chin, he then stood, grabbed his tattered coat, threw his gun under his arm and strode out, leaving the door open behind him.

Anderson stood at the doorway and watched as the stockman walked across to the blacks' camp, where he was warmly greeted by a group of old men and children. Anderson heard them call him by name, 'Charlie', as they patted him on the back.

The same small boy whom Anderson had seen at the creek earlier, now joined the group with Kilmeister. The stockman crouched down and spoke to the boy, who giggled and pushed him before running and hiding behind one of the elders. Kilmeister pretended to chase him, before he laughed and turned away. He waved to the boy and the rest of the group before walking out of Anderson's view, across to where his hobbled horse stood picking at the grass. The boy followed him, and another child, slightly taller than the first, trailed behind.

'Charlie,' called the boy.

Kilmeister turned and looked down at the boy. 'Yair, young chap.'

'Charlie, I pat horse.'

'Sure, you can pat the horse.' The convict nodded as he slipped the bridle over the horse's head. 'What's yer name, though?'

'Charley.'

'No, not my name. What's yer name?'

'Me Charley.'

'Oh, yer Charley too?' The boy nodded enthusiastically. 'And what's his name?' Kilmeister pointed to the other child, who, although older, was obviously shy and stood back a few metres, his eyes downcast.

'Him Charley.'

'Oh, so I'm Charlie, yer Charley, and he's Charley.'

The boy smiled and again nodded, this time even more enthusiastically. Kilmeister bent down, picked up the little boy and held his hand out to allow him to pat the white blaze of the bay gelding.

'And what'd her name be?' Kilmeister nodded toward a young woman who had followed them and was standing a short distance away, watching.

'Martha.'

'She yer mother?'

The boy nodded.

'Hmmm,' the stockman murmured as he looked the woman up and down. 'Hallo, Martha.'

The woman looked at him but gave no acknowledgement other than a nervous half smile.

Kilmeister let Charley slide down his leg to the ground. 'Does the other Charley want to pat the horse too?' He held out his hand toward the child, who shook his head and took a few steps backwards. 'Oh well, maybe tomorrow.'

Kilmeister saddled his horse while the two boys stood and watched. 'I'll see ya later,' he said, mounting his horse. The two Charleys waved as he urged his mount over to where the young woman stood, several yards away. She backed away nervously as the powerful animal approached her bare feet. 'And I'll be seeing you later too, Martha.' He smiled down at her.

The stockman turned his mount and rode past the hut, where Anderson still stood in the doorway. 'I won't be back 'til late, round sunset. Grab them hobbles for me, would ya?' the stockmen asked, pointing to where he had left them in the grass.

Anderson nodded, but as the stockman turned to ride away he called, 'Kilmeister!'

The stockman reined his mount. 'Yair, what?'

Anderson hesitated. He wanted to say, *'Don't go! Don't leave me here alone with all these blacks!'* He wanted so much to say it but couldn't bring himself to ask that of Kilmeister. He couldn't bear the thought of the ridicule such a request would bring. And Kilmeister wouldn't stay for him anyway. So instead he said, 'Nuthin'.' He then stepped back into the hut and slowly pushed the leather hinged door closed.

So Charles Kilmeister, twenty-three-year-old 'rope maker' of Bristol, England, transported for life in 1833 for housebreaking, rode away, leaving George Anderson alone in a hut on a remote cattle station with forty-four Aborigines camped outside.

* * *

Anderson sat on the slightly rickety bench seat, with his elbows on the table and his hands propped under his bearded chin. His beard was a product of practicality rather than fashion, and was consistent with his tendency to do whatever was easiest. As was usual among the convicts of the district, he took little care with his appearance, trimming his beard short only when it became annoying or hot during the summer months. The skin of the exposed parts of his face had been quite pale when he was transported, but after years in the harsh climate of the colony was now quite tanned and weather-beaten, highlighting the small pink scar on his temple.

Kilmeister had been gone for over an hour but Anderson had not been able to bring himself to open the shutters at the front of the hut. It was normally one of the first things he did each morning, along with emptying the bed pots which this morning remained unemptied under the low bunks. The odour pervaded the room but he remained oblivious to it. His gaze was fixed on the back of the door which separated him from the two things that made his mind and heart race. Ipeta was on the other side of the door, but she was part of a mob of blacks that came from a totally different world – a world that was totally unknown to him. Kilmeister was familiar and confident with them, but for Anderson, virtually everything about them was unknown; and now, isolated amongst them, his previous anxiety about them was overlaid with fear.

He had never been so conscious of his isolation. His role as hut-keeper meant that he spent most of his days alone at the station, but he had never really minded that. Although he hated his life as a convict, he had learnt to live with the loneliness and was content in his own company, away from the tormenting gibes of Kilmeister and his like. There were generally plenty of duties around the huts for him to attend to, and when there weren't, or when his laziness overtook him, he easily amused himself relaxing by the creek or wandering around the immediate area.

He had heard stories, though, about lonely hutkeepers being killed by wild blacks on isolated stations such as this, and he never found the confidence or courage to venture far from the huts. He did, however, find considerable consolation in the fact that his transfer to this station meant he was at least far away from Henry Dangar, who lived in the Hunter Valley. That consolation suddenly seemed rather insignificant now, though, as he became more aware than ever that the nearest neighbour was fifteen miles away, and the nearest town and policeman over one hundred and fifty miles away. He was alone in one of the most remote frontier districts in the British Empire.

Despite his fear, he so wanted to open that door in the hope he might see her again. He sat there for he didn't know how long. He had the cow to milk, the wood to chop and the cleaning up to be done, as well as various other tasks, but he ignored them all. His mind leapt between images of her standing dripping wet by the creek and thoughts of 'wild, murderous blacks'.

Eventually, from somewhere, he found the courage to force his feet to carry him over to the door of the small, crudely made hut. He lifted the wooden latch and carefully pulled the door a few inches toward him. It was a task that required two hands, as the leather hinges and earthen floor did not allow the door to swing freely. He looked out. Less than half of the blacks were there – some of the women, a few old men and the children. The tension of fear immediately eased from his body. None of them took any notice of him as he gradually opened the door wider to take in the whole scene.

The two stockmen's huts stood a few yards apart and were built facing the creek to the north, which wandered across the floor of the low valley. The larger of the two slab huts was occupied by the station superintendent, William Hobbs, while the smaller, more crudely built one was occupied by the assigned convicts, from the doorway of which Anderson now surveyed the blacks' camp.

The camp was spread in a rough semi-circle, starting near the eastern side of the stockmen's huts and extending across to the trees which lined the southern side of the creek. The trees provided a solid upright at one end of those huts which were built amongst them. Near the centre of the camp was a large fire, which was presently burning very low. The women and the older girls worked on the huts, which were basically circular with cone-shaped roofs. The girls brought branches, grasses and reeds from the creek, which the women would then carefully twist together into the roofs. The old men sat around the fire, talking. One of them was making what appeared to be a type of wooden tool. The children were playing a game which Anderson didn't recognise, except he noticed they were laughing and seemed to be enjoying it every bit as much as English children enjoyed their games.

He looked for Ipeta but couldn't see her. The children he had been watching now ceased their game and ran across to the trees on the creek bank before disappearing from view over the edge of the steep bank. His gaze returned to the women working on the huts, amazed at the skill and speed with which the huts were taking shape. As he watched them his attention was taken by a young woman who appeared from beneath a pile of branches which she dropped onto the ground beside one of the huts. It was her. His heart leapt and he closed the door a little. He wanted to observe her without being detected.

He watched while she helped another woman finish the roof of the hut they were working on. He observed the curves of her nakedness as she bent to gather the long native grasses and branches from the ground. He watched her casually twist and weave them together, and he watched her reach up to place them on the roof before carefully tying them into place with the reeds. He watched while she smiled and chatted with her workmate, wishing it was he she was smiling at and chatting with. He remained totally engrossed in her until he noticed a small boy walking toward him. It was young Charley. He was soaking wet and his smile beamed ahead of him as he walked. He was hardly a threatening sight. Anderson opened the door as the boy approached.

'Hallo, what ya name?'

'George. What's yours?'

'Me Charley. Comem me, George.' The boy held out his hand as a signal for him to follow.

Anderson hesitated, though he was ashamed of his hesitation; but he couldn't help feeling some fear about leaving the sanctuary of the hut. He reassured himself with the fact it was only the women, children and old men who were there, and he would at least be closer to Ipeta. Charley led him toward the blacks' camp and past his mother, Martha, who had been standing at the edge of the camp, watching her son. The boy smiled up at her. Martha shook her head gently as she smiled back.

Charley took the hutkeeper to where the old men sat around the smouldering fire. They all stood as he and the boy approached.

Anderson's heart leapt. Old they may have been, but they were all very big men, and one of them was huge. They held out their hands to Anderson as Charley pointed to each in turn.

'Sandy … Joey … Daddy.' Anderson shook hands with them, amazed at their familiarity with what he believed was only a white man's custom. Charley pointed to Anderson. 'Dat George.'

'George,' they all repeated with varying degrees of success.

They all sat down, motioning for Anderson to do the same. Then Sandy said something to the boy which was totally unintelligible to Anderson. The boy ran over toward his mother, while Anderson turned his gaze back to the three imposing looking men sitting around the fire with him. Daddy was the huge one and quite clearly the oldest, with hair so grey it was almost white. He had a massive chest that was marked with lines of raised scars. The same type of scar lines also marked his shoulders and upper arms. All his features were large: his broad, flat nose; his dark brown eyes; the open pores of his black skin; his thick lips and his hands. The convict had felt his tiny English hand disappear when grasped by that of the massive native of this most remote part of the world.

Sandy was not nearly as old as Daddy, and could probably be more accurately described as mature aged. A striking looking brass plate hung from his neck and across his chest. Anderson could only wonder where he obtained such a thing, but he noted, with a tinge of fear, that it actually added to the already fearsome appearance engendered by his size, powerfully muscled chest and deep-set black eyes - eyes which Anderson found totally inscrutable and therefore somewhat unnerving. He also had the same raised scar lines as Daddy on his chest and shoulders. As he sat there, Anderson became increasingly nervous, to the point of being plain scared. He was sitting alone in the middle of a mob of wild blacks with some of the biggest men he had ever seen in his life. How had he come to be in such a situation?

Anderson's thoughts were disrupted by the return of young Charley, whose smiling face immediately provided him with a degree of comfort. The boy gave something to each of the elders and then handed one to Anderson. It looked like some sort of food. This was confirmed for Anderson when Sandy broke a piece off and began to eat it. Joey, who to Anderson's amazement wore a tartan cap, also took a bite, before he motioned to Anderson to do the same. He hesitated only momentarily, believing that if these imposing masses of manhood were going to kill him, it would be by a less cowardly and underhanded method than poisoning him with a gift of food. The Englishman ate. It was a type of bread or damper, and although cooked a little black on the outside was quite soft and pleasant tasting inside.

Anderson nodded and made some appreciative murmurs. 'Thank you.'

His hosts nodded.

'It good, George?' asked Charley, who was standing beside Anderson.

'Yair, it's good, Charley.' Anderson's curiosity got the better of him. 'Why can ya speak English, Charley?'

The boy looked confused by the question. 'Uh?'

'Why can ya speak English?' Anderson repeated. Seeing the same blank look on the boy's face, he added, 'How can ya talk like a whitefella?'

The boy's face lit up even more than usual. 'I makem good whitefella talk, eh George?'

'Yair, ya be good at whitefella talk; but how can ya talk like whitefella?'

The boy tilted his head to one side, still confused.

'Who taught ya whitefella talk? Who say whitefella talk to ya?'

'Charley say hisself.' The boy beamed proudly.

Anderson smiled then motioned toward his hosts. 'Do they talk whitefella talk?'

'Nah,' Charley replied, shaking his head.

When Anderson finished his food, Charley grabbed him by the arm. 'Come, George,' he said, dragging the convict to his feet.

Anderson nodded to the elders. 'Thank you.'

Charley led him off toward the creek, and it was only then that Anderson noticed the other blacks had stopped working on the huts and were watching him. He and the boy continued straight past the hut where Ipeta stood. The convict only dared to glance at her, but he noticed that she too was watching him – and that was enough to make his heart jump again and his face flush. He followed Charley down the bank of the creek.

'George playem Charley. Pleease?' pleaded the boy, joining his hands under his chin.

He reminded Anderson of the black cherubs in those old paintings which hung in the church in London he had attended in his other life, in a world so far away.

'Sure.' The convict smiled then sat on the steep slope of the bank, before removing his boots and following the young boy into the cool waters of the creek.

* * *

Late that afternoon as Anderson was, as usual, alone in the hut preparing the evening meal, he heard the familiar sound of a horse approaching the hut. Knowing it would be Kilmeister, he hurried to straighten up the hut and clear up the breakfast plates. He had found time to milk the cow, with Charley's help; to chop the firewood, with Charley's help; and to begin cooking, but he had neglected the less essential cleaning tasks.

The stockman opened the door and looked around the hut. 'And what've ya been doing all day, Anderson?'

'Nuthin'.'

'Yair, nuthin'; that'd be right. Is supper ready yet?'

'It'll be ready directly.'

'Good. I'll just tend me horse and wash up.'

Kilmeister closed the door and returned shortly after.

'After I finish eating I'll be going out to see the blacks,' he advised, leaning his gun against the wall, beside his bunk.

'I'll come over too – if that's all right?'

'I thought you'd be too bleedin' scared of them.' Kilmeister sat at the table as Anderson placed his supper in front of him.

'They seem quiet enough.' Anderson did not want to seem too anxious.

'They are, and they'll be good for this dull old place.'

'Mmmm,' Anderson murmured as he sat down at the table with his own meal. His day with the blacks had left him curious about many things. Their arrival was by far the most exciting thing that had happened in his time on the station, and though he wouldn't normally ask Kilmeister anything, on this occasion he allowed himself. 'Do ya know why it is that some of the blacks can speak English, like little Charley?'

'So that's what you've been doing. You've be talkin' to the blacks all day.'

'Well, why?'

'Eaton and the other chaps at McIntyre's and Wiseman's been teaching them. They been up there, on and off, for ages. I seen them many times meself; even had one of them gins one night at McIntyre's. But I told ya that before.' The stockman filled his mouth with bread and beef stew and continued. 'That's how I know they're peaceful and won't hurt no-one. Eaton thought they'd be safer up here, so I asked them to come up. They'll liven up this boring place a little, and while we're protecting them, we get to have some of their gins.'

Ignoring the last comment, Anderson responded to the answer to his question. 'I didn't know they was at McIntyre's and Wiseman's so long they learnt English. I suppose that's where that old chap, Joey, got his tartan cap from. Oh, and that's why they shake hands. I was very much surprised at how big they are, especially that old Daddy,' babbled Anderson, forgetting himself for a moment in a highly uncharacteristic display of enthusiasm.

Kilmeister had certainly never seen such behaviour from the normally reticent hutkeeper. 'My oath, you have met them all, ain't ya?

He's huge, all right. He's some sort of witch doctor - knows all the magic and stuff. Did ya meet King Sandy, too?'

'I met one of them named Sandy, with a brass breast plate, along with Daddy and Joey, but I didn't know he was their king.'

'Well, he ain't really. He's just called King Sandy. They don't really have a king. All that lot are the elders. They're the leaders. Anyway, come on, let's go and see them. I dare say it'll be better than sitting around here listening to you all bleedin' night. I fancy getting meself one of them young gins.' Kilmeister wiped his chin on the back of his sleeve, got to his feet and strode out into the night, closely followed by an eager George Anderson.

It was probably the first time the two of them had chosen to be in each other's company in the five months Anderson had been on the station. They were both part of a convict system which sentenced first time petty thieves to transportation for life, in the name of justice, thus providing a supply of labour to sustain the expansion of the Empire. The harshness of the system often forged strong bonds between its victims, but there was no bond between Anderson and Kilmeister. They had never got on, and although their circumstances made them often tolerate each other out of necessity, there was an underlying animosity which ran deep into their hearts.

CHAPTER TWO

K ilmeister was preparing to leave the hut rather later than usual, having had the company of one of the young Weraerai women for the evening, when he nodded toward the door. 'Horses. That'll be Hobbs, for sure.'

Anderson listened for a moment before replying. 'I reckon he's gonna be fearful upset about the blacks being here.'

'It won't be no bother. Leave it to me,' retorted Kilmeister as he opened the door to confirm the return of the station superintendent, William Hobbs, a twenty-six-year-old free settler from Somerset, England. With him were convict stockman Andrew Burrowes, a twenty-five-year-old groom from county Sligo in Ireland, transported for life for highway robbery; as well as two young Aboriginal stockmen from the Peel River district, brothers Yintayintin and Kuimunga, known to the whites as Davey and Billy.

Hobbs had been in Dangar's employ for less than two years, but he had already established himself as the squatter's principal superintendent, being in charge of his four cattle stations in the north. It was a responsible position for a young man, but Hobbs was ambitious and diligent, and the remote frontier districts of the colony were a young man's domain.

Hobbs cantered his mount up to the stockmen's hut, where Kilmeister now stood at the door. The superintendent leapt from his horse and confronted the convict. 'What in the hell is going on here, Kilmeister? What are they doing here?'

'It's all right, Mr Hobbs, they're peaceful. They shan't hurt us.'

'What are they doing here?' Hobbs repeated. 'They'll just be bringing trouble.'

Kilmeister stepped back into the hut, and Hobbs followed him.

'They shan't be no bother, Mr Hobbs. These are the blacks from up on McIntyre's run. You know they've been up there for many months past and never hurt no-one, sir. They're almost domesticated like. And they'll liven this dull old place up a bit, sir.'

'I know precisely who they are, Kilmeister, but I'm sure I don't have to be reminding you that you're not here for a good time. The blacks have to go, and that's the end of it.'

'But, sir, they —— '

Hobbs cut him short. 'Listen, man, I won't waste my time arguing with you about it. They have to go. You invited them, so you tell them they have to be off this station by sunset.'

Despite the strong relationship that had developed between the two men over two years of working together on isolated cattle stations on the young colony's very frontier, Hobbs was very much the boss. His word was law – he knew it, and the assigned convicts knew it.

'Yes, Mr Hobbs. Sorry, sir.'

The superintendent turned to leave.

'Excuse me, sir,' Kilmeister asked cautiously. Hobbs stopped at the door and looked back at the stockman, who continued. 'But does it help at all that they be unarmed, sir?'

'They're unarmed!' Hobbs shook his head. 'You just don't understand, do you, Charlie?'

'Understand what, sir?'

'I'm not just worried about us; I'm worried about them as well, and the trouble it would cause if anything happened to them here. Look, we both know there have been a great number of blacks killed in this district, but from what I've been hearing of recent times it's only getting worse – much worse. You obviously aren't aware of just how bad things are.'

'Maybe I am, sir.'

'Good gracious, you couldn't be, or you wouldn't be damn fool enough to allow the blacks to come here.'

'But, Mr Hobbs, sir —— '

'Charlie, just sit down and listen to me for a minute.' Kilmeister did as he was told, and Hobbs continued as he took a seat opposite the stockman. 'We stayed at Newton's last night, and Tom Foster has been told the whole drive against the blacks has just increased since Major Nunn and his troopers went back to Sydney. There are bands of stockmen just riding around the district killing blacks, because apparently Major Nunn told them he couldn't be coming up here all the time to sort out their problems with the blacks and that they'd have to fend for themselves. And that's what they've been doing – "fending for themselves" by killing any they come across.'

Kilmeister was well aware of what was happening with the slaughter of the blacks. He got around the district regularly, and word of the killings spread quickly among the stockmen, despite the distances involved. Regardless of his good relationship with Hobbs, however, he had never shared such information with the superintendent.

'Mr Hobbs, sir, like I said, I knew there'd been some trouble with them, but that's part of the reason these ones are here, sir.'

'What do you mean?'

'Well, Mr Hobbs, sir, that's why Eaton told these blacks to come down here, on account of many of their tribe already being killed. He thought they'd be safer down here, sir, like where it's a bit more out of the way. Safer than up there, where all the locals know they are there and —— '

'And what about when someone tells them they're down here? I'm not wanting any problems here, and them being unarmed may only make it worse. They shan't be able to defend themselves at all.' Hobbs paused and looked intently at his trusted stockman. 'Look, all the stations are going well at the moment, and I have it that Mr Dangar is very pleased, so I'm not going to be placing that all at risk. And besides, Mr Dangar hates the blacks. They have to go. Is that understood?' Hobbs stood to leave.

'Yes, Mr Hobbs. Mr Hobbs?'

'Yes, Charlie.'

'Would you please at least come out and meet them afore I tell them they have to go, because they're really friendly coves, ain't they, Anderson?'

George Anderson had stood by the door in total silence to this point, but as he opened his mouth to agree, Hobbs cut him off.

'Charlie, you dare me to my teeth; they have to go, and that's it.' William Hobbs strode out the door and across to his own hut.

Although Anderson had very much wanted Kilmeister to succeed in his attempt to persuade Hobbs to let the blacks stay, he couldn't help enjoy the sight of Hobbs berating the stockman. Anderson knew Hobbs to be a good, decent man, but he couldn't help feeling frustrated by his decision to send the blacks away, and at Kilmeister's failure to convince him to change his mind. He was tired of Kilmeister's know-all attitude and nasty, bullying streak, so he took his disappointment out on the self-assured stockmen.

''obbs weren't no bother, eh Charlie!' he teased.

'Shut yer bleedin' hole, Anderson,' Kilmeister snapped. 'Anyway, I ain't finished yet.'

* * *

William Hobbs sat in his hut, turning his conversation with Kilmeister over in his mind. He did feel genuine concern for the blacks, but letting them stay just wasn't worth the risk. He understood Mr Dangar was very satisfied with his performance, and Mr Dangar was one of the largest property owners in the colony. The Myall Creek station was just part of his extensive pastoral holdings, and although its boundaries were not clearly defined, it sprawled across some forty thousand acres, through valleys and across hillsides, following watercourses to the edge of the low, tree-covered mountains. It and the Lower Station were the most remote of Dangar's property holdings; so remote that they and the other stations scattered across the Big River district were beyond the Limits of Location of the colony.

Dangar's brief history lesson, when he sent him there, had taught Hobbs that this referred to the boundaries to which official government administration extended. It was, however, still part of Crown Land claimed for the British Government by Governor Phillip in 1788, and accordingly, as the Colonial Government could neither grant nor sell the land to the squatters, those occupying the land were required to pay a fee of a mere ten pound a year. This fee enabled the squatters to occupy whatever land they wished and ensured the government received a financial benefit from that occupation. It was a system which was supported by the assignment of convicts to the squatters for labour and which Dangar believed worked very well. While Hobbs remained Dangar's principal superintendent it could be a system from which Hobbs could also benefit greatly. He therefore felt more than justified in his belief that he couldn't place it all in jeopardy by allowing the blacks to stay, just in case something went wrong.

But what about the blacks? he thought. He realised they must be in dire fear for their lives, given the massacres by the government-dispatched troopers led by Major Nunn, and carried on since their departure by bands of local stockmen. Hobbs sat there at the table in his hut, watching a large spider crawl slowly up the wall and onto the bark roof.

Outside, Kilmeister had headed to the Aborigines' camp, where he had exchanged greetings with various members of the group before taking young Charley by the hand and escorting him over to his horse. He chatted cheerily to the boy and put him up on the hobbled animal. Later, when Hobbs finally emerged from his hut, Kilmeister whispered briefly in Charley's ear, and the boy hurried over to greet the station superintendent.

'Hallo, Midder Boss. Me Charley.'

Hobbs was momentarily taken aback. 'Hallo, Charley. How would you be?'

'Me good. Plenty good day, Midder.' The boy smiled.

Hobbs shook his head in disbelief. 'Yes, Charley, it's a very good day.'

'Mr Hobbs, you comem our camp, eatem food, pleease.'

Hobbs looked over at Kilmeister, who immediately turned away, rubbing the back of his head.

'You'd be unbelievable, Kilmeister,' the station superintendent called, with a half smile.

* * *

The Aboriginal group camped at the Myall Creek station was from the Weraerai tribe, which formed part of the great Kamilaroi nation. At the time of the arrival of the white man, the Kamilaroi had numbered nearly fifteen thousand, and their lands extended from the Hunter Valley in the south to beyond the Queensland border. That evening, their camp saw something of a special feast, as the Weraerai, with encouragement from Kilmeister, wanted to do all they could to impress the 'boss man', Mr Hobbs, who held their immediate safety in his hands.

All the whites – Hobbs, Kilmeister, Anderson and Burrowes – attended, along with their black stockmen, Davey and Billy. Anderson watched as the entire mob of blacks gathered with them around the large fire. They were mainly women and children, with several youths, a few old men and a handful of warrior aged men. In the cool of the late autumn evening, many of the Weraerai had kangaroo or possum skins draped over their shoulders, much to Anderson's disappointment. He preferred the day time when the women went totally naked.

The hutkeeper had supplied some beef and flour to supplement the kangaroo, possum, lizards, berries and yams provided by the hosts. The food was therefore plentiful, and quite different for those of the visitors prepared to try their hosts' favourite delicacies.

Throughout the meal Anderson's attention was focused on Ipeta, who was sitting nearly opposite him on the far side of the fire. Near him was his boss, William Hobbs, who sat next to the elders, where Davey had asked him to sit, having explained that when talking to "blackfellas" he should sit beside them, not in front of them. Hobbs was not particularly interested in instruction on such niceties of Aboriginal culture, but considering the circumstances he was quite prepared to do as requested by his black stockman.

Burrowes and Kilmeister sat between Hobbs and Anderson while Davey and Billy acted as translators. Although their own dialect was slightly different, as they were all part of the Kamilaroi people, the language was similar enough to allow the conversation to flow quite fluently.

'Davey, tell them I fancy this kangaroo meat,' instructed Hobbs.

'King Sandy say it's bery good meat,' Davey replied.

'Indeed it is.' Hobbs nodded to King Sandy, who began talking to Davey and some of the Weraerai boys, including young Charley; the shy, older Charley; and two ten-year-olds, Jimmy and Johnny, who were inseparable friends.

Hobbs observed the expressions on the faces of the wide-eyed young boys, but given that they had their backs to the fire it was difficult to see much more than the whites of their eyes and the flashing white of their smiles. As King Sandy continued with his story he became increasingly animated, and the children and Davey increasingly amused. This allowed Anderson to feel much more relaxed in the presence of the imposing Weraerai warrior than he had been when he first met him the previous morning. He was still just as large and powerful looking, and his eyes just as black and piercing, but in the brief two days he had known him, Anderson had already come to realise King Sandy was a friendly, peaceful man who, along with old Daddy and Joey, was revered by his people.

As the children began to laugh aloud and point at young Charley's father, Sandy, Hobbs wondered what King Sandy could possibly be talking about, and so asked Davey.

'He tellin' about today, boss, when dey huntin' dat roo. Dey all get round roo down de creek further and dey all chasin' it. Roo gotem bad leg, so dey catchin' it near de creek bank. Den Sandy, Charley's dad, he divem at it. He miss it and fallem on ground.'

Davey paused while King Sandy continued, now getting to his feet. Bobby, one of the few other mature men in the group, joined him beside the fire to act out the incident which was causing so much mirth.

Smiling broadly, Davey turned to Hobbs and explained, 'Bobby, he Sandy. King Sandy, he roo.'

Hobbs nodded his understanding as Bobby began to leap after King Sandy, who repeatedly jumped aside, allowing Bobby to fall flat on the ground, only to look up with a shocked expression on his face. Meanwhile the object of the fun, Sandy, who was being teasingly pushed from all sides by his tribespeople, seemed to be enjoying the entertainment as much as everyone else.

King Sandy provided a further brief explanation and then casually stepped aside as Bobby leapt at him again. This time when Bobby landed on the ground he rolled around holding his leg in mock pain, which had all the Weraerai laughing merrily, particularly the children. Davey composed himself long enough to explain to the whites that Sandy had dived again at the roo, missed, and this time had slipped down a rocky part of the creek bank into the water, grazing his leg as he did so.

The story and the antics of King Sandy and Bobby brought smiles to all the white visitors. Young Charley, though, rather suddenly ceased his laughter and jumped to his feet. He then ran over to his father, Sandy, gave him a brief but very tight hug, before giving his deeply grazed knee an affectionate pat. That done, he ran back to join his young friends, who were still laughing as King Sandy and Bobby repeated their performance. Hobbs noted the blacks, like most people, believed in milking a good joke for all its worth.

The whole scene left Hobbs contemplating. He couldn't help but be surprised at the good humour of the blacks, given their precarious situation. He understood little of their nature. He did his best, though, to keep in the spirit of the proceedings; and when King Sandy finally resumed his seat, he asked Davey how they eventually caught the roo. After checking with King Sandy, Davey explained that King Sandy had stunned it with a throwing stick before the others grabbed it.

Davey then explained, 'Dey lucky dey gotem dat one today. Dey only caughtem dat fella roo because it gotem bad leg. Dat first roo dey catchem for plenty, plenty days, boss.'

'Why would that be, Davey. I thought they'd be eating roo all the time?' Burrowes asked, somewhat naively.

Hobbs looked at him, having already come to some understanding of the blacks' situation. 'Well, Andy, I daresay being without spears would be a problem for them. I'd be pretty sure it would be hard to catch roos without spears.' The superintendent then looked at Davey for confirmation of his theory.

Davey nodded. 'Dat right, boss; and dere not so many roos now as before, before de cattle come 'ere.'

'There still be lots of roos round here though, Davey,' added Kilmeister, joining in.

'Yair, but not so many like before, and cattle eatem and flatten de long grass. Not so easy creepem on roo no more wif no long grass to hidem blackfella,' Davey explained.

'Hmmm,' murmured Hobbs. 'It's not surprising, then, that this was the first one they've had for days.' He paused, his brow furrowing, before he added, 'How are they surviving without weapons? Ask them, Davey.'

Davey did as instructed, even though he knew the answer himself. King Sandy and Old Daddy gave a lengthy answer, which Davey translated. 'Bit tough sometimes now, boss, but dey all right. De gins getem some tucker, like berries and yams and roots and tubers, and dey make like bread wit de grass seeds, catchem fish and possums and birds and snakes - de tings we eatem just now. Lots of tings, boss, but not as much as before.' Davey then added, of his own accord, 'And de whitefellas give 'em some tings, too.'

Kilmeister interjected. 'The chaps at McIntyre's and Wiseman's would help them out with some flour and sugar and that.' His voice tailed off as he added, 'Like in exchange for some of their women.' He turned to Burrowes and winked.

Hobbs either did not hear the last part of Kilmeister's comment or chose to ignore it. 'Terrible business,' he mumbled to no-one in particular, beginning to think about the blacks' situation and how the cattle were driving their natural food away. Their weapons had been taken from them, so they couldn't hunt, and they had then ended up depending on the whites for handouts. He wondered how such a situation could end, before allowing himself to be distracted from his gloomy thoughts by the sound of Daddy's voice, who was telling a story to the group of young children.

'What's he saying, Davey?' Hobbs inquired, hoping to find some simple solution to the predicament in which, he was now realising, they all found themselves. He was already aware that he was going to have a great deal of difficulty adhering to his original decision to send the Weraerai away. It was certainly the safest decision from his own point of view, and it would enable him to get the problem out of sight and pretend it didn't exist. There was something in Hobbs' nature, however, which wouldn't allow such a decision to sit easily with him. If he was going to resolve the matter, he felt he needed to understand more about the problem itself, so he listened to Davey intently.

'He say deir people been through plenty tough times before, boss, and he tellem young fellas story about dat.'

'Tell us, thanks, Davey.'

'Yair, boss.'

Daddy continued on in his calm, measured tones, and Davey translated as he went. 'Long time before, boss, dere was terrible bad drought. All de rivers and creeks dry up till dere just few green water holes. All over de land turnem dry and de grass brown. Deir whole ari dry and brown.'

It was a description with which Hobbs was somewhat familiar. It had been many months since it last rained in the Big River district, and although the creeks and rivers still flowed freely, the land had become parched and brown. It was a matter which was causing significant concern to the station superintendent, and he couldn't help but hope the description which Daddy was giving was not a regular occurrence in the district. He therefore sought some clarification as to where exactly Daddy was talking about.

'Hold on, Davey, what's their 'ari'?' Hobbs interrupted.

'Dis land here deir ari, boss,' Davey replied before seeking further clarification from Old Daddy, who responded in his usual manner, though this time he waved his arms around slowly and pointed into the distance in various directions. 'From here downem de creek to de Big River, close up Newton's station, boss. Den up de river pastem Wiseman's and McIntyre's and up to de mountains, boss.'

'So, all this land where all these stations are belongs to them?' Hobbs asked.

Davey passed on the young superintendent's question to the giant, grey-haired old doctor, who looked straight at Hobbs.

'Girr ngurrmba walaaybaa nhalay Weaeraigu.'

Davey translated. 'He say dis is the birthplace and land of de Weraerai, boss.' Daddy continued and Davey again translated. 'He say dis land not belongem to us, we belongem to dis land. We part of dis land, same as de trees, de hills, de rivers and de animals. We all part of dis land.'

A brief silence fell over the Weraerai's British guests.

It took several moments before Hobbs remembered he had interrupted the old man's story. 'Davey, ask Daddy to go on with his story.'

Old Daddy continued and Davey translated. 'All de land was dry and brown, all de food was gone and de people bery hungry, boss. Den Baiame, de great spirit ancestor, an' his sons Booma-ooma-nowi and Ghinda-inda-mui, dey frow de rocks an' de stones in de dry rivers and creeks an' dey makem de shape of de big fish traps. Baiame showem how workem de fish traps. Dat night de people have corroboree – dat's special big dance, boss,' Davey added, anticipating the next question from Hobbs, who had just started to lean forward toward his young stockman. 'Special for Baiame.'

Davey continued the translation. 'Den Baiame showem de elders how makem de rain come. Plenty long time de ground rumble under de stampin' feet of de elders as dey dancem in de dust of de dry ground. De dust rose up past de clappin' boomerangs and de dancers bery tired, boss. Dey frow 'emselves down by de fire and sleepem. While dey sleepem de dust clouds risem up round Bahloo – dat's de moon, boss – and Bahloo fill dem wit' rain. De dancers was woke up by de rain on dere faces and it keepem rainin' for plenty, plenty days. De rivers and creeks flood all over de top of de fish traps. Slowly, slowly de water go down and de people bery happy cause de traps all full of dem fish – plenty, plenty fish. De people go in and killem de fish with deir spears and sticks, or just catch dem in deir hands. De people, dey bery happy cause dey gotem lots food. Dey bery fankful Baiame 'cause dey not hungry no more and now dey knowem how buildem de fish traps.'

The old man paused. Hobbs sat in silence for a short time before addressing his black stockman. 'Davey, tell Daddy I think that's a fine story.'

Davey did so, and Old Daddy said something to him in response. Davey then turned back to Hobbs. 'He wantem showem ya how dey buildem de fish trap right here in de creek. He say can dey showem ya tomorrow?'

All of a sudden Hobbs felt rather like a trapped fish himself. 'Oh ... um ... all right, I'll be down in the morning; but I have much work to be done around the place. Tell him thank you, that would be good.'

Anderson had been following the conversation very closely, and watching his boss's reactions to the blacks, looking for any indication as to whether or not Hobbs was likely to let the blacks stay. Throughout the discussion he had switched his gaze from the group adjacent to him, across to the other side of the circle, to where Ipeta sat. He had stared at her for lengthy periods, and at times thought she was looking back at him, but the poor light and the distance made it impossible for him to be sure.

He *was* sure of one thing, though – she looked every bit as beautiful, sitting there now, wrapped in possum skins, as she had when he saw her standing wet and naked by the creek the previous morning. The flickering firelight caught the white of her smile shining through the darkness, and the hutkeeper's heart was aflame. He was sure she was looking at him now. But why would she bother looking at him? Surely if she was going to be looking at any of the whites it would be Hobbs, or perhaps even Burrowes, but certainly not him. But as he turned and looked over at her again, there could be no mistake – she was looking back at him.

He couldn't drag his eyes away from her for more than a moment, but he did manage to observe that Hobbs was now deep in conversation with Davey and a small group of the blacks that included young Charley, who was sitting on Hobbs' knee with one arm slung around his neck; Charley's mother; Martha; and father, Sandy. The conversation was clearly amusing, and Charley was obviously doing a fine job of entertaining them.

Anderson noticed that Kilmeister and Burrowes, also, were deep in conversation, in rather hushed tones.

He looked back to Ipeta as she sat talking and laughing with a group of her friends, her family, her tribespeople. Anderson didn't know who they were or what they meant to her, he just knew he wanted to be someone in her life too. He was now convinced she was the most beautiful woman he had ever seen.

'And what would you be lookin' at, Anderson?' Kilmeister shattered his trance. 'Picking yerself out a gin for the night, are ya?'

Anderson turned and glared at him but Kilmeister continued, oblivious to the hutkeeper's reaction. 'Me and Burrowes were just talkin' about them ourselves. We both think that one over there is the best.' He pointed straight at Ipeta. 'I'll have her warmin' me bed afore long, you can be sure of that.'

The words cut through Anderson like a knife. It took all his restraint to not throw himself at Kilmeister and shut his filthy little mouth.

Kilmeister continued, still oblivious to the effect his comments were having on Anderson. 'Her name's Ipeta, and I fancy she's bloody good lookin'. Martha's pretty friggin' good too.' The stockman motioned toward Charley's mother. 'They've both got husbands, but that don't stop them from lettin' us take them if we want them. They know if they want us to protect them they have to let us have their women. Actually, we were just discussin' whether Hobbs would be wanting one for himself or not. It would be good if he would, because he'd be happy to have the blacks stay once he'd tried their gins. But we don't think we ought suggest it.'

'Aye, knowing what he's like, I daren't be saying anything about it,' added Burrowes. 'If he wants to grab one himself, well that's grand; but I don't think we ought be suggesting it to him. In fact, Charlie, if you're gonna get a gin, I think you'd better wait until Hobbs goes to bed afore ye be doin' anything.'

'Yair, I think you're right. Knowin' Hobbs, he wouldn't want to know anything about it. Anyway, Anderson, which one do ya fancy yerself?'

'None of 'em,' muttered Anderson.

'Too shy, eh George? Ya probably wouldn't bleedin' know what to do with one anyway,' teased Kilmeister. 'Have ya ever had a woman, eh George?'

Anderson gritted his teeth and ignored the question.

'They're there for the takin',' Kilmeister continued. 'Shame to be seein' them go to waste.'

Continuing to ignore Kilmeister, Anderson looked over to see

Hobbs getting to his feet, lifting young Charley up with him as he did so. 'Goodnight, and thank you all.' He nodded and smiled at the elders.

Davey also thanked them, joined in chorus by young Charley as he did so. The elders nodded, and Hobbs smiled at the young boy's confidence, before turning to the three convicts and the black stockmen. 'Come on, you chaps, we'd better be heading in.'

They quickly took their leave of the blacks and followed the station superintendent over to the huts. Just as Hobbs got to the door of his hut he was joined by Kilmeister, with Burrowes close behind. Anderson, Davey and Billy continued on into their hut.

'Mr Hobbs, sir.' Kilmeister addressed his boss in a faltering voice.

Hobbs turned. 'Yes, Charlie?'

'The blacks, sir – can they be stayin', sir, just for a short while?'

Hobbs paused, lowering his head and staring at the ground. He couldn't help feeling some resentment at the dilemma in which the stockman had placed him. He didn't feel he could take it out on the blacks though. 'They ought to stay for a few days, until we sort out what's the best thing to do with them.'

'Thanks, Mr Hobbs. Ya won't regret it, sir.'

Kilmeister waited until Hobbs had entered his cabin and closed the door behind him. He then turned and winked at Burrowes, who said quietly, 'Yer a great gasser, Charlie; you've conned Hobbs again.'

'Nothin' to do with it. He trusts me. I'm gonna tell the blacks. Ya comin'?'

'No, I'll be headin' to bed.'

'Ya sure? The blacks will be real grateful.'

'Aye, to be sure they will; but another night, when thing's are a bit more settled.' Burrowes then turned and began walking toward the convicts' hut.

'I'm gonna get meself that Ipeta,' Kilmeister mumbled as he hurried across to the Weraerai camp, where he headed straight to the elders. 'It's all right, ya can stay,' he blurted out excitedly.

Old Daddy, King Sandy and Joey looked at him, then at each other. Kilmeister looked around and spotted young Charley being herded off to 'bed' by his mother.

'Hey, Charley, come here.'

Charley hurried over, closely followed by Martha.

'Charley, tell them you can stay. Mr Hobbs said you can stay.'

Charley translated, and the relieved elders immediately took Kilmeister by the hand and shook it vigorously.

'Dey say tank you, Charlie. Dey bery happy.'

'Yair, I can see that.'

The elders called out to the surrounding members of the clan, who were immediately overcome with joy.

'Tanks, Charlie,' said young Charley, smiling as Martha took him by the hand and led him away.

Kilmeister accepted the thanks of the grateful Weraerai and immediately walked over to where Ipeta was standing with a small group.

'You, come with me,' he said, aided by hand signals, before grabbing her by the wrist. Ipeta pulled away and yelled at him angrily. Kilmeister hesitated.

'Charlie.' He turned to see King Sandy, with one of the other young women standing beside him. 'Charlie,' King Sandy called again, patting the young woman on the shoulder and motioning her toward Kilmeister.

'Oh, thanks, King Sandy.' Kilmeister nodded to the tribal elder then looked back at Ipeta, who glared at him before turning and walking away. Kilmeister smiled. 'Another night yer mine,' he muttered after her, taking the other young woman by the wrist and leading her off to the convicts' hut.

CHAPTER THREE

G eorge Anderson knocked on the door of the superintendent's
hut.

'It's me, Mr 'obbs, with your breakfast.'

'Come in, George.'

Anderson had spent a rather disturbed night in the small, crowded
stockmen's hut, with his bed only a couple of feet from Kilmeister
and the young gin. A plethora of conflicting thoughts and feelings
had overwhelmed him. Never before had he been placed in such a
situation, although many times on the convict ship he was in close
proximity to copulating men. Initially the reaction that provoked in
him was repulsion, but as the trip wore on it tended more toward simple annoyance at having his precious sleep – in the cramped, stinking
conditions — disturbed.

Now, though, with a woman involved in the sex act, it fired
entirely different feelings in him. The pleasure of those feelings
was completely extinguished, however, by the involvement of the
despised Kilmeister, particularly as he was rather aggressive with the
gin, which Anderson found abhorrent.

He had lain in the darkness of the hut wrestling with these feelings, the only distraction from them being the stifled giggles of Davey and Billy. Finally there was silence, but he couldn't sleep. His mind had drifted back to his life in London and to the crime which had seen him transported for life to the colony. He so regretted the greed and stupidity which had allowed him to be led by Norman and Tucker into carrying out such a deed. He bitterly resented their treachery and the justice system which saw *him* transported and *them* free to walk the streets of London. He had wondered, for a moment, what petty crime Norman might be up to now.

The bitterness in his heart faded, though, as his mind began to return to the present and to thoughts of Ipeta. She was still very much on his mind as he entered the superintendent's hut, which was reflective of its occupant – clean, tidy and organised. Unlike the general convict population of the district, Hobbs did pay some attention to his appearance; he was clean shaven and his full head of fair hair was neatly trimmed and combed. His face was also neat, orderly and well proportioned, giving him the overall appearance of being well groomed and pleasant looking, especially when compared to the scruffy looking hutkeeper who now placed his breakfast of bread and eggs on the table. 'Morning, Mr 'obbs.'

'Morning, George.'

'Did ya sleep well, sir?'

Hobbs was about to start eating, but instead paused and looked up at Anderson. 'Well, no, not the best. I spent a fair time lying awake thinking about the blacks. It's rather worrying, really.'

'I suppose it is, sir,' Anderson replied, though the situation was simple in his view – the blacks should stay.

'It is, George.'

Hobbs was not in the habit of discussing issues weighing on his mind with the assigned convicts, though he might occasionally discuss a stock related matter with Kilmeister or Burrowes. In this case, though, as he felt it affected all of them, and he knew Kilmeister to be completely prejudiced in his view, he was prepared to open up a little to Anderson. He was, of course, totally unaware of the fact that the hutkeeper's feelings for Ipeta made him every bit as biased as Kilmeister.

'I just don't know. With these bands of stockmen riding around the countryside, I don't know if they'd be safer here with us, or whether I should be just avoiding the risk of any trouble here at Mr Dangar's and be just sending them away. You know, then whatever happens to them happens, but it won't be causing any bother here.'

'They should be safe 'ere, shouldn't they, Mr 'obbs?'

'Yair, hopefully they should be. We've also got the problem of them not having any weapons to hunt with, though. I daresay we won't be able to just keep giving them food. And I suppose I'm concerned that if they did have weapons they could turn on us.'

'Ya think they would, sir? They seem very peaceful.'

'Yair, I know they seem like very peaceful people, but you never know ... ' The worried expression on Hobbs' face slowly gave way to a smile. 'That Charley, he's a funny little chap, isn't he? He really reminds me of a young lad I once knew; lived near me back in Somerset. Same sort of confident, cheeky little chap. Always had a smile on his face, and smart as they come. His English is remarkable, isn't it?'

'Yair, it is, sir.'

'How old would you believe him to be, George?'

'Dunno, Mr 'obbs.'

'About six, I'd say – same age as my young neighbour was when I left England to come out here. Strange, isn't it? Most of the younger blacks speak some English – not as well as young Charley, but some – whereas the adults and the elders hardly speak it at all.'

'Yair, it is, sir,' Anderson again agreed with his boss.

'Anyway, George, are the others ready yet?'

'Just having their breakfast, Mr 'obbs.'

'Good, because if I'm to be going down to the creek this morning to build fish traps or whatever, I don't want work around the place to stop. Send them in here as soon as they finish eating.'

'Yes, sir.'

Anderson left Hobbs to his breakfast and stepped back out into the cool, crisp air of the autumn morning. As he retraced the footprints left by his boots in the night's dew, he looked over to the blacks' camp. Filtered by the trees lining the creek, the morning sun scattered shafts of light across the ground. One of the blacks was stirring the embers of the campfire and adding some kindling. The sounds of children playing in the water could already be heard coming from beyond the creek bank. Anderson hesitated at the door of the hut for a moment, hoping to catch a glimpse of Ipeta – but there was no sign of her amongst the morning's early risers. He opened the door and entered. Burrowes, Davey and Billy sat at the small wooden table eating breakfast. Kilmeister was still in bed, the young Aboriginal woman lying beside him.

'Kilmeister, you'd better be gettin' up. Mr 'obbs wants to see all of ya in his hut in a few minutes,' advised Anderson.

'Aye, come on, Charlie, move your arse. Get up,' urged Burrowes. 'And yer'd better be getting yer wee friend out of here afore Mr Hobbs sees her.'

'Yair, all right.' Kilmeister struggled out of bed. 'Come on you, off ya go.' He pulled the young woman by the arm and pushed her toward the door. Anderson opened it for her and she wandered, naked, into the morning, back to her people.

'Yer'd better hurry up, Charlie,' Burrowes repeated.

'All right, leave me alone; I didn't get much sleep last night, ya know.'

'Aye, we know that; and neither did we,' returned Burrowes.

'She couldn't get enough of me, that young thing.'

'That weren't quite the way I heard it,' Burrowes scoffed as he stood up, having finished his breakfast. 'Yer ready, Davey, Billy?'

'Yair, boss.'

Kilmeister hurried to get his clothes on, while gulping a few mouthfuls of his breakfast.

'Come on, Charlie, we're goin'. We ain't waitin' for you.' Burrowes headed out into the morning light with the two black stockmen at his side.

'Wait up, I'm coming,' Kilmeister called after them, grabbing his coat and following.

Shortly afterwards, George Anderson had just finished cleaning up the breakfast plates and was picking up Davey's and Billy's blankets from the earthen floor, where they slept, when Hobbs entered.

'Have you finished cleaning up in here, George?'

'Yair, nearly, Mr 'obbs.'

'Good, because I've sent the others off to move some cattle down the bottom end of the station, but I've kept Davey with me while I go building fish traps. Thought you should come along too. You can clean my hut up later if you wish.'

'Thanks, Mr 'obbs, that'd be good.'

Anderson hurriedly finished folding the blankets while Hobbs stood at the door. The convict was too delighted to even think about the motives behind Hobbs' kind offer, which were in fact twofold. Although Hobbs was unaware of the extent of Kilmeister's taunting of Anderson, he was aware that, as the new chum and the hutkeeper, Anderson was left out of things at times and hadn't quite fitted in with the others. He also knew of his floggings at the hands of Mr Dangar, and he felt for him.

Hobbs' other motive was less altruistic. He in fact shared a little of Anderson's initial nervousness around the blacks, and it was only when he had stepped outside his hut a few minutes earlier, to be confronted by a sea of smiling black faces, that he realised he was to be the only white man on this fish trap building excursion. Even though Davey had been on Dangar's stations for years and Hobbs knew him very well, he was every bit as black as the Weraerai. Anderson might not have been a great warrior, but Hobbs felt he was at least the right colour.

'Ever been fishing, George?'

'Yair, Mr 'obbs, a few times in the Thames. Never caught nuthin' much, though. It were a bit dirty, I suppose.'

'Ah, yes. Well this'll be my first time, so it ought to be interesting. Come on, ya ready?'

'Yes, sir.'

The superintendent and the hutkeeper joined Davey, who had been waiting outside, and walked across to the Weraerai camp. They were immediately greeted by the elders. Daddy wrapped his massive arm around Hobbs, smiling and saying something that was totally unintelligible to the superintendent.

'He says, "Hallo, Midder Boss. Come, we showem ya how catchem plenty, plenty fish",' Davey translated.

The elders immediately started walking across to the creek with Hobbs and Davey.

'Dey want takem us down de creek, boss.'

'Fine, Davey, wherever they like,' replied Hobbs, 'but I can't believe that they want to go building fish traps in the middle of a drought, when it hasn't rained for months.'

'Don't worry, boss, it always rainem sometime.'

Anderson followed closely behind and was immediately joined by young Charley and Martha. As they walked beside the trees at the top of the creek bank, Anderson noticed Sandy – whom he had discovered the previous night was Charley's father –walking just behind them. Although he had then been the object of much fun at the hands of King Sandy, he worried Anderson slightly because he was also very strongly built, with similar dark eyes to King Sandy, and because he was one of the very few young men in the clan. The great majority of them were women and children, along with a few old men, with whom Anderson was already comfortable. The young men had obviously been out hunting that first day he had been at the camp, and although they had been there in the evenings, he hadn't had much to do with them yet, so he was still quite anxious around them.

'Hallo, Jackey-Jackey,' chirped Charley, looking up at Anderson.

'Hallo, Charley. What did you call me?'

'Jackey-Jackey.'

'You're silly, Charley.' The hutkeeper smiled. 'I'm George.'

'We callem ya Jackey-Jackey. Good name, eh George?'

'Yair, if you think so.' Anderson laughed.

'Jackey-Jackey our friend?'

'Yair, I hope so, Charley.'

'Jackey-Jackey?'

'Yair, Charley?' But before the boy could ask his question, Anderson asked one of his own. He motioned toward Martha. 'Is that ya mother?'

The child nodded. 'Dat Martha.'

Anderson nodded to Martha. 'Mornin', Martha.'

Much to Anderson's surprise, she responded by uttering his new name, 'Jackey-Jackey', and smiled.

Charley pointed to his father. 'Dat bubaa, Sandy.'

'Jackey-Jackey,' said Sandy, smiling.

Anderson immediately felt a little relieved. 'Mornin', Sandy.'

'How's Sandy's leg?' Anderson asked Charley, referring to the injury which had been the cause of so much mirth around the campfire the previous evening.

'It good,' replied Charley without bothering to check with his father.

They walked on, following Hobbs and the elders as they made their way further down the creek. Anderson kept glancing back over his shoulder as they weaved their way through some trees on the edge of the bank; and what he was hoping to see, he saw. Ipeta was walking with the group just behind them. The fact that he had been hoping and half expecting her to be there didn't stop his heart from leaping, as it did virtually every time he saw her. His mind raced with thoughts of actually spending some time with her, or at least near her. If he could find the courage, he might even attempt talking to her.

The creek began a large meander to the left but the Weraerai party continued straight ahead across country. Here the grass was thigh height, as it was an area where the cattle had not grazed for some time. The Weraerai immediately sorted themselves into single file as they continued on. Hobbs and Anderson fell in with them, but a curious Hobbs turned to Davey, who was walking behind him.

'Why are they walking in a single line, Davey?'

'Snakes, boss,' was Davey's simple reply.

Hobbs considered this for a moment, before asking, 'But how does walking in a single line help with snakes?'

'Snakes always runem away, boss. If ya in one line, snake can runem away. If ya beside udder fella, ya scare snake into udder fella's legs and snake bitem udder fella – or worse, udder fella scarem snake into your legs and him bitem you.'

'Oh, I see,' replied Hobbs, glancing back at Davey, who was walking with his head down so Hobbs couldn't detect the grin which the superintendent knew would be there.

Shortly after, the leaders of the party arrived at the point where the creek meandered back to the right. After stopping on the top of the bank, the elders started talking among themselves and pointing to various parts of the creek. At the spot at which they had arrived, the creek widened out into quite a large pool before narrowing through a rocky section. The banks remained quite steep on both sides, but due to the long dry spell the water level was fairly low.

The elders gave directions as the others arrived, and Anderson noted that only about half the mob had come on their fishing expedition.

'Come, Jackey-Jackey, ya helpem us?' Charley called as he jumped into the water.

'Yair, of course I'll help ya. What are we doin' first?'

'We getem rocks, makem de fish traps.'

Anderson clambered down to the edge of the creek, where he sat down to remove his boots. Hobbs had already done so, and was wading into the water with Davey and King Sandy.

'It's rather cool, George.'

'It all right, boss,' Davey chimed in.

The rest of the group spread out, collecting rocks from the creek bed and the edges of the bank. They worked together with the assistance of their new English friends, bringing the rocks to where the creek narrowed, at which point, being too old for the manual lifting, Daddy and Joey gave directions as to their placement..

As they wandered back and forth, young Charley started working and playing with Hobbs. Anderson took the opportunity to work as closely to Ipeta as he could without making it obvious he was following her. He wasn't sure, but he thought she had glanced at him a few times, and appeared to him to be particularly aware of his presence – or so he hoped.

He stood with a pile of rocks in his arms, watching her as she carefully placed some rocks which she had just dropped into the water at the required spot. As she wedged the last rock into place she looked up at Anderson.

'Hallo, Jackey-Jackey.' She smiled.

'Hallo, Ipeta. You … you speak English,' stammered a shocked but delighted Anderson.

Ipeta smiled again and shook her head.

'Oh, sorry. I thought ya must speak English. Just a few words, eh?'

She looked at him blankly.

Anderson moved his left hand slightly from the rocks which he cradled in his arms and held his thumb and index finger slightly apart. A rock dropped from his grasp as he did so.

'You speak a little bit of English. He motioned to her and raised his voice slightly. 'You speak little bit English.'

Ipeta nodded as she took a couple of steps toward the convict and stood in front of him. She took two rocks from the pile he still held, and as she did so her hand brushed his arm. It was the first time in too many years that he had so much as been touched by a woman – not that he was conscious of that fact at the time, it just felt strange to him. Strange, but so wonderful, and it stirred in him feelings that were unknown but wonderfully exciting. She looked up at him. She was very different looking to white women, he thought, but she was oh so beautiful.

She turned and carefully placed the rocks alongside those she had just arranged. Ipeta then looked up and motioned for him to put the rocks down in front of her. He hesitated. He wanted her to take them out of his arms herself and touch his arm again – a touch that to him had been the most sensual caress. She motioned again for him to put the rocks down. He finally did so, and together they began to arrange them into a wall.

He watched her as they worked together, gathering the rocks and building their wall to link up with the other walls. He watched her and was stirred by both her beauty and her nakedness. Both were so extraordinary to him, so foreign but so arousing. They were as nought, though, beside the moment when she touched – no, *held* – his arm.

They were crouched in shallow water, carefully placing their rocks in the wall, when the sound of laughter came from the other end of the pool. To gain his attention, Ipeta gently grasped his forearm as she pointed to young Charley and the inseparable Johnny and Jimmy, who were clowning with Hobbs. Anderson looked at them briefly but quickly dropped his eyes to his arm, upon which rested her hand. He looked at the silky smooth skin of her slender fingers from which a wonderful warmth emanated, flowing through his veins. The back of his neck tingled, his loins stirred. He wished she would leave her hand there always. She turned and looked at him to see if he was sharing her mirth but saw he was not looking at the children but at her hand. Ipeta gave him a slightly quizzical half smile, leaving her hand on his arm for just a moment longer. She then tenderly squeezed his arm and, much to Anderson's disappointment, removed her hand and continued working.

* * *

Hobbs sat on the bank, pulling on his boots and surveying the complex arrangement of dams and pools they had built. Young Charley, who had been his companion throughout most of the morning, was leaning on his shoulder.

'Fine, Davey, so what happens now?' Hobbs asked.

'We comem back when de rains come, boss. Den we have plenty, plenty fish.'

'Sounds good. Hopefully we'll get some rain soon; we certainly need it. What if they want to catch fish today? Ask Daddy if this is the only way they catch fish.'

Davey found it slightly frustrating that Hobbs continually had him ask questions of the elders that he knew the answers to himself. He felt as if Hobbs couldn't believe that he would know anything about any of these "blackfella things". In the five years he'd been in Henry Dangar's service, no one – including Hobbs – had been the least bit interested in asking him about "blackfella ways". They had only been interested in teaching him about "whitefella ways"; and though he had learnt a lot about whitefella ways, he was still a blackfella. He might not know as much about the Bora as the elders, but he sure knew how to catch a fish. Despite this frustration, he had great respect for both Hobbs and the Weraerai elders and so passed the question on to Daddy.

As he did so, though, the practical joker in him thought that one day he might just have a bit of fun with these translations. He would wait until his brother Billy was around, though, because there was no point in having a great joke if you had no one to share it with.

He therefore translated Daddy's reply accurately. 'Daddy say dey gotem plenty, plenty ways to catchem de fish. Dey havem a line and stone hook like him seen some of de whitefellas usin'. Dey usem de nets dey makem outta de branches and twigs, and dey use de spears when dey got dem. Him say dis bery good way catchem plenty, plenty fish for 'morrow, boss; and him say you always be hungry 'morrow. Him say dat he wanted to showem you de way Baiame teachem his ancestors.'

'Yes, Davey, I understand that; and thank him very much for me, would you? Come on, George, we'd best get back.'

'Comin', Mr 'obbs.'

Anderson turned to his new workmate. 'Bye, Ipeta.'

'Bye, Jackey-Jackey.' And her smile lit up his life.

As Anderson and Hobbs walked back along the creek bank together they hardly spoke a word, as they were both deep in thought. They had entirely different matters on their minds, however. Anderson was deeply engrossed in thoughts of Ipeta, but those thoughts were tainted with some confusion over having such feelings for a black woman.

Hobbs, on the other hand, was trying to reconcile his personal ambition with his compassionate nature. His ambition did not want to allow the risk of any problems with the blacks occurring on Mr Dangar's station, and therefore he wanted to send them away. His humane nature, though, was wrestling with the dangers these amiable people faced if he did so. As was his wont, he couldn't make a decision, and so he forced the matter from his mind and focused on the day's immediate tasks.

CHAPTER FOUR

The following evening the Weraerai camp again played host to their white visitors, but on this occasion the seating arrangements were quite different. Rather than the guests sitting together next to the elders, they were now scattered throughout the circle surrounding the campfire. Only Hobbs sat with the elders. Perhaps their mutual positions of authority provided them with a type of bond; but quite apart from that, Hobbs appeared, to Anderson at least, to be developing a genuine interest in the Weraerai way of life. He was more motivated, however, by a hope that he might somehow find an answer to his dilemma. Hobbs continued to use Davey as an interpreter, while young Charley used Hobbs' knee as his base as he wandered from group to group, making sure he didn't miss out on anything and ensuring that no-one missed out on their share of his humour and happiness.

'Daddy, Joey – can you tell me why your people move about all the time? Wouldn't it be better to stay in one place and build proper huts?' inquired Hobbs.

It was yet another question Davey could have answered himself, still he passed it on and translated the elders' response. 'Dey movem about for food, boss. If dey stay in one place dey eatem all de food in dat place, den nuthin' to eat, boss. Dey movem someplace else, den when dey come back, dere is food dere again. Some foods good in some place at different times, likem when it cold or hot. And, boss, all round deir ari are special places dey visit and talkem with de creator beings and de spirit ancestors.'

'And is the reason they have so few things so that they have less to carry as they move about?'

Davey decided to answer this himself, as he was keen to show Hobbs he knew plenty about being a 'blackfella'. 'Yair, boss, dat right; and dey havem all dey need, boss. Blackfellas not needem much, boss.'

'Yair, they certainly don't seem to need much.' Hobbs nodded.

'And de tings don't belongem to eachfella. Everyting belongem everyfella. Everyting belongem all mob.'

Hobbs was about to make further enquiries but was interrupted by a low droning sound coming from two long, hollowed-out pieces of wood being played by two of the men of the clan. They were accompanied by the clapping of short, thick pieces of wood, together with what Hobbs knew to be boomerangs. A group of five of the young adult males, led by King Sandy and Ipeta's husband, emerged from the darkness and started dancing around the fire. Hobbs was at first taken aback by their fearsome appearance. They were all very heavily painted with white on their legs, across their bodies and down their arms. Reddish-brown ochre formed patterns through the white, while their faces had a line of white dots across their noses and foreheads. Small branches were tucked into reeds tied around their calves.

Hobbs initial reaction was shared by Anderson, who found the performance of the ancient dance, with its chanting and stamping to the rhythms of the clapping sticks, so primitive and confronting it was almost intimidating. He was also aware he would have found it even more confronting had he not known the participants. He looked at Ipeta, who sat near him with Martha and Sandy. She looked back at him. He found nothing primitive or confronting in her.

Burrowes also sat close by, watching as the dancing continued. A short time later Kilmeister wandered over to join them. He had seen the Weraerai dancing when they had been at McIntyre's, so he was quite comfortable with the whole spectacle, and had seen McIntyre's men dance with them at times.

'What do ya think, Andy? Should we join in?' he asked.

'Ah, I dunno. Do you think they'd be mindin' if we did?'

'Nah, they won't mind. Hey Davey, it'll be all right if we join in, shan't it?' Kilmeister called across the campfire.

'Yair, no problems, boss. It not Bora dance, it only story about de blue tongue lizard fella. Billy likem dancin'. Hey Billy, you showem Charlie how dancem like blackfella,' Davey called to his younger brother, who was busy talking to one of the young girls.

Billy got to his feet, and as the music continued he motioned to Kilmeister to join them.

Kilmeister did so, calling to Burrowes, 'Come on, Andy, you bloody Irish are supposed to be pretty good on yer feet.'

'Aye, we are indeed, but not that sort of dancin'. But I'll be havin' a wee try anyway,' he replied, jumping to his feet.

Billy showed Kilmeister and Burrowes some basic steps, much to the amusement of the whole camp, while King Sandy and the others continued a far more complex dance around them.

Hobbs turned to Davey. 'Davey, can you ask Daddy if they have this sort of dancing very often?'

'Sure, boss.'

Daddy gave his usual lengthy reply while Hobbs waited patiently for an answer.

'Him says dey havem plenty, plenty types of dancin', boss. Dey havem dances dat tellem stories of de Bora. Stories teachem young fellas big lessons about life. Dey havem dances for plenty, plenty tings; special tings likem when de young fellas dey becomem big fellas. Him say before, dey used to havem bery, bery big corroborees.

Plenty, plenty tribes from de Kamilaroi people comem and it go for days. Plenty, plenty dancers and each mob tryin' to do better dan udder fellas.'

'It must have been a spectacular sight; but what does he mean 'before'? Before what?'

'Before "wunda" comem dis place – before "whitefella" comem, boss.'

'Oh.'

Around the fire the dancing continued. More of the Weraerai had now joined in, as King Sandy's dance had finished.

'Boss, it all right if me go joinem dem for while?' Davey asked, seeking a break from his translating duties.

'Yair, sure; I'll be heading in now, anyway. I have a report to write for Mr Dangar. Thank them for me, Davey. Very good, King Sandy,' he called as he took leave of his hosts. 'And don't you chaps be forgetting there's work to be done tomorrow,' he advised his convict workers.

'Yes, Mr Hobbs.'

'Good night, boss.'

Young Charley went running after the superintendent. 'Midder Boss.' As Hobbs turned the boy jumped into his arms. 'You no sayem goodnight Charley.'

'Oh, I am sorry. Goodnight, Charley. You'd better get some sleep, my young friend.'

'Yair, Midder Boss. Goodnight.' Charley hugged Hobbs tightly before sliding to the ground and running back to where his parents sat with Anderson and Ipeta, some little distance behind the main group around the fire.

'Mr Hobbs, he nice man, Jackey-Jackey,' enthused Charley as he jumped onto his father's knee.

'Yair, he is, Charley,' replied Anderson.

Martha spoke to Charley, and Charley replied.

'What did she ask ya, Charley?' Anderson inquired.

'She askem what we say.'

Martha nodded and smiled at Anderson.

'Yair, Mr 'obbs good man,' Anderson nodded in reply.

A few moments later Martha whispered something to Charley, who immediately turned to Anderson. 'Goodnight, Jackey-Jackey. Me goem sleep.'

Martha and Sandy both got to their feet and carried their young son off toward their hut, leaving Ipeta alone with the man whose heart she held in the palm of her hand. Together they sat beneath the silent stars of the clear autumn night – stars which tonight somehow seemed brighter than usual to George Anderson. He returned his gaze to Ipeta, contemplating her while the flickering glow of the flames fondled the velvet skin of her face. Her eyes turned to meet his gaze, and slowly her soft, full lips parted to a smile which shone against her black skin like the crescent moon in the night sky above. The pulsating rhythms of the dance swirled around them, and Anderson was immersed in feelings which fired his desires as never before and melted his sensitivities about the colour of her skin. He knew what he wanted, but he didn't know how, or if he could allow himself, to have it.

The dancing near them continued for some time, during which Sandy and Martha returned; and although he acknowledged them, Anderson remained almost oblivious to their presence.

In another section of the camp, in the darkness of the shadows cast by the trees and the huts, Burrowes, Kilmeister and Billy sat in close company with three young women. After Hobbs had retired for the evening, Burrowes recovered the secret stash of rum which he and Kilmeister kept hidden from Hobbs at the back of their hut. They would normally only indulge when Hobbs was away, but as they felt this was a special occasion they had decided to share it round a little with their sexual quarry.

Kilmeister lay his head in the near naked lap of one of the girls. He lifted the possum skins draped over her shoulders to look at her breasts, only a few inches from his face. The smooth black skin of her young breasts contrasted with the white, pock-marked skin of his face.

'Ah, beautiful, ain't they, Andy?'

'Aye, beautiful, to be sure.' Burrowes smiled. 'But Charlie, we'd best be askin' the elders about these gins. That's why ye nearly got into strife afore. You know what Eaton told us about their customs.'

Having had this mob of Weraerai camped on his station for many months, Andrew Eaton had learnt enough about them to know they had a very complex system of rules about marriage and relationships. He had also learnt that although the Weraerai were prepared to lend their women to the whites, to ensure they were all protected, there were only certain women they would lend and they would do so only with the woman's consent. Eaton also knew that they resented most strongly the white men just taking their women, and that the taking and raping of Aboriginal women had been the cause of various bloody clashes in the remote district. He had therefore told Kilmeister and Burrowes, when he sent the Weraerai up to their station, that they should always ask the elders if they could have a particular gin. In his semi-drunken state, however, Kilmeister was not interested in such cultural niceties.

'Ah, bugger what Eaton says. What are the blacks gonna do about it, anyway?'

'Listen, you stupid bastard. We'd be wantin' the blacks to stay, aye?'

'Aye,' Kilmeister mocked in reply.

'Well, the last thing we'd be wantin' is any trouble at all with them, or Hobbs will be sendin' them away.'

'All right, all right,' Kilmeister conceded.

'Besides, the gins can get into bother themselves with their mob.' Burrowes turned to Billy. 'Billy, will you go and ask the elders if it's all right if we have these gins?

Billy disentangled himself from the embrace of a young girl he had already had the foresight to ask the elders about, and got to his feet to do the stockmen's bidding.

The music and dancing continued on around the fire, on which a new pile of dead branches was now thrown. The tinder dry leaves crackled and hissed as they fed the blaze, and the fingers of the flame reached into the night sky. This sudden burst of heat further inflamed the passions of the stockmen – passions which had already been ignited by the music, the rum and the semi-naked women.

By the time Billy returned from seeing the elders and nodded, 'It all right, boss,' Kilmeister had already slipped his hand beneath the possum skin draped across the young woman's lap.

Billy bent down and whispered something to his girl. He then took her by the hand and led her off, deeper into the shadows, before he was given any more errands to run.

Burrowes took a mouthful of rum before handing it to Kilmeister, who sat up and took a swig himself. As he did so he glanced beyond the bottom of the bottle tilted to his mouth and saw Anderson with Ipeta, closer to the fire. 'Bleedin' hell. What's that damned arse doin' with my gin?' he muttered while getting to his feet. 'Hey, Anderson,' he called as he strode over to where Anderson and his companions sat, 'I told ya I fancied her. She's mine. You damned well keep away from her.'

Totally taken aback, Anderson bit back. 'No!'

'Listen, she needs a man, not a bleedin' woman like you.'

Kilmeister immediately grabbed Ipeta by the arm and started pulling her to her feet. She resisted, clinging to Anderson's arm.

'Leave her alone, Kilmeister,' snapped Anderson, pulling Ipeta down beside him.

'Bugger you, Anderson!'

Sandy calmly got to his feet, towering over Kilmeister, glared at him and shook his head.

'Just leave her alone, Charlie,' repeated Anderson, also getting to his feet.

Sandy pointed to the girl Kilmeister had left sitting in the shadows nearby and called her over. Kilmeister said nothing as he took the young woman by the wrist and led her off to the stockmen's hut.

Anderson looked up at the massive Weraerai warrior standing beside him, nodded, 'Thanks, Sandy,' and together they resumed their seats on the ground.

CHAPTER FIVE

Hunter Valley, New South Wales.

A group of ten well-dressed men and women sat around a long, finely set dining table as two convict women removed plates from in front of them. Henry Dangar, former government surveyor and now wealthy squatter, was playing host to a group of his fellow squatters. He sat at the head of the table, dressed in the fashion of the day: a double-breasted frock coat made in London from the colony's finest superfine merino wool, with a velvet collar; a high-collared, white shirt, the front of which was covered by a purple silk cravat, held in place by a chained emerald cravat pin; a black waistcoat of embroidered silk; and dark grey, woollen trousers, featuring the latest development in London fashion – a fly.

'I don't know how you do it, Dangar,' commented the similarly attired Robert Scott, magistrate and one of the largest landholders in the colony. His wealth, lifestyle and flamboyance had seen him bestowed with the title of 'Count Bobby' by the colony's monied elite.

'Do what, Scott?'

'How you always manage to have only the very best convict cooks assigned to you. That lamb was absolutely superb.'

'A-ha! That's an acquired skill I won't be sharing with you, my friend,' joked Dangar, getting to his feet. 'And if you ladies will excuse us, we shall adjourn for a cigar. We have some business to discuss.'

The men politely took their leave of the women and wandered into the adjoining sitting room, where Henry Dangar offered cigars to his guests. The room was large, with a fireplace at one end, the timber in which now burnt quite strongly, as the convict help had anticipated the master and his guests moving there after dining. It was furnished with two lounges and several lounge chairs, loosely arranged around a low table near the middle of the room. At one end of the table was a high-backed chair with purple and gold striped velvet upholstery across the seat. On the walls hung a variety of paintings: one of the new colony's main street, George Street, running up from the harbour and the Rocks; one of the Thames in London; as well as an array of family portraits. A piano stood in one corner, and a timber desk in another. Against the long wall, opposite the large windows that looked out onto the veranda and the garden, was a sideboard at which Henry Dangar now stood pouring port from a crystal decanter.

'Now, tell me, Scott,' he began, 'how did your meeting with our new Governor go?'

'Not very well, Dangar; not well at all, in fact,' responded Robert Scott. 'To start with, it was only a very brief, informal meeting; but apart from that, Gipps made it very clear that one of his major priorities is "to ensure that the natives of this colony are protected and treated fairly". I mean, really!'

'What nonsense!' Dangar shook his head. 'But we were afraid of that, from what we'd heard previously about Gipps. It is apparent, then, that he won't be assisting us at all in resolving our problems with the blacks.'

'Look, Gipps is a naive fool, like the rest of his Whig colleagues. They've all got their heads in the clouds, so you can be quite sure he will be no assistance whatever.'

James Glennie, another Hunter Valley landholder and squatter, with a station in the Big River district, joined in. 'Scott, did you not acquaint him with the fact that these savages are obstructing the expansion of the colony; that they spear cattle, they rush cattle, they attack stockmen; and that many men in these remote districts live in the most dire fear of them?'

'Of course I did, but the man's a fool, as I said,' snapped Scott.

'It sounds like he's going to be even more of a hindrance to us than we first suspected,' mused Dangar, handing Scott a glass of port.

'Undoubtedly.' Scott nodded. 'What amazes me, though, is with all the money the Australian Agricultural Company has poured into the expansion of this colony over the last dozen or so years, would you not believe that their investors would be unable to influence the British Government to ensure they sent out another reasonable man like we've had in the past? I mean, Brisbane and Darling were at least practical men, content to let things sort themselves out in the interior; even Bourke, when we had our deputation to him about the blacks' depredations, simply said, "Protect yourselves, gentlemen". And, of course, we did.'

'Precisely,' Glennie agreed. 'But also, those Governors weren't afraid to commit troopers and police to assist, on occasion.'

Dangar examined the tip of his cigar. 'Anyway, gentlemen, there's no good us concerning ourselves now with what the British Government *should* have done. What we have to do is determine how we resolve our problem with the blacks.'

'Well, we'll just have to continue to drive them out of the Big River district, just as we drove them out of this valley,' responded Scott. 'Settled a few myself, you know – or have I told you that story?'

'You've told me – several times, in fact, Scott.' Glennie smiled.

'Well, you haven't told me,' said Dangar. 'And, by Jove, I would most definitely like to hear it; but should we not resolve this matter first, if we may?'

'Certainly,' nodded Scott, 'but I'm given to understand that some progress is continuing to be made in the district anyway.'

'What do you mean?' inquired Glennie.

'Well, since Major Nunn's little excursion up there, I am given to understand that some of the local men have been continuing the drive against the blacks in the district.'

'Yes,' Dangar nodded, 'I had heard that myself. Young Fleming is involved, isn't he?'

'So I believe; and those of my men who rode with Nunn are certainly assisting,' Scott added.

'Well, then there couldn't be too many of the blacks left up there – are there?' inquired Glennie. 'Because from what I have been given to believe, Major Nunn and his troopers killed hundreds of them.'

'Apparently they did; but let's face the facts: one black is too many blacks, and there are still a great number of them up there, believe me. Hundreds and hundreds, in fact probably more,' Dangar responded.

'Thousands,' muttered Scott before rapidly draining his port glass.

'I understood, according to original estimates, there were only a few hundred in the whole district,' Glennie persisted.

'Yes, well, those estimates were wrong. There were thousands of them up there. You see, the problem is that people always forget how big this colony is; and just because the blacks are spread out across it, people think there aren't many of them; but, I am most reliably informed, there are thousands of them out there,' Scott explained.

'But Fleming and the others are making some progress with it, are they?' asked Glennie.

'Yes, or so I understand. You see, Nunn showed our men up there how to handle the damn blacks. You simply assemble as large a party of men as possible, get all the weapons you can and then hunt them down relentlessly. Obviously, however, it's going to be a much slower process without Nunn. I mean, he had nearly thirty of his own troopers with him, as well as about twenty of our stockmen. So that was a very large party of men who could obviously be very effective in sorting the blacks out. Now, without Nunn and his troopers, our men are in smaller groups but are still apparently making some progress, or so I'm given to understand.' Scott peered into his empty glass.

'Well, what we really need is for Nunn and his men to be dispatched back to the district until the job is completed,' Glennie observed.

'Well, unfortunately, from what Scott has told us, that is just not going to happen; not while that fool Gipps is here, anyway. You two might have been able to persuade our acting Governor, Snodgrass, to dispatch Nunn to the district, but with Gipps here we are obviously just going to have to rely on the likes of Fleming and the others,' Dangar pointed out.

'Yes, and they'll just have to make whatever progress they can – for now, at least.' Scott nodded, again peering into his empty glass. 'It is just ridiculous, though, isn't it? Here we have a government sitting back in London that wants the British Empire expanded. They set up a colony out here, they provide us with a supply of convict labour, they invest millions of pounds, and they make millions of pounds from the sheep and cattle and everything else, yet when it comes to the hard work of actually expanding the colony, it's left to men of vision and drive – men like ourselves.' Scott puffed on his cigar before continuing.' And what do they do? Send us out an idealistic fool like George Gipps, who wants to try to impede us by protecting the blacks, who get in the way of that expansion.'

'Precisely, Scott,' Dangar enthused. 'And I think anyone would have to admit we've done a fine job, too. Why, just look at our expansion on this northern side of the colony alone. We've opened up the Hunter Valley all the way up to the Big River in just, what, twelve or fourteen years?'

'About fourteen, I'd say,' replied Glennie.

'And that's a distance of nearly three hundred miles, I would estimate,' added Dangar.

'Yes, easily,' agreed Scott. 'Anyway, where were we … Yes, I was going to tell you about my contribution to eliminating the damn blacks from our Hunter Valley here.'

'Ah yes, certainly, Scott, go on; I'd love to hear it. Another port, gentlemen?' asked Dangar, getting to his feet.

'Yes, yes, thank you. Well, it was about twelve years ago, the spring of twenty-six to be precise, and I was acting in my capacity as magistrate, investigating some trouble with the blacks at Lethbridge's property. I was out with a group of troopers and local stockmen scouring the countryside for the culprits, when we came across this mob of the savages ... '

CHAPTER SIX

R ain had been falling heavily all night. The earth was sodden, and small rivulets formed in the soil and ran down from the ridges into Myall Creek. The level of the creek had risen part way up the steep bank as it wound its way past the Weraerai camp and the stockmen's huts, continuing around the rocky base of the ridge to the west. The rain had now eased to a fine mist as a young boy ran across from the Weraerai camp to the hut of the station superintendent.

William Hobbs had just risen and was nearly dressed when there was a knock at the door. He slipped on his coat before opening it.

Despite the fact the Weraerai had now been camped on the station for over two weeks, Hobbs had at no stage made the decision to let them stay. He just hadn't been able to find it in his heart to make the decision to send them away. A large part of the reason for that was the small boy who now stood at his door.

'Mornin', Midder Boss.'

'Good morning, Charley.'

'Come, Midder Boss, we goem fishin'.'

'Charley, we need this rain, but I don't fancy fishing in it.'

'It all right. Lookem, Midder Boss,' chirped Charley, pointing to where the morning sun was trying to break through the thinning clouds. 'Come fishin' with Charley, pleease. Elders want showem ya dey catchem fish.'

'Oh, all right, Charley, I'll come for a little while, but then I have work to do. Be a good chap and see how George is going with my breakfast.'

'Sure, Midder Boss.'

'Thanks, Charley.'

Charley bounced across the few metres between the huts, knocked on the door, disappeared inside momentarily and within a minute was back at Hobbs' hut.

'That was quick, Charley.'

'Jackey-Jackey sayem it be five minutes.'

'Oh, good, thanks, Charley.'

'Midder Boss?'

'Yes, Charley.'

'How longem five minutes?'

'Not very long, Charley. Sit down and wait for George and you'll find out.'

Charley sat down at the table opposite Hobbs and watched in silent fascination for a few moments as the superintendent laid his rifle on the table and began cleaning it. Charley was, by now, perfectly comfortable in the superintendent's hut, as he had become a very regular visitor

'What ya doin', Midder Boss?'

'Just cleaning my gun.' Hobbs quickly changed the subject. 'Hey, do you think we'll catch plenty of fish this morning?'

'Yep. We catchem plenty, plenty guya after de rain.'

'"Guya"? That's "fish", isn't it, Charley?'

'Yair, Midder Boss.' Charley beamed.

Their conversation continued briefly until there was a knock at the door.

'It's just me, sir.'

'Come in, George.'

'Hallo, Jackey-Jackey.'

Anderson entered. 'Good mornin', Mr 'obbs. Hallo, Charley.'

'Just put it down there, George. I'm nearly finished. Now, Charley, that would be five minutes. Well, actually, it was a bit less than five minutes, I suspect, but for your purposes I think that it would be close enough.'

'Pardon, Midder Boss?' said the boy, screwing up his face.

'Never mind, Charley. That was five minutes.'

'Tanks, Midder Boss. Jackey-Jackey, you catchem fish wit us?'

Anderson looked at the boy, then at Hobbs. 'That'll be up to Mr 'obbs, Charley.'

'Can Jackey-Jackey come wit us, pleease, Midder Boss.'

'Well, it should be all right.' Hobbs thought for a moment. 'Yair, I believe we could all go along. An hour or two won't do any harm. Tell the others, would you, George? We'll go as soon as we finish breakfast.'

'Yes, sir. Thank you, sir.'

* * *

Half an hour later the group of Weraerai and their white colleagues arrived at the spot where the river widened before narrowing at the point where they had built the fish traps nearly two weeks before. The traps were full of fish, and the whites removed their boots as the Weraerai waded into the water.

'Hey, Davey,' called Hobbs, 'how do we catch them?'

The young black stockman smiled. 'Easy, boss, wif ya hands. No spears, so catchem wif ya hands.'

'Oh!' Hobbs then turned to his men. 'This won't be easy.'

With that, Hobbs and his convicts followed the Weraerai in amongst the stone traps, where they quickly joined them diving and lunging around, grabbing at the entrapped fish.

Anderson and Ipeta shared in the fun and the challenge of trying to catch the fish caught in the trap they had built together. Kilmeister,

Burrowes and Davey tried to herd the fish into the smallest corner of another trap. There was plenty of wrestling and yelling from the young stockmen, but they were initially quite ineffective fishermen.

Hobbs teamed up with Daddy, King Sandy and young Charley, and their group enjoyed immediate success as King Sandy's experience saw him quickly wrap his hands around a large cod, which he threw to Hobbs, who, much to his own surprise, caught it. Daddy wasn't much help, being too old and slow to actually catch the fish himself, but he was very good at giving instructions, yelling encouragement, waving his arms around and enthusiastically congratulating those who were successful.

It took some time but eventually Hobbs was the first of the whites to actually catch a good size perch, which he quickly held aloft to the cheers of all.

Anderson tried to focus on catching the fish but found it far more enjoyable to take every opportunity he could to get his hands on Ipeta rather than their aquatic quarry. As she lunged about in pursuit of a catch, he lunged about also, but at first only seemed to come up with her hands clasped in his. She eventually managed to get him to concentrate on the task at hand long enough for them to seize a large perch together.

Each time a fish was caught a cry of delight rose from the captor, who immediately handed it to one of three Aboriginal women who remained standing on the edge of the creek with a type of net bag into which the fish were quickly dispatched. After nearly an hour, fish bulged from the net bags and only the smallest and most elusive of them remained in the traps. The clothes of the stockmen were drenched.

'Come on, you chaps, we'd better be going and getting dry, we've got work to do,' Hobbs directed as he walked out of the creek and onto the bank. 'Thank the elders for me, Davey.'

Kilmeister followed his boss out of the water, patting King Sandy on the back as he did. 'Thanks, King Sandy. That was good.'

'Aye, good, to be sure,' echoed Burrowes.

Anderson hung back with the Weraerai as the others put on their boots and began to climb the bank. 'Mr 'obbs, I'll just help with the fish and get some sorted out for supper tonight,' he called, desperately hoping the superintendent would accept his feeble excuse to stay behind with Ipeta and her people.

'All right, George, that'll be fine. We probably won't be back until after sunset now that we're getting such a late start. Don't you forget about that firewood for my hut, though.'

'I won't, Mr 'obbs,' he called back.

As the stockmen wandered off and disappeared amongst the trees, Anderson waded over to Daddy and took the great old man by the hand.

'Thanks, Daddy,'

The old man smiled and nodded. 'Jackey-Jackey.'

Anderson then turned and waved his thanks to King Sandy and Joey. As he did so he became aware of just how cold and wet his shirt felt against his skin now that he had stopped jumping around in pursuit of the fish. He stood there amongst the naked Weraerai and pulled his still buttoned shirt off over his head to let the autumn sun warm his back. It was the first time the Weraerai had seen him without his shirt, and they were immediately struck by the multitude of deep scars across his back.

'Jackey-Jackey, ya back, plenty, plenty scars,' said Charley.

Daddy immediately spoke to the boy.

'Daddy say you bery brave warrior havem plenty, plenty scars.'

As Charley spoke, Daddy proudly motioned to the scars on his own arms, chest and shoulders.

Anderson shook his head. 'No, Charley, I'm not brave. I didn't want these. I was flogged.'

'Flogged? What dat?' asked Charley.

'Ah, it means being beaten … hit with a whip … like a stick with, ah, reeds on it.'

'Did it hurt, Jackey-Jackey?' the child asked.

'Yair, Charley, it hurt very much. Twice I were hit fifty times across the back.' He cringed at the memory of the pain and the injustice.

'Who done dat to ya?' Charley asked.

Anderson spat the words, 'Mr Dangar,' then immediately turned and walked toward his beautiful Ipeta. As he looked at her the bitter thoughts of his floggings slowly drained from his mind, to be replaced by thoughts of how wonderful she looked at that moment, with her black, naked body wet and glistening in the morning sun, and those soft brown eyes that played on his heart strings. He looked at her and thought how much his forlorn, seemingly hopeless existence had changed since those floggings. How his life, which he had believed was over, was now filled with these overwhelming feelings of hope. He had not thought these feelings through to any logical conclusions – they remained only vague, yet potent, emotions – but they permeated his consciousness and filled his soul.

As the rest of the fishing party moved off toward the camp, Anderson again held back with Ipeta. Charley turned to call them as he climbed the bank, but Martha directed his head to the front and kept him moving forward, leaving Anderson and Ipeta standing knee-deep in the water.

Ipeta took Anderson by the shoulders and slowly turned him until his back was to her. She then gently ran her fingers along the vicious scars. He allowed her to do so for just a moment, before turning to face her again. She said something to him in her language, but he wasn't interested in working out what it was, such were his sensitivities on the matter. He was totally oblivious to the effect the discovery of his hated scars had just had on Ipeta and her people.

Anderson and Ipeta wandered slowly back along the western side of the creek until they reached the foot of the ridge nearly half a mile to the west of the huts. Ipeta took him by the hand and, pointing up the ridge, said, 'Yawurr thulu.'

Anderson had no idea what she had said, but he assumed she wanted to walk up the ridge for some reason. In no hurry to get back to his duties, he was happy to go wherever she wanted to take him.

They began to climb the side of the ridge, which varied from gently sloping to quite steep on the edge of the gullies which ran across it. The only sound was that of the multitude of different birds that inhabited the area.

'Thirrithurri,' she said, smiling, as they watched a small black and white bird flitting around on a nearby bush.

Anderson smiled back at her and mumbled an attempt at pronouncing what was apparently the bird's name. He was aware that she had recently become intent on speaking to him in her own language and trying to teach it to him. She did this despite the fact that she continued to try her best with English, which he took every opportunity to work on with her. However, his slightly lazy streak meant he wasn't particularly interested in learning her language, but his feelings for her were such that he always feigned some sort of interest whenever she tried to teach him, which she now continued to do.

'Gilaa,' she said, pointing to a group of pink and grey parrots which fed on grass seeds further up the slope.

'Gilaa,' he repeated, bringing that smile to her face which needed only the slightest provocation to appear. He smiled back at her as he mumbled, 'Yair, they're more bloody birds.'

She looked at him, a little confused, with her head tilted slightly to the side.

'Thigaraa,' he said, remembering that was the word for 'bird', though he wasn't the least bit inclined to learn the names of all the different types of birds, no matter how strong his passion for her.

She nodded and smiled again.

They wandered into one of the gullies which overlooked the creek. Here Ipeta stopped and began picking small red berries from a bush. When she had a good handful she took Anderson's hand. He loved it when she touched him. She held his hand out, palm upwards, slowly pouring about half of the berries into it.

'Yawurr,' she said.

'Berries,' he said.

She took a couple of them from her hand and held them between her fingers in front of his mouth. Anderson opened his mouth, smiling as she dropped them onto his tongue. He chewed them and swallowed.

'Mmmm, spicy.'

She tilted her head to the side again.

'Good,' he said, nodding, having no idea how to explain 'spicy' to her.

She then ate some of the berries herself, before attempting to put the last few into Anderson's mouth; but he held her hand and playfully bit her finger as she did so. She laughed and pushed him away. He grabbed her hand and held it to his chest.

CHAPTER SEVEN

I t was the middle of the morning and the Weraerai elders were sitting around the campfire, where they had been since first light. Most of the young men were out hunting with their limited weapons, and many of the women were also away, collecting a few of their dietary staples. The elder children had accompanied them, learning survival skills developed over thousands of years, including details on tracking, hunting and food sources. The youngest children stayed around the camp with the other women, who carried out maintenance work on the huts.

The elders remained deep in discussion of the problems confronting their clan, trying to reach a decision on how they could be resolved. The Weraerai lived by a complex system of law and lifestyle, established by the Great Spirit Father, Baiame. This system encompassed laws on marriage and relationships; property; crime and morality; diplomacy and trade with other tribes; and conservation of the clan's resources, including the protection of hatcheries and nurseries. It provided guidelines for the protection of the tribe's most valuable knowledge. To ensure the accuracy and reliability of such knowledge, it was kept secret and only passed on to those who would understand, appreciate and protect it. It was secret men's business and secret women's business. The system of law also taught disciplines of mind, body and soul, and respect for all life and the precedence of the greater good of the community and cosmos over individual need or desire.

The arrival of white men in their district a couple of years earlier, with their cattle, sheep, horses, guns and disregard for their system of law and lifestyle, had shattered the Weraerai. Their law required them to seek consent before they entered another clan's land, and to light a smoke fire to let the estate owners know they were there and wished to enter their land. To do otherwise was viewed as either extremely rude or an act of aggression.

The Weraerai believed in sharing everything with the other members of their clan, so consequently they found the greed of the white men, who had so many possessions, extremely offensive. Under their law, animals belonged to whichever clan's estate they wandered onto. While animals remained on a particular clan's land they belonged to them, but when they moved onto a neighbouring clan's land, ownership passed to the neighbouring clan. But the white man showed no respect for their law, and treated the land as if no-one had owned it until they claimed it for themselves. The white men treated the cattle and sheep as their own despite the fact they were on Weraerai land.

Now the Weraerai desperately sought a solution to the conflict which this behaviour had caused, and the resultant mass destruction of their people. The focus of the elders' discussions now centred on issues vital to the survival of their people. They were trying to decide whether they should stay at the Myall Creek station or return to McIntyre's, where they had lived in safety for many months. Additionally, they were discussing how they should behave toward the white men, particularly those on the Myall Creek Station.

Joey had removed his prized tartan cap from his head and was fidgeting with it as he ventured, 'I think we will be safe if we stay here.'

Daddy thought for a moment before nodding. 'Yes, Hobbs is a good man, a good boss. He will protect us.'

'Eaton said we would be safe here, but Charlie doesn't treat our women like he should. Not like Eaton did,' King Sandy expressed with some concern.

As was their way, there was silence while the elders thought about each other's comments.

Joey then added, 'But Jackey-Jackey is good to us all, and his scars show he is a brave warrior.'

King Sandy hesitated briefly before observing thoughtfully, 'He must be brave, but they don't treat him like he's a brave warrior.'

'Yes, but he and Charlie don't like each other,' replied Joey.

The others nodded, then the discussion continued on to the matter of the whites' use of the women. Like many indigenous cultures across the world, the Aborigines did not associate sexual intercourse with pregnancy, and they had a different attitude to sexual relationships to that being taught by Christian missionaries like the Reverend Threlkeld, in some of the less remote districts to the south. For the Weraerai, there were occasions when, if a man's wife consented, she may be lent to a friendly visitor who didn't have a wife. This was a practice, though, which had rapidly become commonplace with the whites due to the Weraerai's parlous situation and their necessity to trade the women's sexual favours for the clan's protection. The Weraerai were well aware of the widespread practice of the whites abducting and raping Aboriginal women and the conflicts that practice had caused. They wished to ensure their clan did not become the target of such a dire practice. The women's favours were the only thing the Weraerai clan had which the whites wanted. The whites had already seized their land, and the clan were desperate to ensure the same did not happen to their women.

The elders discussed their concern about Kilmeister, who seemed rather inclined to ignore the correct customs in seeking consent before taking a young woman.

Old Daddy defended the stockman's behaviour from King Sandy's criticisms, though. 'It is just that he doesn't fully understand our ways yet,' said the white-haired old man.

But King Sandy pushed his point. 'He should understand our ways by now. He's very friendly when he wants something but his behaviour toward our people worries me.'

The discussion continued, and the issue of whether their safety might be further assured if Hobbs had a woman was debated at some length. From there the topics began to meander like the creek next to which they sat.

After the men returned from hunting, Ipeta's husband, a man of middle age, was called to join them. He did as requested and sat in the dirt beside the elders. He listened intently to them before expressing his views. The dialogue continued beside the dying embers of the fire. The last remnants of smoke drifted into the late autumn sky, where a brown eagle circled soundlessly.

CHAPTER EIGHT

Hobbs and the stockmen had been away since early morning, and it was now past midday. George Anderson worked alone in the stockmen's hut making shelves to more easily store his various foodstuffs and cooking utensils. Amidst the banging of his hammer, he thought he heard a faint knock at the door. He put down his hammer, walked across and opened it. Before him stood the woman who had occupied his every waking thought for the two weeks since he had seen her naked and dripping wet on that first morning.

'Hallo, Jackey-Jackey.' Ipeta smiled.

Anderson was taken a little by surprise at her coming to his hut and, although delighted to see her, was unsure how to react. He stepped back and motioned for her to come in.

'Hallo, Ipeta,' he said, smiling. She entered the hut and he closed the door behind her. 'It's good you came to see me, but why you come here?' he asked, his words accompanied by the hand gestures which had become a natural part of his communication with her.

She looked at him quizzically, and as she did so he thought how out of place she looked in the hut. Primitive and all as it was, it was a white man's hut and a symbol of the British Empire, of a white man's civilization. She was part of a culture he knew not how old, but incalculably older than his and so dramatically different. He looked at her standing silently before him, black, beautiful and naked. Her nakedness was something he had had a great deal of difficulty getting used to, although outside, amid the nakedness of her own people, under the trees, by the creek, it seemed almost natural, and he was less stirred by it recently than he had been when he first saw her. Here, however, in a white man's hut, *his* hut, alone with him, there was nothing natural about her nakedness, it was simply, purely erotic – more erotic than anything George Anderson had ever experienced. He broke the brief silence.

'Ipeta, what do you want?' he asked gently.

'Jackey-Jackey maliyaa Ipeta?' she uttered slowly.

'Yes, I'm your friend.' Anderson nodded.

'Jackey-Jackey wantem Ipeta?'

His heart leapt at the possibility. His whole body craved her, but he wasn't sure of her meaning so he asked again. 'Sorry, Ipeta, I don't understand.'

'Murri —— '

'Your people – yes, go on.'

'Murri say Jackey-Jackey wantem Ipeta. Ipeta comem to Jackey-Jackey.'

A wave of pure passion swept over him. 'Oh yes, Jackey-Jackey wants Ipeta, oh so much.' He hesitated. 'But not now.' *Not like this,* he thought, *not in the cold light of day.* He wanted her so badly he ached for her, but he felt he couldn't have her. It would make him no better than Kilmeister, using the blacks. His whole body burnt for her. Maybe at night in the darkness, in the heat of the fire and excitement of the music and dancing, but not now; not like this.

She moved closer to him, so close her naked breasts brushed the front of his shirt. She looked up into his eyes, took his hand and smiled her smile at him, softly, sensually, and like a leaf on an autumn breeze, his resistance blew away. He took her, held her to him, felt the

bliss of her mouth beneath his lips and the wonders of her woman-
hood flowed over him.

* * *

He lay beside her on his narrow little bed, his passion satisfied. He
held her. He held her more tightly than he could remember ever
holding anyone or anything. He lay there, holding her to his chest
and looking up at the bark and sapling roof above him. He lay there
remembering. He remembered the misery and hopelessness of his
life since he had first been arrested and dragged off to face the horrors of Newgate Prison, before being thrown into that overcrowded
prison hulk on the edge of the Thames. He remembered being forced
in chains into the bowels of the convict ship and setting sail from
the shores of the motherland 'for the term of his natural life'. He
remembered that ship so well; the smell of human excrement, sweat
and suffering came so strongly to him now that he rubbed his nose
unconsciously. He remembered the cramped conditions, the men
copulating in the night, the suffering, the floggings; and he remembered the clanking of chains and the endless arguing, fighting and
bullying. He remembered just hoping it would all stop, hoping his
life would end and make it all stop; but it didn't stop, it just went on
interminably, month after month.

He remembered, when he finally arrived in New South Wales,
being assigned to Henry Dangar, who continually mistreated him
and had him flogged unjustly for trivial offences. He remembered the
smug look on Dangar's face as he stood watching as he was flogged.
He remembered the agony of that lash, and the deep, deep misery and
hopelessness which pervaded his thoughts. He remembered believing
he would never again experience a moment of happiness in his life.
He looked down at Ipeta, at his ebony angel lying on his chest, and
wondered how he had ever come to such joy. He rolled toward her,
held her even more tightly, and he sobbed and sobbed.

CHAPTER NINE

Thursday 7 June 1838.

William Hobbs was saddling his horse early in the morning in preparation for his ride to Dangar's lower station some sixty miles down river to the north-west. He was to check on the progress of Burrowes and Charles Reid, a ticket-of-leave convict stockman who had recently arrived at the station with a mob of cattle. Hobbs had sent the pair of them off two days earlier to take the cattle to the lower station.

As he slung his pack across the back of the horse, his now almost constant shadow appeared beside him.

'Good morning, Charley. How are you, young chap?'

'I good. Midder Boss, you goem away now?'

'Yair, but as I told you yesterday, I won't be away long. I have to go to see how Andy's going with those cattle.'

'How longem you go?'

'About a week, Charley. That's seven days.'

'I no like ya goem, Midder Boss. I miss ya.'

'I'll miss you too, my little friend, but I'll see you when I get back.'

The boy put his arms up to Hobbs, and the superintendent bent down and picked up the child, who hugged him tightly around the neck.

'Come on, Charley, I'd better be going to say goodbye to the others.' Hobbs carried the boy for a few strides before allowing him to jump to the ground beside him. He took his hand and together they strolled over to the Weraerai camp, where Hobbs was farewelled by all.

As he returned to his horse, Kilmeister emerged from the hut. 'Are you all set to go then, Mr Hobbs?'

'Yair, certainly am, Charlie. Now, I expect you chaps here to keep up your duties; and don't be forgetting about moving that mob on the other side of the creek. That'll have to be in the next day or two – no later.'

'It'll be fine, sir. You know I'll look after everythin',' Kilmeister assured him.

Anderson appeared, axe in hand, from around the side of the hut, where he had been chopping wood. He usually didn't like it when Hobbs went away, as Kilmeister bullied him less when Hobbs was around, but on this occasion he had been looking forward to the boss leaving so he could spend more unfettered time with Ipeta.

'Bye, Mr 'obbs,' he called as Hobbs mounted his horse.

'Bye, George. You keep up your duties now.'

'Yes, Mr 'obbs.'

Hobbs turned his mount and trotted off along the creek. Several of the young boys, including Charley, Johnny and Jimmy, ran alongside, waving and yelling their goodbyes.

* * *

That evening, Andrew Burrowes and Charles Reid arrived with their cattle at Bell's station, about thirty-five miles downriver from

Dangar's. John Russell, the station overseer, was a thirty-three-year-old former convict who had been transported for seven years in 1827 for stealing a harness.

'Top of the evenin' to you, John,' called Burrowes as Russell emerged from the hut. 'And how would ye be?'

'Good, Andy. Just movin' that mob downriver, are ya?'

'Aye, down to our lower station. Will it be all right to yard them here for the night?' asked Burrowes.

'Sure, I'll just get one of the chaps to give ya a hand,' offered Russell, turning back to the open doorway behind him.

A tall young man soon emerged from the hut. He was Edward Foley, a twenty-eight-year-old Irish convict stockman transported for life in 1832 for "assaulting a dwelling", in a futile protest against an English landlord. He was assigned to the Fleming family on the Hawkesbury but was now with young John Fleming at his Mungie Bundie property further down the river.

'Ed here will give ya a hand,' called Russell before re-entering the hut.

Once Burrowes, Reid and Foley had the cattle securely yarded, the three men headed into the stockmen's hut. On entering the hut, Burrowes was quite taken aback. He had expected to see only Russell and the hutkeeper, John Deady, another Irish convict. Instead he found the small hut crowded with stockmen who were all heavily armed with muskets and pistols. They were: George Palliser, a twenty-eight-year-old former convict, now head stockmen at Bell's Noogera Creek property some thirty miles away; William Hawkins, a twenty-nine-year-old convict on a ticket-of-leave, and head stockmen at Robert Lethbridge's Noogera Creek station; Charles Telluse, a thirty-year-old convict stockman assigned to James Glennie (one of Henry Dangar's dinner guests in the Hunter Valley) at his Gineroi station; John 'Black' Johnstone, a twenty-eight-year-old English-born negro, a former convict and now stockman at the Coxes' Durra Durra run about twenty five miles south of Bells'; and James Parry, a twenty-two-year-old Irish convict and hutkeeper at Daniel Eaton's Biniguy run about seven miles downstream. Only a few of them were known to Burrowes, and less to Reid, as they were from stations right across Big River country.

The host overseer, John Russell, was cleaning a sword while seated at the large table in the middle of the room. Russell was a thickset, rough-hewn type, with a body that appeared to have been hacked from an iron bark tree, and a jagged, bristly head lodged carelessly on top. His shirt sleeves were rolled to the elbow, revealing burly forearms covered in thick black hair. He looked up and motioned toward Burrowes and Reid as they entered.

'These chaps are Burrowes and Reid; they're Dangar's men from up river.'

Russell did not bother to introduce those that Burrowes and Reid didn't already know, and the group only briefly interrupted their conversation to acknowledge the new arrivals before Telluse asked Russell, 'So, John, how many of us do ya think we'll get together this time?'

'As many as we can. Probably eleven or twelve, maybe a couple more.

'Jem Lamb should be able to join us, but we'll know more about numbers when Fleming gets here, tonight or tomorrow mornin',' Russell replied.

'Well, do ya think that'll be enough?' asked Telluse.

'Should be, but these damn blacks can be a treacherous lot; and as Nunn showed us, the more men we have, the better,' added Russell.

'Any idea where we'll find some blacks this time?' inquired Palliser. 'There aren't too many of them left round here.'

'There's still plenty around,' Russell assured him. 'We ain't got rid of all of them yet. I'm not sure exactly where we'll find 'em but we normally manage to find some. Fleming has just been out after a mob of 'em, so he should have some idea.'

'Fleming seems to spend considerable time chasin' blacks, don't he?' Parry suggested.

'My oath he does, Jem. I reckon Fleming's killed even more blacks than me,' replied Russell. 'Ya know what these rich young squatters are like, though. They've got more bleedin' time on their hands than we workin' men.'

Burrowes and Reid listened in silence, chewing on a meal of meat and bread which Deady had provided them, as the conversation turned to how good the lives of the wealthy squatters were and how tough things were for them. By the time Dangar's men had finished their meal, the stockmen were trying to outdo each other with horror stories of their days in chain gangs, on prison ships and in various gaols. Burrowes had his own stories but he didn't share them as the others talked of brutal, sadistic gaolers and violently disturbed convicts. They told tales of the motherland, of bear baiting and cock fighting, and they told of black massacres.

Finally there was a break in the conversation which allowed Parry to ask, 'John, what if we can't find any blacks?'

'Bit anxious, are ya, lad? Don't worry, son, we'll find some. It might take a day or two but we'll find them,' Russell assured him.

There was a moment of silence, before Russell turned to Burrowes and Reid standing quietly in the corner. 'What about you blokes – any blacks up your way?'

Burrowes answered without thinking. 'Aye, there's a mob of about forty of them camped at the Myall Creek station.' His words hung in the air momentarily as every man in the room turned to look at him. He immediately wished he could take those words back; but he couldn't, so he fumblingly tried to recover the situation. 'Aye, but they've been there for weeks, so they couldn't possibly have caused any problems down this way. And they're really quiet and peaceful. They're livin' right next to our huts and not causin' any problems.'

'Hmmm, about forty, ya say, eh?' Russell asked as he casually scratched his thick black four-day growth.

'Aye, about that,' Burrowes replied hesitantly.

'Yair, well I think we might go and check on them anyway.'

'But they're peaceful and not doin' any harm,' Burrowes again assured him.

'Not yet they're not, but they're bleedin' treacherous vermin,' Russell continued.

Burrowes tried again. 'This mob are domesticated, though.'

Russell ignored the comment. 'And who's down on your station now, anyway?' he asked, getting up from the table and walking across to the fireplace, where Foley and Parry stood.

'Charlie Kilmeister and Anderson, the hutkeeper,' Burrowes replied.

'Anderson. He's the new chum, ain't he?'

'Aye.'

'What about ya boss, Hobbs, ain't he there?' Russell continued his inquiries as he moved away from the fire and around the table toward Dangar's men. Although Russell was not a tall man, his powerful build made him an imposing figure. He was the district's renowned hard man, and Burrowes fidgeted nervously with his plate in the face of his interrogation.

'He'll be followin' us down river directly. He'll be a day or two behind us.'

'Hmmm. These blacks are domesticated, ya say?' Russell persisted.

'Aye, real domesticated like, and unarmed. They be no trouble at all,' Burrowes insisted. 'They haven't even got many adult males amongst 'em. They're mainly women and wee ones, and a few old men.'

Reid looked at Burrowes and shook his head slightly. He knew Burrowes was trying to make up for what he had let slip, but he had a horrible feeling that Burrowes was now only making it worse for the Weraerai clan that he sought to protect.

'Anyway, it's about time we all got some sleep; we've got a big day tomorrow, ain't we lads?' Russell announced. 'We're goin' a huntin' blacks.'

The announcement was met with mirthful agreement from the others in the hut.

As the men sorted out their sleeping places on the floor, Burrowes and Reid noticed Deady and one of the stockmen disappear together into the tiny ante room at the end of the hut in which there was only one bed.

Burrowes nudged Reid and whispered, 'Looks like them lads need a nice warm gin.'

'They wouldn't know what to do with one,' Reid responded, before adding, 'There's almost as much of that goes on 'round here as there was in gaol.'

'Aye, to be sure; but give me a nice warm gin any day.'

'Listen, Andy, after what's been said tonight, I think it could be a while afore you have a nice warm gin again.'

'Nah.' Burrowes hesitated for a moment before trying to reassure both Reid and himself. 'It'll be all right. Kilmeister will look after 'em.'

CHAPTER TEN

Friday 8 June 1838.

B urrowes sat astride his horse outside the cattle yard as Reid rode in and drove the cattle out. Deady watched from the door of the hut as several of the stockmen filed past him and wandered off in various directions to round up their hobbled horses.

'See you chaps later,' Burrowes called. 'Thanks for puttin' us up.'

'No bother. Looks like rain, though,' Deady observed.

Burrowes looked skyward and saw dark clouds rapidly closing in from the south. 'Aye, to be sure; we'd better get moving. Come on, Charlie.'

Charles Reid trotted his mount up to join Burrowes. 'When are that lot setting off after the blacks?' he asked as they settled in behind the cattle.

'Soon, but it seems they're going to wait a wee while for John Fleming.'

'I hope they don't go up to Myall Creek.'

'Aye, so do I.'

* * *

The rain was falling steadily late in the afternoon as the two stock-men neared John Fleming's Mungie Bundie station. Quite suddenly their cattle scattered in front of them as a lone horseman came riding through the middle of the beasts. Horse and rider made an eerie sight in the dull afternoon light, with the steam rising from the sweating animal into the cold, wet air, shrouding both the rider and his mount in a cloudy grey haze.

As the rider, a tall young man wearing a long overcoat, cantered his mount up to them, Burrowes noticed a sword slung from his belt and a carbine in his saddle.

The rider jerked his mount to a halt beside them. 'Have you chaps been at Bell's?' he asked urgently.

'Aye, we were there overnight,' Burrowes answered.

'Are there a group of stockmen there?'

'Aye, they were just roundin' up their horses when we left this mornin', but they were goin' to be waitin' around for a wee while.'

'Well, maybe this rain has held 'em up. I've just been off chasing blacks and this little mare of mine is just about knocked up, so I hope they've got a fresh horse down there.' And with that he kicked his exhausted looking mount into a canter and disappeared off along the track toward Bell's.

Reid turned to Burrowes. 'Who was that?'

'Don't know for sure, but at a guess I'd say that was Mr John Fleming.'

* * *

George Anderson stood at the door of the hut watching the dark clouds drifting across the sky. He rubbed his back against the rough door frame, scratching an itch that occurred regularly as a result of a small part of his scarring that had remained obstinately slow to heal completely. As the clouds closed in, the rain began to tumble down, and Anderson watched as various members of the Weraerai clan ducked into their shelters to avoid a drenching. He called out to attract their attention and waved to invite them into his hut which, despite a few leaks, provided more solid shelter than the Weraerai's temporary huts. Ipeta, Sandy, Martha and Charley were already in the hut with Davey and Billy. Several others now came to join them, including Bobby, one of the young men of the clan. With him were his three-year-old daughter and his wife, who carried their young baby in her arms.

'Tanks, Jackey-Jackey,' said a smiling Bobby.

'That's all right,' replied Anderson, placing a welcoming hand on his shoulder.

Kilmeister was in Hobbs' hut, where he had spent a lot of time since the superintendent left for the lower station. While he remained there, Anderson was comfortable having Ipeta in the stockmen's hut with him – something he wouldn't do when Kilmeister was around.

The rain increased and the hut gradually became more crowded as the Weraerai came in, pleased to make the most of the opportunity to see inside the white man's hut, which some of them had not yet had the chance to do.

'Davey, tell some of 'em to go over to 'obbs' hut with Kilmeister. He's got more room in there,' requested Anderson, gently shaking his head at the crowd that was now crushing into the hut.

'Yair, boss,' replied Davey, immediately instructing the last group of arrivals, who then disappeared out the door and over to the superintendent's hut.

The crush was immediately relieved, but a few minutes later the Weraerai returned and another group left to inspect Hobbs' hut. Shortly afterwards, the process was repeated.

'Davey, what are they doin'? asked Anderson, totally bemused.

'Nuthin' boss, dey lookem at both dem huts.'

'Oh, right.' Anderson smiled, realising the Weraerai were far more interested in seeing the white men's huts than staying out of the rain.

'Dey just see which one dey like best, boss.'

'Which one do you like best, Davey?'

'Mr 'obbs' hut, boss. It big.'

'Yair, ain't it?'

'Plenty room sharem wit ma family, boss. Sharem wit me brudders.'

'You're a bit different to us, Davey. You blackfellas share everything.'

'Dat right, boss. You whitefellas no sharem nuffin'. You just take tings; tings no belongem ya.'

'Yair, but I took something that weren't mine once and I got sent 'ere for life.'

'Mmmm.' Davey nodded. There was a brief silence between the pair before he added, 'You likem 'ere, boss?'

Anderson hesitated, looked at Ipeta, thought for a moment and answered, 'Davey, I hated every minute I been in this bleedin' colony until the last few weeks.'

He was about to continue but hesitated again, scratching his closely cropped beard. He became lost in his thoughts. He didn't know how to explain it; and even if he could, he was quite sure Davey wouldn't understand anyway. He recognised fully the deep joy Ipeta had brought to his lonely, wretched existence. He realised, though, that there was something more to this strange state of calm and happiness in which he currently found himself. It had something to do with the fact that since he had been arrested he had been treated like filth by everyone he came in contact with – police, gaolers and squatters alike. Even other convicts harassed and taunted him. He was the new chum, the lowly hutkeeper who never quite fitted in.

Somehow, though, amongst the Weraerai he was treated with respect, particularly since they had seen the scars on his back. He even had his own special name, 'Jackey-Jackey', of which he had become rather proud. He was now somebody, not just a piece of dirt. He didn't understand it fully, he just knew it made him feel good about himself; and that, combined with the affection of the lovely, gentle Ipeta, made him happier than he would ever have thought possible. He was very aware, though, that he did not really understand how she felt about him. She showered her affection upon him but he didn't know why. He wasn't sure to what extent it was due to the protection he and the others on the station offered to her people. He knew that was the reason the other gins slept with the whites; but they showed them no affection. He looked down at her as she sat at the table beside where he stood. There was something special between them, he was sure of it. A wave of pure joy engulfed him. He reached down to Ipeta's hand resting on the wooden table in front of her. She looked up at him as he gently squeezed it. He smiled, mouthed 'thank you', then walked out of the hut and stood in the rain.

Ipeta went to the door, looked out at him and smiled, shaking her head slowly. George Anderson stood – arms outstretched, palms upturned – staring up at the slate grey sky above, oblivious to the bitter winter rain biting at his skin. He murmured skywards, 'Thank you.'

CHAPTER ELEVEN

Saturday 9 June 1838.

William Mace, ticket-of-leave overseer of Dight's station, and John Bates, his convict hutkeeper, arrived at Dr Newton's station at the junction of Myall Creek and the Big River early in the morning. They rode up to the stockmen's hut, where they were greeted by Thomas Foster, Newton's superintendent. Foster was only a few years older than his friend William Hobbs, but there were premature streaks of grey in both his hair and his full beard.

'Good mornin', Mr Foster.'

'Good morning, Bill, John.'

'Pleased to see some more decent rain. We certainly need it,' remarked Mace.

'Yair, and looks like there's still some more around. Nice to see you chaps, anyway. Come in, come in,' Foster urged.

Mace and Bates dismounted and followed Foster into the hut, where the convict hutkeeper Robert Sexton quickly set about preparing a cup of tea for the guests.

'Good to see you again, Bill. John, how are ya, my old mate?' Sexton shook Bates' hand vigorously. He was using the word 'old' in both its senses, for at forty-five, John Bates was the oldest European in the Big River district. He had been transported for fourteen years, leaving behind in England a wife and seven children. He possessed a father's kindness and was slightly out of place in a young man's frontier. Sexton was one of his few friends, as they shared the bond of being hutkeepers.

The two friends caught up briefly before Foster interjected. 'And what brings you two across the river this morning? Please, sit down,' he invited.

The visitors sat at the table as Mace replied. 'Well, Mr Hobbs dropped into our station a couple of days back and he mentioned there were a mob of blacks camped up at his place. I asked him if I might be able to borrow three or four of them for a couple of days to help out with cuttin' some bark for us; and knowin' ya needed some cut yerself, I thought ya might wanna come up with me to fetch them.'

'Yes, my word, that would be rather handy, but,' Foster hesitated, 'what did Mr Hobbs say the blacks were like?'

'He said they're real peaceful. It's that mob that have been round here for ages, stayin' at McIntyre's and Wiseman's.'

'Oh, right. Yair, I've heard about them but I've never seen them. Actually, I've never seen any blacks around, but it'd certainly be helpful if they could cut some bark for us. Was it all right with Mr Hobbs if we borrowed them?' asked Foster.

'He said it was fine with him and to just go up and see Kilmeister and he'd organise the blacks,' Mace answered, before adding, 'Look, Mr Foster, they shan't be no trouble. Mr Hobbs says they're a really quiet mob, and I saw them a few times myself when they were at McIntyre's, and they had no trouble with them there.'

'Well, if you're sure, we could certainly do with a hand with that bark. All right, I'll just get organised and get my horse saddled while you have your cup of tea.'

'Fine, Mr Foster, take ya time, no rush.'

* * *

About twenty minutes later, William Mace and Thomas Foster were ready to set off for the Myall Creek station.

'We'll have to stay up there overnight, of course, Sexton, so we'll be back tomorrow afternoon sometime,' advised Foster.

'Will it be all right if I stay here a while to catch up with Sexton?' Bates asked Mace.

'Yair, of course,' came the reply.

The rain had started falling again as Foster and Mace turned and rode away from the huts of Dr Newton's station, while a few miles to the north a group of convict stockmen now led by the wealthy young squatter John Fleming were riding toward Newton's. Their number had now increased to ten from the seven that had stayed the Thursday night at Bell's station.

Apart from Fleming, they had now been joined by James Lamb, assigned convict stockman from Cobb's station, just across the river from Bell's; and John Blake, an Irish convict stockman from James Glennie's station, where the group had spent the previous night. They rode through the rain and crossed Myall Creek to the outskirts of Newton's property, with Fleming and Russell riding at the head.

The rain had eased again by late morning, when they galloped up to the gate adjacent to the Newton station huts, from which Robert Sexton and John Bates quickly emerged.

'Good mornin',' called Sexton, somewhat surprised by the number and manner of the horsemen.

'You fellas know if there are any blacks round here?' Russell inquired brusquely.

'No, none around here,' returned Sexton.

'Ya sure?' snapped Russell as his excited mount twisted from side to side.

'Yair, there's none at all,' Sexton insisted.

'Could you fetch me a light for my pipe?' Fleming cut in, pulling a pipe from the pocket of his overcoat.

'Yes, sir,' replied Sexton, returning to the hut.

'Now, what about you?' Fleming motioned for Bates to come over to where he remained mounted. 'Do you know if there are any blacks around here?'

'I don't know of any, sir,' Bates replied coolly as he walked across to the young squatter.

'Are you sure about that?' Fleming persisted.

'Sir, there's none that I know of.'

'We were told there were a mob of them around here,' Russell continued.

Bates held his ground. 'Not here, that I know.'

Sexton returned with a light from the fire and handed it to Fleming, who lit his pipe. Smoke immediately wafted around him as an anxious pair of eyes watched from between the rails of the stockyard. They belonged to young Johnny Murphy, a fourteen-year-old lad in the care of Dr Newton, who was staying at the station. Johnny had never seen such a large, intimidating group of stockmen. All were heavily armed with pistols and short muskets, and a couple carried swords. To the boy, they looked like policeman. Johnny also noticed that one had several pairs of handcuffs slung from the front of his saddle, while another rode a big, beautiful black horse; though it, like the other horses, was mud-splattered and soaking wet with sweat and rain. Johnny watched and listened as the questioning of Bates and Sexton continued.

'We heard there were a few blacks up 'ere cuttin' bark,' probed Russell astride his striking black mount.

'Not here there ain't,' insisted Sexton, quite incredulous that these men could already know of Foster and Mace's intention to bring some bark cutters down from Myall Creek.

'We've heard there's a mob up at Dangar's,' Fleming continued.

'Yair, well I understand there's some up there, sir,' conceded Sexton.

Fleming turned to Russell. 'Well, we can head up there tomorrow, but let's get up to Hall's first.'

And with that, he knocked his pipe against the side of his saddle, turned his mount and led the stockmen away.

* * *

It was mid-afternoon when Foster and Mace arrived at the Myall Creek station. Ipeta and Martha were standing with young Charley near the door of the stockmen's hut when they rode up. They immediately stepped back inside the door as the strangers approached.

'Jackey-Jackey, men,' blurted young Charley excitedly.

'Thanks, Charley,' replied Anderson, moving to the door.

'Good day, George. Is Charlie Kilmeister around?' Foster asked as he drew his mount up to the front of the hut.

'Hallo, Mr Foster. Yair, he's just in the other hut,' Anderson replied before asking, 'What brings you up this way?'

'Mr Hobbs dropped into Mace here's station a couple of days back and informed him you had some blacks about the place. He said we could borrow a few for a couple of days to assist in cutting some bark for us.'

Anderson didn't know Mace but nodded to him before looking down at young Charley, who was standing beside him, leaning against his leg. 'Go get Charlie, would ya?' he asked the boy.

Charley ran across to Hobbs' hut just as Kilmeister appeared in the doorway. He exchanged greetings and pleasantries with the visitors before inviting them into the stockmen's hut.

Foster and Mace dismounted and followed Kilmeister into the hut while Anderson, still standing at the door, motioned to Ipeta, Martha and Sandy to leave. They immediately did so, squeezing past Foster and Mace as they entered. The two white men were slightly taken aback by the appearance and proximity of the blacks.

Noticing their reaction, Kilmeister smiled. 'Don't ya be worryin' about them, they're harmless.'

'Well, those gins certainly look harmless; bloody nice, in fact,' responded Mace. 'But I'm not too sure about that big fella.'

'That's Sandy. He's a bit scary lookin', all right.' Kilmeister laughed. 'But he ain't no bother once ya get to know him.'

'Well, I'm pleased to hear that,' chimed in Foster, 'because the blacks are the reason we've come up here.'

'Really? Hey, Anderson, about time ya got that fire started, ain't it? Mr Foster and Bill are cold and wet.'

'That's what I were just gonna do,' Anderson replied, closing the door and walking over to the fireplace. He looked at Kilmeister, who had his back to him, and shook his head before proceeding to light the fire.

Kilmeister continued his discussion with the visitors. 'Sorry, Mr Foster. Go on about why you're here.'

As Foster explained to Kilmeister the purpose of their visit, Anderson crouched over the fireplace feeding some kindling and finely split logs into the low flames. The rain, although much needed, had presented Anderson with the problem of keeping the wood dry. He had brought extra wood inside but it occupied space in the small hut, which was already overcrowded with three low beds, the table and bench seats in the middle of the room, the food stores, the fireplace and Anderson's cooking bench. Trying to find a place to stack some firewood to keep it dry was difficult, especially given the occasionally leaky roof.

As the flames grew, however, Anderson's thoughts were not focused on such trivial housekeeping matters as firewood. They switched between curiosity about Foster and Mace's request, and annoyance at the torments of Kilmeister, who was now asking Foster about the number of boys he would need for the bark cutting.

'Only three, maybe four, of their older boys. We won't be in need of any men,' Foster replied.

'Well, this mob ain't got many men anyway, but there are quite a few boys, so it shan't be no bother. As soon as ya dry off a bit, we'll go out and talk to the blacks about it.'

'Good. Thanks, Charlie,' replied Foster, getting up from the table and going across to the fire which was now burning strongly.

'So these blacks ain't no trouble, eh?' asked Mace.

'Nah, none at all. It's good havin' them round the place. They liven things up a bit, ya know?' said Kilmeister.

'I'd be bloody sure they would. A nice gin would be good on these cold nights, too, eh?' remarked Mace.

Kilmeister laughed. 'My oath.'

'I wouldn't mind those two that just left. I'd fancy either of them, but that young one was real good lookin',' Mace continued.

'That's Anderson's whore,' taunted Kilmeister.

'Shut ya hole, Kilmeister,' Anderson muttered through gritted teeth as he fed larger logs onto the fire. The animosity between the two had grown since Anderson's relationship with Ipeta had developed, and Hobbs' absence had only intensified it.

'Oh, lucky George, eh!' Mace smiled.

'Nah, she might be good lookin' but she's a whore,' spat Kilmeister.

Anderson's face reddened with rage and his fists clenched as he stood up, but he managed to control himself, remembering Foster's presence. Hitting Kilmeister in front of a superintendent could land him in trouble yet again, so instead he spat back, 'Well, if she's a whore, how come she wouldn't 'ave you when ya kept trying to get 'er?'

Kilmeister glared at the young hutkeeper. 'I wouldn't touch that whore.'

'Nah, she wouldn't touch you.'

'Shut yer bleedin' hole, ya maggot,' snapped Kilmeister, moving toward Anderson, 'or I'll —— '

'All right, all right. Calm down, you two,' Foster intervened.

The hut became silent for a moment as Kilmeister gathered himself. He, too, was very aware of not crossing the line in front of Foster, so he changed the subject instantly.

'Mr Foster, why don't ya take that coat off and leave it in front of the fire? You can borrow Mr Hobbs' old coat while we go and see the blacks.'

'Yes, that'd be good. Thanks.'

Foster slipped off his coat before following Kilmeister out the door and across to Hobbs' hut. When they entered, Foster was a little taken aback to see two gins sitting at the table. One was breast-feeding a small baby while a young girl, about four years old, stood by her side.

She looked up as Kilmeister and Foster entered and gave the stranger a hesitant half-smile. Kilmeister ignored their presence, while Foster, though quite surprised to see them in Hobbs' hut, said nothing about them as he accepted the coat the stockman handed him.

'Thanks.'

'Come on, Mr Foster, we'll go and have a talk to the blacks, then eat with them.'

They returned to the stockmen's hut just long enough for Kilmeister to poke his head in the door and say to Mace, 'Come on, Bill, we're goin' to see the blacks.' Then, turning to Anderson, he asked, 'Where's Davey and Billy?'

Anderson glared at him and shrugged. 'Dunno.'

Kilmeister, however, quickly spotted the young black stockmen at the nearby stockyards and called them over.

It was late in the afternoon as they walked across to the Weraerai camp. The fire in the middle of the camp burnt strongly in the fading light, casting what was to Foster a strange orange glow over the blacks sitting around it. The elders stood as the group approached, and Foster was immediately taken by the size of them, particularly the massive old man, Daddy. He was still taking in the size of the man when he heard Kilmeister speak.

'Daddy, this boss man.' The giant thrust out his hand, grabbed Foster's and shook it as it had never before been shaken. Kilmeister then continued. 'King Sandy, Joey, this boss man.' They also shook the superintendent's hand strongly, but not with quite the same enthusiasm as Daddy. Kilmeister introduced Mace then they all took their places around the warming flames of the Weraerai fire.

'Davey, tell them that Mr Foster and Mace have stations down on the Big River and they'll be wanting three or four young fellas to go with them to cut some bark for a few days.'

As Davey passed on Kilmeister's message, looks of concern became etched into the elders' faces, and quite an intense conversation started amongst them.

'What's the problem, Davey?' asked Kilmeister.

'Dey worry 'bout lettin' young fellas go wifout' em, boss.'

'Tell them not to worry about that. Mr Foster will look after 'em, won't ya, Mr Foster?' Kilmeister said reassuringly.

'Yes, yes, of course,' Foster responded quickly, a little surprised that the blacks' nervousness seemed to exceed his own.

Kilmeister turned back to Davey. 'See? Tell them they'll be all right. Mr Foster's a good man. Tell them,' he insisted.

Davey passed the assurances on to the elders, who, after further concerned discussion interspersed with prompting from Davey and Kilmeister, finally nodded and smiled.

'Good, good,' Kilmeister said, also nodding.

By the time George Anderson emerged from the hut to stroll across and join the others, the setting sun had cast a stunning rainbow against the eerie light of the evening sky. The rainbow curved from high in the darkening sky to just beyond the ridge to the west, like a spectacular heavenly herald come to earth. Anderson paused to absorb its beauty; as he did, he tried to recall the old sailors' dictum about a rainbow at night which he had heard as a child. It was either good news or an ominous warning. He couldn't recall which, so he put it from his mind and wandered over and joined the others around the Weraerai fire.

A meal of beef, fish, lizards, yams and damper was distributed around the group. Foster and Mace declared it the best food they'd had 'in ages'. They sat and ate and talked and laughed, unaware it was to be their last meal together, for twenty-four hours later Death would come to the Weraerai camp.

At that moment, Death, in the form of a young squatter and his gang, was some twelve miles away, across the Big River at a station on Bingara Creek owned by Fleming's grandfather, George Hall. There the resident convict stockman, James Oates, had been enlisted to join them. Commonly known as 'Hall's Jemmy', Oates had been transported for life in 1829, at the age of nineteen, for assault and robbery. The group remained overnight at Hall's station, their number having now grown to eleven.

CHAPTER TWELVE

Sunday 10 June 1838.

George Anderson strolled out into the cool, crisp winter morning. The rain clouds having finally cleared, the sun rose into a sapphire blue sky above the gently rolling hills to the east of the station. Anderson sauntered slowly across to the creek, bucket in hand, as part of his morning duties. As he walked, he looked toward the hut Ipeta shared with her husband, hoping she would come and join him at the creek to say her morning 'hallo'. She normally did so on the mornings she didn't stay with him in his hut, and although they only spent a few minutes together at such times, he felt it had recently become their special quiet time together alone, and he treasured it.

He walked in amongst the trees to the top of the creek bank, where he stood waiting patiently, looking through the trees to her hut. He only had to wait a few moments before she appeared, emerging with possum skins wrapped around her shoulders. She came to him through the dappled light of the leaf-filtered sun, the warmth from her smile enveloping him in spite of the cold morning air.

'Good morning, Ipeta.'

'Good morning, Jackey-Jackey.' Her pronunciation was almost perfect.

She stood before him and gave him her hand, which he took tenderly and raised to his face. She opened the palm of her hand and held his cheek briefly, before he slowly slid her hand across to his mouth. He kissed her fingers gently, oh so gently, just as she had taught him. Their eyes – eyes that connected worlds – never broke contact. He, the convict outcast from the most powerful empire on the planet, and she, the tribeswoman of its oldest civilization.

He wanted to know why she cared for him so.

'Ipeta, you're so good to me, so kind. Why are ya so good to me?'

She tilted her head slightly to the side, indicating to her lover she didn't understand. *How could she?* he thought.

'Me good?' she asked.

'Yes, ya good; ya so very good.' Anderson smiled. 'But why? Why are ya so good to me? Because we protect ya? Why?'

'Why?' Ipeta tilted her head again.

'How do I explain "why"?' the convict mumbled to himself in happy frustration.

Without further prompting, though, Ipeta took his hand and pressed it against his chest. 'Jackey-Jackey good man.'

Anderson smiled, knowing it was as much of an answer as he was ever likely to get; and as he looked into her deep brown eyes he realised it was probably the best answer he could ever get. He just hoped it was true.

While they stood there amongst the trees in the morning light, by the gently flowing waters of Myall Creek, he allowed himself to wonder if they would ever be together at a time when he was free from his convict servitude, and Ipeta free from the fear that suffocated her people's lives. The fact that Ipeta had a husband didn't enter his head. He stood there dreaming, savouring the cherished moments of their special time together, while twelve miles away, at Hall's station, Death was stirring.

* * *

After a leisurely breakfast and brief chat with Kilmeister and Anderson, Foster and Mace, accompanied by Kilmeister, walked outside to saddle their horses.

'Charlie, could you see if the blacks are ready to go?' asked Foster.

'Sure, Mr Foster, won't be a moment. Davey,' he called to the young translator, who quickly emerged from around the side of the hut and followed Kilmeister across to the Weraerai camp. They returned before Foster had finished saddling his horse.

'Ya don't mind takin' a few extras with ya, do ya, Mr Foster?'

'What do you mean?'

'Well, they're scared of whitefellas, Mr Foster, and the elders are a bit worried about lettin' just three or four of their young fellas go off by themselves with no-one to look after 'em.'

Foster was hesitant. 'How many want to come?'

Kilmeister turned and pointed across to where the elders stood with a group of the Weraerai men and older boys. The group in fact included most of the clan's adult men. 'That mob there, sir; not Daddy and Joey, but King Sandy and the others. About ten altogether.'

'That's too many. We don't need that many, and I don't propose setting off into the bush with a mob of blacks I don't know,' Foster explained.

'They shan't be no bother, sir. As ya seen last night, they're a real peaceful lot. And besides, sir, they've only got a couple of tomahawks to cut the bark with.'

Foster remained silent for a few moments while he finished saddling his horse. He then turned to Mace, who stood holding his mount a few metres away.

'What do you think, Bill?' Foster asked.

'Well, as you say, we don't need that many; but if Charlie thinks they'll be all right, they shouldn't be no trouble. They seemed friendly last night,' Mace replied.

'I'm not saying they're not friendly; they are perfectly friendly. It's just that … Oh, all right,' Foster relented.

Kilmeister immediately waved to the Weraerai group to come over, which they did.

'Davey, tell them it's all right, they can all go.'

Davey passed the message on and translated the reply from King Sandy. 'He say tanks, Charlie, and he askem if rest of mob be all right here.'

'Of course they'll be all right. I'll look after 'em,' Kilmeister reassured

them.

'Are they ready to go?' asked Foster.

Davey responded without hesitation. 'Yes, dey ready.'

'Good. Well, we'll go, then,' said Foster, mounting his horse.

As Foster sat astride his mount, young Charley hurried over and pulled his trouser leg. 'Charley come too, pleease.'

Foster looked down at the boy's smiling face. 'Hallo, Charley. No, I'm sorry, young chap, you can't; you're too young. Maybe another time, eh?'

George Anderson stood at the door of the hut, watching as the ten Weraerai tribesman said their goodbyes to their families. Those leaving included King Sandy and ten-year-old Jimmy, who now said goodbye to his best friend, Johnny. It was the first time the two ten-year-olds had been separated since either of them could remember. Martha and Sandy's friend Bobby was also going. He picked up his three-year-old daughter and held her high above his head. Holding her in one arm, he then put his other arm around his young wife and kissed the forehead of the baby son she held in her arms. As Anderson watched these tender scenes of family life, he was filled with envy.

It was mid-morning when Foster and Mace set off with their ten

Weraerai bark cutters striding along beside them. They left behind them two old men, Daddy and Joey; two young men, Sandy and Tommy; and thirty women, children and babies, including Ipeta, Martha, young Charley and Johnny.

At about the same time, Fleming's gang emerged from the stock-men's hut at Hall's station, armed with pistols, carbines and swords. They mounted and headed for Myall Creek.

* * *

Shortly after midday, Charles Kilmeister was out on the station performing his daily duties with Davey and Billy, while George Anderson remained at the hut. A shirtless Anderson was chopping firewood, his muscles wet with sweat as he expertly wielded the axe. Young Charley stood watching him while chattering away, as was his custom. Bobby's three-year-old daughter stood beside Charley, holding his hand and listening to every word the older boy said.

'You good at dat, Jackey-Jackey,' Charley observed as the axe split another piece of wood straight down the middle, 'just like my bubba.'

'"Bubaa"– that's "father", ain't it?' Ipeta had been making some progress despite Anderson's mental inertia.

'Dat right, Jackey-Jackey.' The boy beamed.

'I'm learnin' a bit, Charley,' the hutkeeper replied, before adding, 'I suppose I should be getting pretty good at chopping wood by now, though. I've been doin' it long enough.' Anderson looked up from his work to see Martha and Bobby's wife, who as always was holding her baby in her arms. The hutkeeper smiled. 'Hallo, Martha.'

'Hallo, Jackey-Jackey,' said Charley's young mother, returning Anderson's smile.

The children turned to their mothers, who spoke to them gently before Charley looked back at Anderson. 'We gotta getem sumfin' eat. Back soon, Jackey-Jackey.'

'Yair, I know ya will.' Anderson grinned.

* * *

It was mid-afternoon, and George Anderson was in the hut preparing supper for the stockmen's imminent return. Charley and his little friend, Bobby's daughter, sat at the table watching him again.

'Jackey-Jackey, Midder Boss back soon?' Charley asked.

'Probably be a few more days. You miss Mr 'obbs, do ya, Charley?'

'Yair, he my friend. Likem you, Jackey-Jackey.'

'Thanks, Charley.'

'I wish he were here,' the boy sighed. 'He good.'

'Yair, he is. About the nicest overseer a convict could have, really.'

'Convict? What dat?'

'You still don't understand that, do ya? Charlie, Andy and me – we're all convicts. But I suppose you can't understand it, because there's nothin' like it – like a gaol or anything – that your people 'ave.'

'Gaol? What dat?'

* * *

Five miles to the west, Death cantered beside Myall Creek.

* * *

By late afternoon, Foster and Mace, along with their ten Weraerai bark cutters, had arrived at Dr Newton's station, some sixteen miles due west of Dangar's. As they approached the huts they were met by a highly anxious young lad, Johnny Murphy, who came running up to them.

'Mr Foster, Mr Foster,' he called as they rode up, 'there were a big party of horsemen here yesterday, just after you left, and they had guns and swords and everything, and they were lookin' for some blacks, and they were gonna go up to Dangar's to get the blacks up there.'

Thomas Foster went pale. 'What? Calm down, Johnny. Who are these men you're talking about?' he asked, jumping from his horse.

'Mr Sexton says they was some of the stockmen from round the district and a squatter was leadin' them. Mr Sexton says his name was John Fleming.'

Knowing Fleming's reputation, Foster needed no more convincing. He immediately turned to Mace. 'We're going to have to send this mob back, straight away.' He then rushed over to King Sandy and, with the help of frantic hand gestures, tried to explain the situation. 'You must go back. There are horsemen looking to kill your mob. Horsemen with guns. You must go back.'

Although King Sandy didn't understand many of the words Foster was using, he quickly picked up on the urgency of the message. Ten-year-old Jimmy then worked out what Foster was saying and began explaining it to King Sandy. A look of sheer horror gripped his face, and quickly spread across the faces of the other men in the group. Bobby let out an audible moan of grief and fear for his wife, his daughter and his baby son.

Realising they now understood, Foster urged them to return immediately. 'Now, you must go back by the mountains, where they won't find you. Stay away from the track we came down on. Go by the mountains.'

Jimmy again acted as interpreter, and the terrified group immediately set off to run the sixteen miles back to Myall Creek.

* * *

But they were already too late. Death had arrived at the top of the ridge, half a mile to the west of the Myall Creek station huts. The sounds of the multitude of birds which inhabited that ridge were silenced, replaced by the snorting and stamping of excited horses as they were reigned to a halt. Silhouetted against a western sky slowly becoming the colour of fire, the demons stared down at the Weraerai camp before kicking their mounts into a gallop. Long black shadows flowed across the tall, wispy grass that covered the side of the ridge, racing toward the camp, while a bloodcurdling yell rose above the sound of crashing hooves.

The Weraerai were gathered around their campfire preparing their evening meal. Inside the stockmen's hut, Anderson was about to serve supper to Kilmeister, Davey and Billy, when the sound of rumbling earth filled the hut.

'What the hell is that?' Anderson asked, his brow furrowed with concern.

'Horses – and lots of 'em, I'd say,' Kilmeister replied, getting to his feet.

Anderson opened the door to see the tranquillity of the Weraerai camp shattered as Death burst upon it. The horsemen galloped through the middle of the Weraerai fire and, waving guns and swords, knocked down huts as women and children shrieked hysterically. Ipeta, Martha and Charley dashed beneath the flailing swords of Russell and Lamb, racing toward the sanctuary of the stockmen's hut. Other panic-stricken Weraerai rushed after them.

Johnny and his younger brother, who had been at the edge of the camp, jumped down into the creek. They looked at each other, terror in their eyes, wondering whether to run or hide. Choosing the latter, they flung themselves up against the side of the bank. The pair pressed themselves into the dirt of the steep bank, their eyes locked on each other in a bond of fear. In the dark shadows their small black bodies were barely discernable. They lay there in silence, their hearts racing as the sounds of chaos and the screams of their people continued above them.

Kilmeister stepped outside the door of the hut as the terrified Weraerai crushed past him and into the hut, imploring him and Anderson to help them. Anderson watched from inside the doorway as Kilmeister walked over and spoke to Fleming and Russell, who had now drawn their mounts to a halt several metres from the hut. The other stockmen had by now formed their horses into a semi-circle around the remaining Weraerai. The powerful animals closed in on the fear-stricken tribespeople, herding them toward the hut.

Anderson stepped hesitantly toward the door as the last few Weraerai crowded into the hut crying, 'Jackey-Jackey, Jackey-Jackey'. Ipeta came and clung to his arm. Other women and children pawed at him, begging him to save them. He tried to reassure them while attempting to overhear what was being said between Kilmeister, Fleming and Russell, but he couldn't make out anything over the wailing and pleading of the terrified women and children.

He watched, though, as several of the horsemen dismounted and shook hands with Kilmeister. Russell took a long tether rope from the front of his saddle and threw it over his shoulder, keeping both hands free for the pistols he wielded. As he approached the hut, Anderson stepped outside and confronted him.

'What are ya goin' to do?' His voice trembled.

'We're just gonna take the blacks over the back of the ridge and frighten them a bit. Now get out of me way.'

With that, Russell pushed past him and entered the hut. He was immediately followed by Lamb, Oates and Foley, causing the cries and shrieks from the terrified Weraerai within the hut to reach a crescendo.

John Fleming remained astride his horse, giving instructions. 'Johnstone, Hawkins, go around to the back of the hut and make sure none of them escape by the window.'

Anderson turned to Kilmeister for help, only to see him hurrying off toward where his hobbled horse was grazing for the night.

'Charlie,' he yelled, panic-stricken, 'where are ya goin'?'

Kilmeister ignored him, and Anderson's gut twisted.

'You,' Fleming called to Anderson, urging his mount over to where the shattered hutkeeper stood staring at the ground in disbelief. Anderson looked up at the young squatter. 'Yair, you. Fetch me a cup of milk.'

'What?' an incredulous Anderson replied.

'You heard me, hutkeeper. Fetch me some milk,' Fleming snapped.

'You heard Mr Fleming, fetch him some milk. And ya can get me some too while you're at it,' bullied Telluse.

Anderson hesitated before shaking his head; then, thinking better of it, he rushed into Hobbs' hut, soon emerging with two cups of milk. As he handed a cup up to Fleming, the young squatter looked down at him.

'Now, are you going to come and join us while we teach these damn blacks a lesson?'

Anderson looked meekly into the cold blue eyes of the young squatter. His jaw quivered, while fear still knotted his gut. 'No, sir, I won't,' he muttered from between clenched teeth, before he turned and strode toward the hut.

'Yair, Kilmeister said you were gutless,' Telluse called after him.

Ned Foley stood at the door, his pistol drawn. Anderson came up beside him and, as he looked into the now dimly lit hut, his heart almost broke. There in front of him, all his Weraerai friends now had their hands tied, palm to palm, with whip-cord. Mothers cradled babies in their arms. Toddlers clutched at their mothers' legs. Young Charley clung to Martha's side, sobbing. Such was the little boy's distress, he didn't even see Anderson at the door. Frail old Daddy and Joey, their hands also tied, had been pushed off to one side. Sandy and Tommy, having had pistols thrust in their faces by Russell and Lamb, were handcuffed. And there was Ipeta. When she saw him, Anderson could see hope replace the fear in her eyes.

'Jackey-Jackey,' she cried.

Martha and Charley saw him too. 'Jackey-Jackey,' they called out in pleading tones.

Anderson glanced at Foley, who was watching him intently. When he tried to step into the hut, Foley, pistol in hand, placed his arm across Anderson's chest. Anderson stopped and stood, watching while Russell took the long tether rope and threaded it through the whip cord binding their hands, linking them to each other and to the rope. Russell then grabbed one end of the rope and started leading the helpless Weraerai out the door past Anderson and Foley.

The youngest of the children were not bound, being either carried by their mothers or clinging to their legs as they shuffled out. The old men, Daddy and Joey, though their hands were bound, were not linked to the tether rope, but, resigned to their fate, they walked placidly alongside their enroped tribespeople.

Ipeta was dragged within a couple of feet from where Anderson stood. When the line stopped moving while Russell handed the end of the rope to the mounted Telluse, she was right in front of her Jackey-Jackey. She looked at him, and he gazed into those beautiful soft brown eyes that had melted his heart the first time he saw her. Looking into those eyes now, into her soul, he saw the terror – the deep, deep terror – at the fate that awaited her. Yet he detected something else, also, amidst that terror as she looked back into his own soul. Was it pity for him that he saw in her eyes? In that instant, with his mind clouded by the inferno of emotions burning inside him, he wasn't sure what he saw.

She shook her head, almost imperceptibly. He didn't understand why. He reached his hand out to her and she raised her bound hands and held his momentarily. It was a moment that seemed like an age to them both, clinging to each other as though clinging to a final thread of hope. The line lurched forward and their grasp was broken. He desperately tried to reclaim her hand, but she was pulled away, staggering, leaving Anderson stunned and staring.

'Jackey-Jackey.' It was young Charley crying out to him as the morbid procession moved on. Anderson looked down at his helpless little friend clinging to Martha's side. Jolted from his trance, he immediately grabbed the boy and pulled him away from the condemned line. As Charley clung to him, Anderson put his hand in the middle of the boy's back and gently held him even closer. But the sobbing child suddenly pulled away and ran crying after his enroped mother, seeking safety in her loving arms. Strangely, though, those usually nurturing arms were pushing him away, back toward Jackey-Jackey, who was crouched on one knee with his arms outstretched, screaming for the boy to come back to him. Confused and distraught, the child fought his mother's rejection, gripping her arm as the rope dragged her forward.

The tail end of the procession passed Anderson and was followed into the middle of the yard by Lamb and Foley. Those who had been guarding the window at the back now returned as Kilmeister rode up on his horse and joined them. Now there were twelve.

Amid the pleading and wailing in front of him, Anderson heard a faint cry behind him. He turned to see Bobby's three-year-old daughter emerging from the hut, calling for her mother. He quickly grabbed the girl before she was seen and put her back inside the hut. He initially pushed her behind the open door, but then thought better of it and shoved the child under his bed.

'Stay there, stay there, don't move,' he ordered, waving his finger at the girl. 'Right? Stay, don't move,' he insisted. The girl looked out at him through reddened, tear-soaked eyes and nodded. 'Good girl,' he said softly, somehow managing a half-smile for the child.

He hurried back outside and stood by the door of the hut. Most of the horsemen were now mounted and had formed a circle around the defenceless Weraerai. Just as Russell was about to mount his horse, Davey, who had followed the procession from the hut, approached him.

'Hey, boss, you givem me one dem gins for me?'

Russell laughed. 'Fancy one for yaself, eh, boy? Sure, have one.' Russell then pulled out his knife and cut one of the young women free, shoving her into Davey's arms.

Disgusted by his own inaction, Anderson was now even more humiliated. Here was Davey, a black, and in grave peril of being dragged off himself, having the courage to try to save one of the gins. He rushed forward toward Russell. 'Can I 'ave one?' He pointed to Ipeta. 'Can I 'ave that one?'

'Ya want one too, eh?' Russell scoffed, before pausing a moment and glancing at Kilmeister, who shook his head. Russell then looked at Ipeta before turning back to Anderson. 'Ya haven't got the bleedin' guts to join us, yet ya want a gin for yaself; and ya want the best of the lot, too. Well, we'll be keepin' her ourselves, won't we, lads?'

It was a question which brought mirthful agreement from the remainder of the gang but which ripped Anderson's heart apart.

'Ya can have this one,' Russell barked as he cut another young woman free and pushed her toward Anderson.

She looked up at Anderson as she landed in his arms. 'Tank you, Jackey-Jackey.'

He smiled feebly but said nothing.

Russell then mounted his massive black horse and, together with the rest of Fleming's henchmen, dragged their hapless victims away. Anderson, along with Davey, Billy and the two young women, stood and watched as the Weraerai were led toward the ridge, their screams and cries for help rising, unheeded, into the evening sky.

Half a mile to the west, toward the top of the ridge, the land dipped away into a gully overlooking the creek and out of the view of the station huts. On the slopes of the gully was a clearing surrounded by eucalypts, myall trees and red berry bushes. It was the type of secluded spot lovers might seek. Here the grim column halted, and an ominous silence hung in the air. The setting sun had painted the evening sky a myriad shades of red, the beauty of which belied the darkness of the deeds taking place beneath it.

'We might have some fun with some of these gins first, eh, lads ... '

* * *

Baby wrenched from mother's arms and thrown to ground ... Sandy and Tommy lunge forward to protect ... Two shots ring out ... Sandy and Tommy fall to ground ... Sandy struggles to feet, sword slashes back of his neck, severs head ... Bobby's wife knocked to ground, her baby grabbed ... Mother wails ... Baby screams as held by legs and head smashed against tree ... Mother slashed with sword ... Terror ... Head hacked off ... Ipeta grabbed, thrown to ground ... *'Have a go at this one'* ... *'Hold her down'*... Rape ... *'It's my turn'* ... *'Stay still, ya black bitch'* ... Boot crushes throat ... *'He said "stay still"'* ... Can't breath ... Raped again ... *'Gimme a sword'* ... *'Save her for later'* ... *'No, kill her'* ... *'She's the scared little hutkeeper's whore'* ... Sword slices her face open, slashes her throat ... Arms hacked off ... Another baby wrenched from hysterical mother ... Horror ... Brains smashed out against rock ... Old Daddy forced to watch helplessly ... *'My go. Give me the sword'* ... Young Charley dragged from Martha's leg. *'Pleease, Mister, don't hurt Char——'* ... Sword raised skyward, catches red glint of sun ... Slash ... Returns skyward, red with Charley's blood ... And again ... Lies bleeding, throat slashed ... Again ... Babies' severed heads ... Shattered skulls ... Mutilated bodies litter gully ... Martha ... *'Save her for tonight'* ... Old Daddy last ... Pushed to knees ... *'Stupid old man'* ... Slash ... Slash ... Head falls to ground ... Others gather round ... Arms and legs hacked off ... *'Cut the arms, legs and heads off all of 'em'* ... Hack ... Hack ... A baby's faint cry ... Heel of boot crushes face ... Silence.

* * *

Their labours thus complete, for now, John Fleming led his assigned assassins off to the west while the red of the setting sun soaked the soil as the blood of twenty eight men, women and children flowed over their tribal land.

Beside her headless corpse lay Ipeta's severed arm. The soft, warm hand that George Anderson had kissed so gently just after sunrise that morning, while dreaming his futile dreams, now, at sunset, lay cold and lifeless, soon to nourish wild dogs.

* * *

Anderson sat on his bed, hoping desperately that the fact he had only heard two shots meant perhaps most of the blacks had been spared. Seated at the table were Billy and the two young women whom Davey and Anderson had managed to save. One of them was nursing Bobby's sobbing three-year–old daughter whom Anderson had hidden under his bed. Billy and the other girl were talking quietly, comforting young Johnny and his brother, who had escaped by hiding in the creek. The pair of them had come to the stockmen's hut a little earlier, in a state of bewildered confusion and fear – emotions currently shared by all in the hut.

Davey had followed the group, not long after the horsemen led the blacks away. Anderson and Billy now anxiously awaited his return, hoping he was safe himself and could provide them with some news of the Weraerai, as well as advice as to what to do with the survivors.

As he sat staring at the dirt floor, a plethora of emotions racing through his mind, heart and body, Anderson was jolted back to reality as the door of the hut was shoved open. It was Davey.

'Dey all dead.'

Anderson remained sitting on his bed, unable to move. The two Aboriginal girls immediately began wailing as Davey repeated his terrible news in their language. As the children cried, Anderson finally forced himself to his feet, when all he wanted to do was lie on his bed and pretend such cruelties did not exist in this world. He walked over to Davey.

'What happened?'

'I go ridge where dey take dem and I hidem in trees. Dey kill 'em all wif deir swords. Cutem deir heads off.'

'Did anyone survive?'

Davey nodded. 'Martha. Dey takem her wit dem.'

'And Ipeta?'

'Sorry, boss, dey killed her. Dey killed all dem. De littluns, too.'

Anderson grasped his face with his hands and groaned. 'Ipeta.' He remained transfixed in silent grief for a moment, before he suddenly turned and strode to the other end of the small hut. 'Aaargh,' he moaned, throwing his head back and clenching his fists. 'The bastards … the bastards.' He swung around to Davey. 'Was Kilmeister with 'em?'

'Yair, he wit dem. Why he doem dat, boss?'

'I don't know, Davey. Why did any of them do it to innocent people and littluns and all? Bloody animals,' he muttered.

'What we doem wid dem?' Billy interjected, motioning toward the distraught young women and children.

'I dunno. What can we do with them?' Anderson asked, half to himself. 'We can't send them off into the night by themselves.'

'What if dey comem back?' Billy asked.

'Dey goem de udder way. Maybe dey not comem back tonight,' Davey suggested.

'What if dey do comem back?' Billy repeated, his voice trembling.

'Well, let's 'ope they don't. See if ya can 'elp these gins, and try to quieten them and these poor kids down, can ya?'

'Yair, boss.'

Davey and his brother sat with the girls and children, trying as best they could to console them. Anderson walked to the door, which Davey had left open, and looked out into the blackening western sky – a sky under which, several miles away, Fleming's gang had made their camp for the night. They sat around the fire reliving their deeds of darkness, between taking their turn to rape Martha, who, still bound, was tied to a nearby tree.

* * *

The stockmen's hut was always cold, but tonight it was especially so. The fire which had burnt quite strongly earlier was now just a pile of glowing embers. The dead night air crept in through the hut's many gaps and cracks. It crawled over the top of the uneven walls beneath the steeply pitched roof. It slithered under the door and between the shutters until it permeated the blackness of the room.

The three children, having cried themselves to sleep, now lay on the earthen floor, huddled between the two girls and Davey and Billy. George Anderson, full of sorrow and regret, lay awake on his bed looking up at the roof. The call of a night bird pierced the silence of the hut. Anderson thought nothing of it but the two girls immediately got to their feet. The sound was heard again, and the girl whom Davey had saved went to the closed shutter and made a call mimicking the night bird. Anderson sat up on his bed and swung his feet to the floor.

'Davey,' he whispered, 'what is it?'

'King Sandy's mob,' Davey whispered back.

The girl repeated the call as Anderson felt for the lamp, while Davey jumped to his feet, went to the door and opened it. The light from the full moon, which had now risen, flooded into the hut. A few moments later Anderson saw King Sandy and Bobby silhouetted in the doorway. The girls rushed to greet them. The other men and boys quickly appeared at the door as the girls briefly told of the horror which had struck their people. Anderson couldn't see the expressions on their faces, as they stood with their backs to the moonlight coming through the doorway, but he heard their moans of grief and despair. Bobby then saw his daughter lying asleep on the floor. He rushed over, picked the little girl up and hugged her as she awoke.

'Bubaa, bubaa,' the delighted child cried as she clung to her father's neck, while tears streamed down the cheeks of the Weraerai warrior. All in the room watched as the father and child hugged each other in elated relief, an isle of joy in a sea of suffering.

The child eased from her father's grip and pointed to Anderson, who stood behind him. 'Jackey-Jackey,' the girl said, followed by some words Anderson did not understand until Bobby, child in one arm, came over and threw his other great arm around the convict hutkeeper.

'Tank you, Jackey-Jackey, tank you.'

Bobby had his daughter safely in his arms, but on a ridge half a mile away, the full moon shone down on the headless bodies of his wife and baby son.

Conversation in the hut quickly became an animated discussion of the safest course of action for the surviving Weraerai. They wanted to go and collect the remains of their people, but Anderson and Davey urged against it. At Anderson's suggestion, it was finally decided their former sanctuary at McIntyre's would be the safest place for them. So, twenty minutes after completing their thirty-two mile return trip to Newton's station, the ten Weraerai men and boys set off again, into the night, along with the two girls and three children, aiming to put as much space as possible between themselves and Myall Creek before the killers inevitable return.

CHAPTER THIRTEEN

Monday 11 June 1838.

E arly the next morning, Thomas Foster was eating breakfast in
the stockmen's hut with Robert Sexton and young Johnny Murphy when they heard the sound of horses approaching at a gallop.
Foster jumped to his feet and went outside to investigate. There he
was greeted by the sight of Fleming's twelve armed horsemen.

'Hallo. What's the matter?' asked the startled superintendent as
the riders drew to a halt.

'Where are the blacks?' demanded an emboldened James Oates.

'God knows where they are now,' replied Foster. He then spotted
Kilmeister amongst the group. 'What, Kilmeister, are you after the
blacks now too?'

'Yair, they rushed me cattle.'

'You didn't mention any problems with them when I was there
yesterday morning,' Foster remarked.

The superintendent then stood aside as several of the horsemen
dismounted and rushed past him into the hut, while others circled

the huts and the stockyards. Kilmeister ignored Foster's comment and followed the others inside.

'Where are the bloody blacks?' Foster heard a voice yell from within. He then retreated to the sanctuary of his own hut to observe the action from there.

Fleming and Russell remained mounted outside the stockmen's hut while those who had gone inside questioned Sexton and Murphy. The remainder scoured the immediate vicinity on horseback.

'It's your bleedin' fault they got away,' Lamb snapped at Sexton, who was still seated at the table with young Murphy. 'You and Foster drove 'em off so we wouldn't catch 'em.'

'We didn't know you was comin' back here,' Sexton protested.

Blake entered the hut at that point, dragging Martha by the wrist.

'Come on, let's get movin',' Lamb urged. 'The blacks ain't here, so let's go find 'em.'

'All right; but what'll I do with her?' Blake asked, releasing his grip on Martha, who immediately huddled on the floor, clinging to the leg of the table.

'Leave her here; we can move faster without her,' instructed Lamb. 'We can get her later, after we catch up with the rest of 'em.'

'Can we leave her here with you?' Blake asked Sexton.

'Sure,' replied the hutkeeper, eager to redeem himself in the eyes of the armed mob, 'but I'd better just check with Mr Foster first.'

Sexton quickly got to his feet and hurried outside to Foster's hut, where the superintendent remained standing well inside his doorway.

'Mr Foster, can they leave that gin with me for a short while?'

'What, leave her here? No, definitely not,' snapped the superintendent.

'They asked —— '

'No, I said,' Foster cut him off. 'That's just asking for trouble.'

Sexton returned to the stockmen's hut and told Blake of Foster's refusal. Blake cursed him, grabbed Martha by the arm and attempted to pull her to her feet; but her other arm was firmly wrapped around the leg of the table, and she clung to it desperately.

'Come on, ya black bitch,' snarled Lamb, kicking her arm free of the table leg.

Martha cried in pain as Blake dragged her to her feet and followed Lamb and the others outside, where Blake mounted his horse before pulling Martha up behind him. Fleming then led his group of assassins off in search of the remaining members of Martha's clan.

* * *

By nine o'clock they had crossed the river and arrived at Dight's station. William Mace, the station overseer, was sitting alone in the hut when he heard them gallop up. Anxious, he got to his feet and went to the door.

'Where are the blacks?' Russell demanded as he and several others slid from their horses.

'What blacks?'

'King Sandy and that lot ya took down to Newton's yesterday.'

'They went back to Dangar's late yesterday,' Mace responded.

'Have a look around, you four; we'll be inside,' Fleming instructed, motioning to Lamb, Johnston, Telluse and Parry. The four rode off as Fleming dismounted and walked to the hut door.

'Yair, come in, sir,' Mace invited, stepping back to allow the young squatter to enter.

The others followed their leader into the hut while Blake pulled Martha from the back of his horse and walked in behind them. Lamb, Johnstone, Telluse and Parry returned a few minutes later and joined the others, so that all twelve were inside the hut with Mace when John Bates, the forty-five-year-old convict hutkeeper, returned with a bucket of water from the nearby creek. Although he had seen their horses outside, he was rather startled when he entered the hut to find the heavily-armed horsemen who had been at Newton's searching for blacks two days before.

'What's going on, Bill?' he asked Mace.

'Nothin', John. Can ya just get these chaps some breakfast?'

'Yair, sure.'

Bates turned but stopped mid-stride when he saw the naked Martha cowering by the fire, her arms wrapped tightly around her legs, apparently trying to make herself as small as possible, hoping to become invisible to her captors. Bates hesitated as he stared at the frightened girl, his kindly heart breaking upon seeing the terror in the eyes gazing up at him from behind her knees. He turned away, though, and started preparing breakfast for his unwelcome visitors.

While he was cooking, James Parry, whom Bates knew, wandered over to him. 'We've had a shot at the blacks, John,' Parry boasted.

'Hmmm?' Bates murmured.

'Yair, we settled 'em.'

Bates ignored the comment and finished cooking breakfast, before serving it to the twelve. Once they had finished eating they immediately prepared to leave.

'What are we gonna do with her?' Blake asked Russell, motioning to Martha, who still sat huddled on the floor by the fire.

'Can we leave her here with ya for a short while, Bill? Help yaself to her if ya like. We all have,' Russell boasted, to the mirth of his abettors.

'Yair, sure, she can stay here,' Mace agreed.

'Thanks. We'll be back for her in a couple of days.'

'Come on, let's go,' directed Fleming.

The stockmen filed out, mounted their horses and rode off to the east, toward Myall Creek, leaving a slightly relieved but still terrified and confused Martha at the hut with Mace and Bates.

During the course of the day, Bates made several attempts to communicate with Martha but she was incapable of responding to a white man, no matter how kind he appeared. Late in the afternoon, while Mace was away, he tried again. He sat down on a chair a couple of metres from where Martha remained huddled next to the fireplace, but still he could illicit no response whatsoever. Finally, he offered her food and water, which she accepted hesitantly. As she chewed slowly on the damper, Bates resumed his seat and sat there contemplating her. Her curly hair was dirty and tangled, with pieces of dry grass and twigs knotted through it. Her body was covered in dirt, dried mud, cuts and grazes. He couldn't see if there were any more wounds on her chest or stomach because they remained hidden behind her knees. It was enough for Bates, though. He knew the butchers would be back. As she finished eating, he got to his feet, walked over to the door of the hut, opened it slowly and stood back.

'Come on, my dear, off you go.' Martha looked up at him and then at the door. 'Go on, go, you poor thing.'

Martha slowly got to her feet and walked over to the door. 'Tank you,' she murmured, before rushing out the door to solitary freedom, never to be seen or heard of again.

* * *

At about the same time, fifteen miles away, Fleming's pack returned to the scene of their crime. They rode toward the gully on the ridge where the dismembered corpses of the twenty-eight Weraerai lay strewn across the ground. Eagle hawks and crows had already started feasting on their remains. A large black crow stood on Ipeta's severed head, its clawed feet amongst the blood-matted hair over her forehead. A cool winter breeze blew across the top of the ridge, ruffling the crow's feathers as it pecked at Ipeta's soft brown eyes. Its beak was full when it took flight upon the approach of the horsemen.

They rode around the site of the carnage they had created just twenty-four hours before. The bodies of women, children, babies and old men littered the clearing.

'Mr Fleming, this is a fearful mess, sir, and Hobbs will be back in a couple of days. From what Kilmeister says, he'll be frightfully upset about this, sir,' ventured James Parry.

'Feeling a little nervous, are you, Jem?' Fleming responded with a smirk. 'Well, that's why we're here. We'll burn them. What do you think, John?'

'Yair, I fancy that'd probably be best,' Russell replied.

'Well, we can do that tomorrow morning. Come on, let's see if that new chum Anderson can get some supper for us.' Fleming turned his mount and led his henchmen down the side of the ridge, toward the stockmen's huts.

George Anderson was inside the hut with Davey and Billy when they rode up. He slowly opened the door a few inches and peered out.

'Anderson, come out here and take this,' called Lamb, slapping his hand on a saddle he had slung across the back of his horse. 'It's Kilmeister's.'

Anderson opened the door fully. 'Where's he?'

'His horse went lame a couple of miles down the creek. He's walkin' back,' Lamb replied, dumping the saddle in the dirt at Anderson's feet, before smiling contemptuously at him and entering the hut with the others. Anderson threw the saddle on the ground around the corner before slowly following them inside. Davey and Billy got up from the table as they entered. Fleming, Russell, Oates and Lamb sat down, while the others milled around the room.

'Now, Anderson, what about some supper for your hungry guests?' Fleming's comment was met with murmurs of approval from his henchmen.

'Yes, sir,' Anderson mumbled.

'And you, young blackfellas, go and look after our horses,' Fleming then instructed.

Davey and Billy, standing in a corner behind a couple of the stockmen, hesitated momentarily.

'Come on, you two, ya heard Mr Fleming. Hurry up,' snapped Russell.

'Yair, burama,' Davey answered as he and Billy stepped between the stockmen and headed toward the door.

'What did ya call me?' Russell barked.

'Burama,' Davey replied. 'It meanum big chief whitefella.'

'Oh, that's all right, then; but he's the chief.' Russell motioned to Fleming.

'Ah, you burama.' Davey smiled at Fleming.

'Yes, boy, I'm burama. Now get moving.'

'And take good care of that big black of mine,' added Russell.

The two young Kamilaroi hurried out, closing the door behind them.

'Yair, burama,' Davey called back, glancing at his brother as they walked away. He then muttered, in his best cockney accent, 'Shine ya boots, guvna.' It was an expression he'd picked up from the convicts, and it caused Billy to burst into laughter, as he always did at his big brother's jokes. Billy's mirth was only increased by his knowledge that 'burama' meant 'dog'.

The two of them tended the horses, while inside the hut Anderson went about preparing supper for the men who had raped and butchered Ipeta. He had more than adequate food on hand because he usually set some aside to supplement what the Weraerai caught themselves. Anderson cooked in total silence while the stockmen sat around recounting details of their deeds of the evening before. An acrid taste rose from his stomach as he overheard their boasting and cruel laughter. He kept working with his back to them, fearful of turning around and letting them see the effect their tales were having on him. He wanted to run from the hut but he dare not.

'And what about that good lookin' young one?' Oates remarked.

'Ya mean Anderson's whore?' Russell mocked. 'Yair, she was a willin' one.'

Russell sat with his back to Anderson, about four feet from where the hutkeeper was cooking. Anderson picked up a large carving knife from the bench and started chopping the beef.

'Yair,' Lamb agreed, 'but we didn't have as much fun with her as we did with that one we kept.'

Russell continued the taunt. 'Nah, Anderson's whore was the best.'

'Yair,' several others chorused.

'Black whores,' Russell spat with disgust.

Anderson continued cooking, fear and hatred burning inside him.

Shortly afterwards, as Anderson was serving the suppers, the door of the hut opened abruptly. It was Kilmeister.

'About time ya got back,' Russell remarked. 'What took ya so long?'

'Nuthin'. It was just a long walk, especially with it gettin' dark.'

Anderson looked past Kilmeister and out the door. It was another spectacular red sunset, just like the evening before. He thought then that he would never enjoy another sunset again. In fact, he was sure he would be haunted by the image of a red sky for as long as he lived. He turned back to his bench and continued serving the guests.

After they had finished eating, the stockmen's conversation turned from boasting about their crimes of the night before, to the where-abouts of more victims. Fleming instructed Anderson, Davey and Billy to sit down at the table, where now only he and Russell remained seated. They obeyed hesitantly.

'All right, Anderson, so where are the two gins we left with you and the young blackfella last night?' Russell demanded.

'I dunno. They went off into the night somewhere.' Anderson's eyes shifted nervously from Russell to Fleming, then down to his own hands clasped on the table.

'What about this King Sandy and the mob that went off with him?'

After a brief pause, Anderson again replied, 'I dunno.'

'Don't give us that, Anderson!'

'I said, I dunno.'

Russell calmly placed his pistol on the table in front of him and then turned his attention to Davey and Billy. 'You two can either tell us where the others are or join the rest of the blacks up on that ridge.'

Davey and Billy remained silent, their heads bowed, staring at the table.

'Where are they?' Russell barked at them.

'Dey gone, boss,' blurted out a terrified Billy.

'Gone? So they *were* here? King Sandy and his mob came back, did they?'

'Yair, boss, dey takem dem gins and dey go agin in de night.'

'Where did they go?' Russell growled as James Lamb grabbed Billy's hair and wrenched his head back.

Kilmeister interjected, not wanting to see Billy hurt. 'They might've gone up to McIntyre's.'

'What?' snapped Russell, turning to Kilmeister.

'They might've gone back to McIntyre's. That's where they were before they come here,' Kilmeister explained. 'Did they go back to McIntyre's, Billy?'

'Yair, boss ... I tink so,' Billy mumbled as Lamb released his hair, shoving his head forward.

Clapping his hands together, Fleming got to his feet. 'Right, then, men. Tomorrow we're off to McIntyre's to find some more blacks.'

'Yair, sounds good to me,' replied Lamb, while the others murmured their support.

Russell leant across the table to Anderson, Davey and Billy. 'And as for you lot, I daren't be sayin' a word of this if I was you; because if ya do, I'll come back here and slit ya bleedin' throats, ya hear?'

They lowered their eyes and nodded.

CHAPTER FOURTEEN

Tuesday 12 June 1838.

G eorge Anderson, bucket in hand, wandered across to the creek, as he did every morning. He strolled past the remnants of the Weraerai camp, gazing at the huts, which were still standing, and particularly at Ipeta's hut, which he had watched her build on that first day. He ambled aimlessly across to the top of the creek bank and stood there in a kind of daze. There he looked over his shoulder, hoping, willing, wishing for Ipeta to emerge from the trees and spend some of that private, quiet time with him that he had cherished so much. He was almost surprised when she didn't appear. He remained there staring at the trees until the intolerable sound of laughter coming from the stockmen's hut forced him back to reality. He fetched the water and returned to the hut to prepare breakfast.

Fleming rose from the table, walked across the hut and opened the door. He was about to step outside but stopped. 'Kilmeister, have you got a leg-rope around here?'

'Yair, sure, Mr Fleming. Anderson, get Mr Fleming the leg-rope,' Kilmeister instructed.

Anderson said nothing, despite the fact he desperately wanted to tell Kilmeister to get it himself. He knew if he did, however, one of them, probably Russell or Lamb, would thrust a pistol in his face and order him to get it. He therefore swallowed the last remaining morsel of his pride and left the hut, returning shortly after with the leg-rope. He handed it to Russell, who was now standing just outside the door of the hut.

'Are ya gunna bury the blacks?' Anderson asked naively.

'Yair, with a good fire,' Russell replied, before stepping back inside the hut. 'Come on, you lot, are ya ready?'

The last of the stockmen, who were just finishing their breakfast, now got to their feet. John Fleming took a large burning stick from the fireplace.

'A couple of you chaps, grab one of these each,' Fleming instructed.

Lamb and Kilmeister both took a smouldering stick from the fireplace, and then they and the others followed Fleming out the door. Once outside, Russell and Fleming called Foley aside.

'Ned, you stay 'ere and look after the weapons. And keep an eye on that Anderson, too. Make sure he knows I'll be havin' his throat slit if he opens his hole,' Russell advised.

Foley smiled. 'I'd be sure he knows that already; but sure, I'll remind him.'

'We won't be long,' Fleming added as he led his accomplices off, carrying the firesticks and the leg-rope.

Foley strolled back into the hut, where Anderson was cleaning up the breakfast plates. The weapons the men had left behind were scattered around the hut, on the beds and on the table.

'Not a bad breakfast, Anderson,' Foley commented pleasantly as he sat down at the table.

Anderson was not interested in the compliment but somehow found it within himself to mutter 'Thanks' in reply. Then, encouraged by Foley's apparently amiable manner, he asked, still hoping she might be out their somewhere, 'Did any of the blacks escape last night?'

'Nah, not one. We got the lot of them. Except, of course, the gin we kept.'

Although Davey had already told him this was Martha, Anderson thought he'd double check. 'Was 'er name Martha, do ya know?'

'Yair, somethin' like that,' Foley replied.

Anderson had already accepted the worst for Ipeta, but this now confirmed it. He was pleased that his friend Martha had survived, but horrified that it was her who had to suffer the repeated attacks the stockmen had been boasting about the previous evening.

'So where is she now?' Anderson asked, anxious about her safety.

'We left her at Dight's, with Mace and Bates.'

'Oh.' There was silence for a few moments before Anderson asked, 'How come, that night, there was only two gun shots?'

'Because we used swords on the rest of them.' And with that, Foley leant over and grabbed a sword which was lying at the other end of the table. He pulled it from its scabbard and waved it in front of Anderson's face. The sword was covered to the hilt in blood.

'Ya see?' Foley sneered.

'Yair,' Anderson murmured, looking away.

'You know they'll kill ya if ya ever tell a word of this,' Foley advised coldly.

'Yair, I know,' Anderson mumbled as he turned away to continue cleaning up the breakfast plates.

* * *

Up on the ridge, Fleming's killers went about the task of concealing their crime. Using the leg-rope, several large logs were dragged into a central location amongst the mutilated corpses of the Weraerai, and thrown on top of a large pile of branches. The firesticks they had brought were then used to set them alight. The demons then fed the flames with the arms, legs, heads and torsoes of the dismembered Weraerai.

Daddy's grey-haired head lay several yards from the conflagration, among some small rocks which littered the ridge. Swarms of ants, crawling in and out of his mouth and eye, had their feast disturbed as the battered boot of a stockmen kicked the tribal doctor's head along the ground to the edge of the fire. Ipeta's mauled arm was picked up and flung into the middle of the blaze, where the hungry flames fed on her black velvet skin. Thick, grey smoke poured into the clear morning sky, the air filling with the stench of burning flesh.

'Come on, you lot, let's get moving; we've got more of these black pests to hunt down,' Fleming called. 'Kilmeister, you stay behind and come up here by and by to check on the fire.'

'Sure, Mr Fleming.'

About an hour after they had left, the killers returned to the huts, and while the others began to round up and saddle their horses, Fleming, Russell and Kilmeister stood outside the huts talking.

'All right, so who's gonna show us the way to McIntyre's? Do those young blacks of yours know the way?' Fleming asked Kilmeister.

'Yair, Mr Fleming, Davey and Billy both know it well.'

'Good. Well, have one of them come out here.'

'Yair, Mr Fleming.'

Kilmeister disappeared into Hobbs' hut, returning a few minutes later with Billy following slowly behind.

'All right, boy, you're coming with us,' ordered Fleming.

The fear of meeting the same fate as his Weraerai cousins immediately flashed across young Billy's eyes. Slowly he shook his head.

'You'll be fine, boy,' Fleming assured him. 'You just do as we say and show us the quickest way to McIntyre's station and we won't hurt you.'

Billy looked at Kilmeister, who nodded and said, 'It'll be all right, Billy.'

'You'll be fine, boy,' Fleming repeated. 'Just do as you're told. We'll even give you a young gin or two if we find any. Now go and get your horse.'

Unconvinced, Billy remained standing still.

'Come on, boy, ya heard Mr Fleming. Hurry up or ya dead,' barked Russell.

Startled, Billy rushed off to get his horse.

A few minutes later the stockmen assembled with their horses. Russell entered the stockmen's hut, where Anderson was still cleaning up.

'We're just leavin' now, Anderson, but Mr Fleming wanted me to make sure you'd got the message about keepin' ya hole shut.'

'Yair,' Anderson murmured, his stomach knotting nervously.

'Ya tell a word about any of this and we'll come back and ya dead! Right?'

Anderson nodded.

Russell turned and strode out the door to join the others, who were now all mounted. Their reluctant guide, Billy, was saying a very drawn out goodbye to his big brother at the door of Hobbs' hut.

'Come on, you, let's go,' Russell shouted to Billy as he mounted his black horse, which Kilmeister was holding for him.

'Don't forget to go up to the fire and make sure it's all consumed,' Fleming instructed.

'I won't, sir; and don't worry about Anderson,' Kilmeister assured Russell and Fleming, 'he won't say nuthin'. I'll be keepin' me eye on him, but he ain't got the guts to say nuthin' anyway.'

Kilmeister then watched his colleagues ride away, leaving him on the station with Anderson and Davey.

Billy mounted his horse and, glancing back at his brother, followed slowly behind the stockmen as they rode around the side of the huts and headed south, in the direction of McIntyre's.

Death was on the move again.

CHAPTER FIFTEEN

Wednesday 13 June 1838.

C oncealed in the bush, King Sandy and his small band of survivors had been watching the stockmen's huts at McIntyre's station since the sun's first rays had begun creeping across the sky. Although it had now fully risen, a thick morning mist still drifted amongst the trees. By now, however, the Weraerai were quite sure that their old friends Andrew Eaton and John Woodward were alone, so they emerged from their hiding place to seek the respite of their former sanctuary. They called out as they approached, and Eaton and Woodward emerged from the hut to greet them.

'King Sandy, hallo,' called Eaton.

'Hallo,' the Weraerai elder called back as he led his people up to the two convicts, who immediately noticed their distress and agitation.

'What's the matter?'

King Sandy started rambling in an unintelligible combination of his native tongue and a slight smattering of English. Eaton and Woodward managed to pick up the repetition of the words 'gandjibalu' (soldiers), 'bumaay' (kill) and 'murri' (people). It was enough for them to be gravely concerned.

'Slow down, King Sandy, slow down,' Eaton said gently, placing his hand on the Weraerai's shoulder. 'Where are the rest of your people?'

'Soldiers,' he replied; then placing his index finger below his left ear, he drew it across his throat toward the other ear. As he did so the two girls and the youngest of the boys began crying.

'Soldiers killed them?' Eaton asked, confused.

Jimmy, the ten-year-old-boy who had helped Foster translate his warning to the bark cutters three evenings before, stepped hesitantly forward to help. He nodded. 'Andy, soldiers killem dem. Dey all dead.'

'What? Where?' Eaton asked, but before he received an answer he had turned to Woodward with his brow furrowed. 'Soldiers? There haven't been any soldiers around here since Major Nunn and his troops a few months ago. I wonder if they're back.'

'I don't think so,' Woodward replied. 'You'd think we would've heard about it if they was.'

'Yair, ya probably right. I suppose it must be some of them stockmen that have been riding round the district.'

'Must be,' Woodward agreed, nodding.

The Weraerai waited anxiously while their white protectors tried to decipher their tale.

'Where did it happen? Down at Myall Creek?' Eaton asked.

Jimmy nodded. 'Mr Hobbs.'

'They should have been safe there,' Eaton mumbled to Woodward.

'I wonder what happened? Kilmeister said he'd look after them.'

'Ya know what a gasser Kilmeister is, though,' Woodward pointed out.

'Yair, but they still should've been safe.'

Urged by King Sandy and the others, little Jimmy spoke up again. 'King Sandy say, "Can we stayem here wit you?"'

Eaton smiled. 'Yair, of course. Sit down and have a rest. I'll see what we've got in the hut for ya to eat. Be back directly.'

Eaton and Woodward went into the hut while the exhausted Weraerai sat down to rest, after three days of almost constant travel. No sooner had they taken their places on the ground, however, than Bobby looked at King Sandy with terror in his eyes. Rising above the silence of the morning, the sound of galloping horses grew from the depths of the mist.

The terrified Weraerai jumped to their feet and rushed into the hut screaming, 'Soldiers, soldiers.'

Eaton hurried to the door and looked out, but the mist and the trees limited his vision to about eighty yards. The sound was unmistakable, though. He turned to the panic-stricken Weraerai. 'Quick! Run, run,' he screamed, waving them to the door.

Bobby picked up his three-year-old daughter, who clung to him as he followed King Sandy, Jimmy and the others out the door. They raced across the clearing that surrounded the hut and into the trees scattered across the hillside beyond.

Eaton and Woodward watched as Fleming's killers burst out of the mist and from between the trees, in pursuit of the fleeing Weraerai.

'There are ya soldiers,' Woodward observed, shaking his head in disgust.

'Poor bastards,' Eaton mumbled anxiously before rushing around the side of the hut. 'Run, run,' he screamed as the Weraerai disappeared from his view, the cloak of Death closing inexorably upon them.

Several shots rang out and Eaton and Woodward followed anxiously on foot as the horsemen disappeared beyond the trees in pursuit of their quarry. They walked in amongst the eucalypts, and there, face down on the ground, lay a young boy, a gaping bullet hole between his shoulder blades. Eaton approached slowly and bent down beside the dead child. He gently rolled him over. It was Jimmy.

CHAPTER SIXTEEN

Thursday 14 June 1838.

T he slaughter of the blacks hung over Myall Creek like the shroud of ghostly grey mist which the cold winter dawn had again breathed upon the station. Anderson went about his duties as a man who has had his heart ripped from his chest. His jaw was set, his eyes were fixed and he said not a word to the traitor. Emptiness filled his day.

CHAPTER SEVENTEEN

Friday 15 June 1838.

T he sound of wood being cut emanated from the back of the stockmen's hut. The long gap between the chops of the axe indicated it was being wielded by a dispirited axeman. It was now mid-afternoon and George Anderson was alone on the station. He knew not of Kilmeister's whereabouts, and Davey had left early in the morning to pick up Billy and two young girls he had with him. Where they had come from was a mystery to Davey and Anderson, as these girls were apparently significantly younger than the two who were with King Sandy's mob when they had set off.

Word had reached them that Billy was over at Wiseman's station, where the remnants of Fleming's gang had set up base for a few days of boozing and bragging about their bloody deeds. Davey was keen to get Billy and the girls away from there as quickly as he could, before the gang changed their minds about their liberty.

As Anderson swung the axe slowly and methodically, the repetitious nature of the work allowed his mind to wander – as it had incessantly over the past few days. He thought of the last time he had been out chopping wood, and looked up, hoping to see the smiling faces of young Charley and Bobby's little daughter appear around the corner of the hut. He stood staring for a moment, before he was snapped from his trance by the sound of approaching horses. It was a sound which he had heard daily during the time he had been on the station, but it was now a sound that made his stomach churn instantly. Walking around the hut to investigate, he quickly realised that it was only a couple of horses approaching. To his further relief, he saw Davey and Billy trotting their mounts toward him. On the back of their horses, young girls clung to each of them.

'Billy, how are ya?' Anderson called. 'Are ya all right?'

'Yair, boss, I good,' Billy replied as he and Davey eased their mounts to a halt beside Anderson.

Davey reached behind him and put his arm around the waist of the young girl. He gently swung her from the back of the horse and let her slide to the ground. The girl was about nine years old, slightly older than her companion, who Billy now lowered to the ground.

'Where did they come from?' Anderson asked. He looked at the young girl, who stood awkwardly, clinging to Davey, who had now dismounted.

'Up Keera Creek, boss,' Billy replied.

'What?' Anderson asked, confused. 'Bring them in, bring them in,' he urged.

Anderson stood back as Davey and Billy helped the two young girls into the hut.

'Why are they limping so badly?' Anderson asked.

Davey and Billy exchanged a few words in Kamilaroi as they sat the girls on Anderson's bunk. Billy then replied, 'Dey cut dem, boss.'

'Who cut them? Where?'

'Dem whitefellas, dey say dem gins too small for dem. Dey cutem dem here, boss,' Billy grabbed his groin, 'wif knife.'

'What?' Anderson gasped in horror. 'The bloody animals ... Are they all right?' he asked, looking at the two girls, who sat with their eyes glued to Billy, obviously aware of what was being discussed.

'Yair, boss, dey cutem dem few days before. Plenty, plenty blood all over dem. Dey all right now,' Billy replied offhandedly.

They don't walk as if they're all right, Anderson thought, but made no comment to Billy, who was now responding to an apparent question from the slightly elder girl.

'Dat Jackey-Jackey,' he said, nodding toward Anderson.

The girl looked at the convict hutkeeper through the distant eyes of the abused. Somehow she managed a half-smile of recognition, while her younger companion just looked at him blankly.

Anderson gave the girls some water to drink before beginning to question Billy. 'What happened when ya went to McIntyre's? Did King Sandy's mob get away?'

'Some did, but dey killem some dem.'

Anderson moaned. 'Oh, no! Who else did those bastards kill?'

'Not see dem all, boss. Dey killem dat little fella, Jimmy. Some de udders run away. Dey shoot dem, goin' bang, bang. Plenty, plenty bang, bang.'

Anderson shook his head in sorrow and disbelief upon hearing of the death of another child. 'Jimmy ... What about King Sandy? Did he get away? And the gins, and Bobby and his little daughter?'

Billy shrugged. 'Dunno, boss, dey all runnin' in de bush. Dey goin' bang, bang wit de guns. Some fallem down like Jimmy, but I no see de udders.'

'Ya didn't see it all?'

'No, boss, I behind dem. Dey kill plenty, plenty blackfellas later, but, boss.'

'What? Where? Not King Sandy's mob?'

'Nah, not King Sandy's mob, udder blackfellas. Dey up Keera Creek and killem lots of blackfellas wit deir guns, and dey chopem deir heads wit dem cobawn knives.' Billy made a gurgling noise in the back of his throat as he slashed his finger across the front of it.

'What, like they did here?'

'Yair, boss, den dey chopem dem up.'

'How many? How many did they kill?'

'Dunno, boss. Lots, like here. Plenty, plenty gins and littluns.'

Anderson turned away and groaned, almost collapsing into the chair by the table. He buried his head in his hands, his mind so filled with appalling images he was oblivious to Billy continuing.

'Dat's where dese young gins was, boss. Dey killem deir mob.'

The words finally registered in Anderson's dazed brain twenty seconds after Billy had spoken them. He nodded and, gradually bringing himself back to a numbed reality, murmured, 'I just hope the rest of King Sandy's mob are all right.'

'I tink dey killem some udders, but I no see dem, boss. I only see Jimmy. And young Johnny, he all right; he hidem in big rocks and dey not see him, just like when he hidem in de creek here. I wink at him when I go past. He smart li'l fella.'

'Yair, he is,' was the only reply Anderson could muster. Then, as the image of cheeky little Johnny again evading Fleming's butchers came into focus in his mind, he managed to look up at Billy and smile. 'Good on him.'

But Anderson had now had enough of the discussion. He got to his feet and walked over to the bench, where he poured some water into a mug. He quickly gulped it down, as though trying to wash away the taste of the talk of death. But it had no effect, so he tried walking outside, hoping the air might clear it from his mind.

The moment he set foot outside the door, though, he saw the scene that confronted him every time he left the hut: the few remaining remnants of the Weraerai camp and the creek where he had spent so much time with Ipeta. He turned and walked to the back of the huts, where he was wandering aimlessly when he again heard the sound of approaching horses. Though he could again tell it was only a couple of horses, they were approaching at a gallop. As he hurried back to the huts, he saw the familiar figures of William Hobbs and Andrew Burrowes mounted on their horses.

Now he was snapped back to reality – the reality of facing William

Hobbs. It was a moment he had spent much time thinking about since the Weraerai had been led away and slaughtered five evenings before. He had wished so often that Hobbs had been there on that terrible evening, for he was sure Hobbs would not have allowed it to happen – even with the squatter Fleming leading the killers. And though he had spent much time thinking about Hobbs' return and knew exactly what he wanted to tell him, he was in a state of total confusion as he watched Hobbs and Burrowes dismount in front of the superintendent's hut. He was unsure of exactly what to say, when to say it, and what the fear that had constantly gnawed at his gut since the massacre would allow him to say.

He arrived at the huts, only to see Hobbs storm into his hut and slam the door behind him.

Burrowes saw Anderson approaching. 'G'day, George,' was his ironic greeting.

'Andy.' Anderson nodded sombrely.

'Mr Hobbs wants to see you.'

'Yair, I figured he would.'

'What the hell happened, George?' Burrowes asked.

'I'll tell ya directly. I'd best go in to see 'obbs first.'

'Where's Kilmeister?'

'That bastard? Dunno.' Anderson shrugged as he passed Burrowes and knocked on the door of the superintendent's hut.

'Come in,' came the agitated voice of William Hobbs from within the hut.

Anderson opened the door and entered. 'Ya wanted to see me, Mr 'obbs?' he asked nervously.

'Of course I want to see you, George. I need someone to tell me what happened. Sit down,' Hobbs commanded, barely able to contain his anger.

Once Anderson was seated, Hobbs continued. 'Now, what happened to the blacks?'

Anderson hesitated. His mind was still racing, still trying to absorb the horrors Billy had just described, while at the same battling his own feelings of guilt and attempting to work out exactly what to tell Hobbs and where to start. He looked down and shrugged. 'I dunno, sir.'

'What? You don't know? Well, you'd better start remembering, George,' Hobbs yelled, getting to his feet and standing over the convict.

Anderson looked up, somewhat shocked at the reaction of his normally placid superintendent. Hobbs was glaring at him, so Anderson immediately dropped his eyes again, and again he hesitated.

'Now, I'll have you tell me precisely what happened,' Hobbs demanded, 'because I've already become acquainted with some of the details on my way back upriver.'

Anderson looked up again, surprised but greatly relieved, momentarily, that someone else had already told Hobbs the tragic news. 'Have ya, sir?'

'Yes, I've heard it from Bates and Foster, but now I want to hear from you how this could possibly have happened.'

'What did they say, sir?' Anderson asked meekly, confused about what exactly Hobbs already knew.

'Never mind what they said, just you tell me what happened.'

Anderson shifted in his seat, trying to scratch that itch against the back of the chair. Beads of sweat began to appear on his forehead. 'Er, well, sir … '

'What happened, Anderson?' Hobbs again demanded, still standing over him.

'Well, sir … um … '

Hobbs gave Anderson some space, returning to his seat on the opposite side of the table. His eyes, though, remained fixed on the witness, who sat in silence with his head bowed.

'How did this happen, George?' Hobbs now asked in an almost soothing tone.

There was silence for a moment more, then Anderson began to speak. 'Well, sir, about five nights ago, sir, a mob of horsemen came gallopin' up to the huts.' As he spoke, Russell's threat to return and kill him flashed across his mind, but he continued nonetheless. 'They rode around the blacks' camp, yellin' and wavin' swords, and all the blacks come runnin' into the hut. They was screamin' and cryin' … They was terrified, sir; and they was grabbin' me and beggin' for help … ' Anderson hesitated.

Hobbs waited for him to continue, quickly becoming aware that Anderson was no longer being evasive but was genuinely struggling in reliving the incident.

'And they was screamin' … I went outside to see what all the riders was doin', and then some of 'em came inside and tied the blacks to a tether rope … Then they led 'em all away, with the littluns trailin' along beside 'em … And then they killed 'em … ' Anderson paused, unable to look up at Hobbs, who now bowed his head and shook it slowly.

The convict and his superintendent sat opposite each other in silence, both looking down at their hands resting on the table in front of them.

Finally Hobbs looked up and, in a quiet voice, asked, 'Where, George? Where did they take them?'

'Over on the ridge, sir.' He pointed, before adding what was both a statement of justification and regret. 'There were nothing I could do to stop 'em, sir. They all had guns and swords, Mr 'obbs.'

Hobbs leant forward and asked bluntly, 'Who were they?'

The sweat on Anderson's brow increased almost instantly. He couldn't bring himself to raise his eyes as he shrugged and said, 'Dunno, sir.' Russell's threats were still too vivid in his memory to allow any other answer.

Hobbs stood again. 'You must know some of them.'

'I don't, sir.'

'A name, Anderson. Just one name … Any name.'

'Sir, I don't know any of 'em. I never seen 'em before. Ya know, sir, I don't get around the district. I never seen 'em before.'

As Hobbs stood thinking, the sound of a lone horse could be heard approaching the huts. He knew Anderson was not telling him the whole truth, but unsure of the best way to proceed with his questioning, he changed the topic. 'Did any of the blacks get away?'

'Davey says they didn't kill Martha, but they took her away with them. And King Sandy and some of —— '

'I know about King Sandy and the mob with him. Foster informed me about that; but how does Davey know they took Martha away?'

'He seen it, sir. He followed them up to the ridge when we heard some gun shots and he watched from behind the trees.'

With a trace of hope in his voice, Hobbs then asked, 'What about young Charley? They can't have killed all the little children.'

Anderson finally raised his head and looked at his boss, knowing full well the pain the answer would cause him. It was a pain Anderson shared as he slowly shook his head. 'Sorry, sir, they killed him. They killed all the others.'

Hobbs turned away abruptly. 'Damn them. Damn them all! Ahhh,' he groaned, before swinging back around to Anderson. 'George, you must have heard at least one name. Who were they?'

'I dunno, sir, I tell ya, honest.'

'Where's Kilmeister?' Although he didn't believe Anderson, he thought he may have more success with his trusted stockman.

'I dunno, sir.'

'Well, that must have been his horse we heard a minute ago. Go and tell him I want to see him, now!'

Relieved his interrogation was over for the time being, Anderson quickly got to his feet and hurried to the door.

'But George, I'll have a name from you, all right? So think about it. I'll be talking to you again directly.'

'Yes, sir,' Anderson mumbled as he walked out.

Andrew Burrowes was still loitering around outside the hut when Anderson emerged. 'Was that Kilmeister that just come back?' Anderson asked him.

'Aye, he'd just be watering his horse.'

'Well, tell 'im 'obbs wants to see 'im straight away, will ya?' Anderson asked as he headed into the stockmen's hut.

'Aye, sure.'

* * *

Charles Kilmeister knocked hesitantly on the door of the superintendent's hut. Hobbs swung the door open. 'Where have you been,
Charlie?'

'Just out on the run, Mr Hobbs, checkin' on the cattle,' the stockman replied.

Hobbs sat down, then motioned for Kilmeister to take the seat
opposite him, just as he had done with Anderson.

'Now, Charlie, I know all about the blacks being murdered. I was
informed about it on my way back upriver, and Anderson's further
acquainted me with the details; but Charlie, how could this happen?'

'Sir, this big party of horsemen with guns and swords came char-
gin' up to the camp and scared all the blacks into our hut. They
followed them inside and they tied them all to a tether rope and took
them away and killed them, Mr Hobbs. There was nothin' I could
do to stop them, sir.'

'Yair, that's exactly what Anderson told me happened, but … '
Hobbs stopped, lost for words. 'I've already decided I'm going to
report this matter to the authorities,' he continued.

'I had nothin' to do with it, Mr Hobbs,' Kilmeister protested, his
voice breaking slightly.

Hobbs ignored the comment. 'Who were they, Charlie?'

'I've never seen them before, sir.'

'But I've been informed that you were seen with them the next day
at Newton's and at Dight's.'

Kilmeister hesitated, fidgeting with the brim of his hat sitting on
the table in front of him. 'Mr Hobbs, I was only with them when I
was lookin' for me cattle, sir. I didn't have nothin' to do with killin'
the blacks, sir, honest.'

'Yes, all right, Charlie, I believe you,' Hobbs conceded. 'Apparently the bastards killed them all, except for Martha. But if you were with them the next day, you must know some of them.'

'I don't, sir. Honest, Mr Hobbs, I was only ridin' with them for a little while when I was lookin' for me cattle. I didn't get any of their names, sir.'

'I find that hard to believe, Charlie. Why would our cattle be all the way over at Dight's? You know most of the stockmen from around the district, anyway. Why wouldn't you know this lot?'

'I dunno, sir.'

'You lot always stick together, don't you? Well, why were you riding with these animals, when they'd murdered the blacks?'

'Like I said, sir, I was lookin' for me cattle, and I was only with them for a little while. Sir, ya gotta believe me,' Kilmeister pleaded, relying on their good relationship to give him some desperately needed credibility. They had spent nearly two years working together in the remote districts of the colony. There had been countless long, boring nights when two, three or four of them had sat around chatting about their lives and dreams. They were times when the normally clear line between the boss and the assigned convicts would become a little blurred and they became just men, reminiscing, boasting and dreaming. They were times that forged friendships and trust.

'Yair, all right, Charlie.' Hobbs nodded, before adding, 'Apparently Davey knows exactly where they killed them.'

'Yair, Mr Hobbs.'

'Go and get him for me.'

'Yes, sir.' Charles Kilmeister immediately jumped to his feet and rushed out the door, calling for Davey.

A few minutes later, Davey hurried over to the superintendent's hut, where Hobbs stood in the doorway.

'Ya wantem me, boss?' he asked.

'Yair, Davey. Anderson says you saw the horsemen kill the blacks.'

'Yair, Midder Boss, over dere,' he answered, pointing to the ridge.

'Come and show me,' Hobbs instructed, closing his door behind him.

Davey led Hobbs over to the middle of the yard and pointed to the ground. 'See, boss, plenty, plenty tracks.'

Hobbs looked down and saw the clear tracks that had been made in the mud that evening and which now made an indelible mark in the landscape. As he and Davey followed the tracks away to the west, Hobbs could clearly see the bare footprints of the Weraerai, with the hoofprints of around a dozen horses on either side of them.

Davey stopped, bent down and pointed to some of the tracks. 'See, boss, dere de littluns' tracks.'

Hobbs looked closely at the various small footprints that Davey pointed out, but said nothing.

As they continued on, for the first time Hobbs began to develop a clear image in his mind of the horror of that evening. The news that his Weraerai friends were dead had upset him enough, but now he was gaining a full understanding of the terror they endured before they died, and it shocked and horrified him.

'Did you see it, did you, Davey?' Hobbs asked without taking his eyes off the prints which followed the main track leading toward Newton's and the other downstream stations.

'Eh, boss?'

'Did you see the killings?'

'Yair, boss. Dey chopem dem heads off. Dey chopem old Daddy's head off.' He slashed his finger across his throat and accompanied it with the same strangled, gurgling sound his brother had used just a little earlier.

'Oh no, they didn't?'

'Yair, boss, and dem arms and dem legs.'

'Oh no!' Hobbs moaned.

'And dey bashem little babies' heads agin' de tree.'

'What?' Hobbs's face contorted. 'Take me up to where it happened.'

'Yair, boss.'

The pair of them followed the tracks in silence. Hobbs had heard enough, so he ceased asking questions. The tracks of the condemned and their murderers now turned off from the main track and ran through the trees on the side of the ridge, at which point they became indiscernible amongst the long grass. Hobbs followed Davey until they emerged from between the gnarled trees which stood as silent sentinels around a large clearing in a gully, part way up the side of the ridge.

However strong Hobbs' disgust had been up to this point, at the details relayed by Davey, it was as nothing compared to his shock at the sight that now lay before him. He immediately shut his eyes and turned away, before opening them again to take in the whole scene.

Fleming's cronies had attempted to use fire to conceal their crime, but the rain had foiled their efforts. In the cool light of day, without his accomplices, Kilmeister had quickly lost the stomach for the task of burning the evidence. The result was a mangled mass of half burnt body parts – torsos, arms, legs and heads – all scattered amongst blackened logs. Crows and eagle-hawks deserted their feast and took flight upon the arrival of Hobbs and his guide, and began circling in the afternoon sky above.

Despite his revulsion, Hobbs forced himself toward the grotesque scene. As he approached, the stench from the half burnt, decaying flesh obliged him to hold his handkerchief to his nose. Walking slowly, he felt something under his foot in the long grass. He stopped and looked down as he lifted his foot, retching at the sight of the baby's head beneath his boot. Recovering himself, he looked back to Davey, who stood in silence at the edge of the clearing.

Hobbs turned and continued to the edge of the funeral fire, where he saw a huge torso he knew could only be that of his jovial old friend Daddy. His resolve to report the atrocity strengthened at the sight. He then made himself pick his way through the mauled and mutilated remains of his Weraerai friends as thousands of large green flies crawled over the putrid flesh and buzzed in the air around him. The combined assault on his senses and emotions left him physically drained, but he was determined to get some idea of the number that had been slain. He counted bodies, the stench engulfing his face. He counted heads, the flies' buzzing invading his ears. He counted women. He counted babies. He counted old men. He counted children - knowing one of them was his friend Charley, his body now lying unrecognisably charred and dismembered amongst the pile of partly burnt corpses and logs.

Hobbs counted twenty-eight before the task became more than he could bear. With his handkerchief still pressed to his face, he hastily retreated back to where Davey was still standing. 'Come on, let's go,' he murmured, heading back toward the huts, with Davey hurrying along behind.

Hobbs strode into his hut, closed the door firmly behind him, sat at the wooden table in the middle of the room and buried his head in his hands, trying to make some sense of what he had just seen. Why would anyone do that to peaceful, innocent people? How did it happen on his station? Surely there must have been something someone could have done to prevent it.

He remained transfixed until he heard the sound of a horse approaching. Sure it would be his friend Thomas Foster, he roused himself and went out to greet him.

'About time you got here, Tom,' Hobbs said as he walked over to Foster's horse.

'Sorry, Bill. It took a bit longer over at the sheep run than I thought it would. What have you found out?'

'It's bloody awful. Davey just took me up to where the bodies are, up on the ridge. You never did see anything like it. They've cut the poor wretches up; cut their heads off, and their arms and legs. They've tried to burn them but the fire's gone out. It's just a mess. It's just the most fearfully brutal thing you can imagine.'

George Anderson stood at the door of the stockmen's hut and watched as Hobbs and Foster wandered over to the superintendent's hut.

'George, make a cup of tea for Mr Foster and myself, would you?'
Hobbs called.

'Yair, Mr 'obbs.'

Once inside, Hobbs and Foster sat down at the table.

'Tom, I just have to report this,' stated Hobbs.

'Look,' replied his friend, 'I understand how you feel, and I've
already acquainted our neighbour, Mr Foot, with the incident, but
you really need to be thinking it through. To start with, it will be just
plain dangerous to report it. You'll be putting your life in danger; and
what do you think Mr Dangar's reaction will be?'

'Well, I daresay he shan't be too happy about any of it – the blacks
even being on the station *or* me reporting it. He hates the blacks. He
thinks they're just a nuisance.'

'Well, there you are. What have you got to gain? And besides, we
all know there have been many blacks killed all over this colony and
nothing ever comes of it. The government never does anything about
it, and then —— '

'Damn it, Tom,' Hobbs cut him off, 'I realise all that.' He got to
his feet and began pacing up and down. 'But the simple fact is that
a whole mob of innocent people, including young children, babies
and my little mate Charley, have been brutally butchered on my station. This wasn't some mob of wild blacks. These people were living
peacefully, directly outside this door.'

'Look, calm down, Bill. Sit down, please,' Foster entreated. Hobbs
reluctantly sat back down as his friend continued. 'I know they were
peaceful. I ate with them the night before it happened, remember?'

'Of course I do; but you haven't seen what I've just seen up on that
ridge. We'll see what you think when I take you up there. Look, I just
cannot sit by and not say anything about it. Anyway, even though Mr
Dangar hates the blacks, I cannot believe he could possibly condone
this sort of brutal slaughter. I cannot believe anyone could justify
butchering those women and little children, and old men like Daddy
and Joey – or any of them, for that matter.'

Foster nodded. 'I know, I know but —— '

'Tom, you only met them once; but believe me, they were good people, kind people. They had a great sense of fun and laughter, for that matter; and that was despite living in constant fear for their lives. And they came here for protection.'

'I accept all that, and I certainly found them all friendly; and King Sandy and the party I took with me were no bother at all. And I agree with you that this sort of thing is terrible, but, my word, I think you should consider it very carefully before proceeding to report it.'

The two men sat in silence for a few moments, when there was a knock at the door.

'Come in,' Hobbs called a little impatiently.

Anderson opened the door, entering somewhat apprehensively. 'Here's your tea, Mr 'obbs, Mr Foster. I'm just gettin' supper now, sir. It'll be ready directly,' said the hutkeeper as he poured the tea.

'George, you know Davey just took me out to where the blacks' bodies are?'

'Yes, sir.'

'Have you been up there?'

'No, sir. I don't wanna go up there, sir.'

'Well, I can understand that. It's just the most fearful thing. What they did to them … You must have been able to do something?'

The words cut Anderson like a knife. It was something he had told himself countless times since the blacks were led away. He began to stutter a reply. 'I-I —— '

'Perhaps you couldn't,' Hobbs continued, cutting him off, 'but you should have at least tried.'

Anderson again started to reply but was this time cut short by Foster. 'Couldn't you at least save young Charley?'

'I tried, Mr Foster, honest I tried,' Anderson protested. 'I held 'im back, but he was so scared, the poor little fella, he went runnin', callin' for his mummy.'

'Well, you should have held him tighter,' Foster countered dismissively.

'I tried, sir, but he were strugglin' to get to his mummy.'

'But he was only a six-year-old boy,' Foster persisted.

'I tried, I tried ... ' Anderson hung his head in despair, realising the futility of trying to convince anyone when he couldn't convince himself.

'All right, George, all right,' Hobbs said soothingly. 'You say you tried - that will have to do.' Anderson stood there in silence, trying to regain his composure, while Hobbs changed the subject. 'Now, what exactly became of King Sandy and his mob?'

'I dunno exactly, sir,' Anderson replied, slowly raising his head. 'I think some of 'em got away.'

'What do you mean? I thought all of his mob got away.'

'Well, I didn't get a chance to tell it all to ya before, Mr 'obbs, but after King Sandy's mob come back here and got the others, they headed off —— '

'Hang on, hang on! What others?'

'The two gins that they gave to Davey and me, sir, and the three littluns.'

'What little ones?' Hobbs asked, becoming increasingly irritated by the fact he seemed not to have been told about much of what had happened.

'Two young fellas, young Johnny and his brother, jumped in the creek and hid when the horsemen first come gallopin' up.'

'Well, good for them.'

'And there were Bobby's young daughter, who I hid under me bed, Mr 'obbs.'

'So you saved her at least, George,' Hobbs responded.

'I suppose so, sir; but I don't know what happened to them down at McIntyre's, because Billy says some of them was killed down there, Mr 'obbs.'

'By the same men?' Hobbs asked incredulously.

'Yes, sir. They made Billy go with them to show them the way, and they chased them down there and killed some more of them.'

Hobbs turned to Foster. 'See why I want to report these animals?'

'I understand why, Bill, it's just a matter of whether it's the wise thing to do.'

Hobbs turned back to Anderson. 'And you don't know how many of them were killed down there?'

'No, sir.'

'What about King Sandy and Johnny? Do you know if they survived?'

'Billy didn't know, sir; but some might have, because he didn't see them dead. But Jimmy was killed, sir.'

'Johnny's little mate? Another child,' Hobbs muttered before again looking to Foster for support. But Foster said nothing. 'Is that all, George? Is there anything else I should know?'

'No, sir.'

'All right, George, you can go.'

'Yes, Mr 'obbs. I'll just finish gettin' supper.'

After Anderson had closed the door behind him, Hobbs continued discussing the matter with Foster. 'Tom, I am resolved to report this, and I am going to need your support on the matter. You're the only one in this district I can depend on.'

'Of course you have my support. I just want you to be fully aware of the risks involved.'

'I am fully aware of the risks involved – to my life and to my position – but these men have most brutally murdered innocent people on my station and I must report it. I just have to ascertain the best way of proceeding. I am unsure if I should report it to Mr Dangar first and let him report it to the authorities, or whether I should just report it directly to them.'

'It's Mr Dangar's property. If you must report it, don't you think you should advise him first?'

'Yes, you're probably right. But what about Mr Foot – you said you'd already advised him.

'Yes, and he's prepared to go down to see the Police Magistrate at Muswellbrook. He's horrified by the whole drive against the blacks. He'll go all the way to Sydney to report it if necessary.'

'Well, good for him. Look, I'll take you up to the ridge in the morning and then we'll decide the best way to proceed.'

'Well, if you're fixed in your determination on this.'

'I am, Tom. I am.'

CHAPTER EIGHTEEN

Saturday 16 June 1838.

William Hobbs stood at the edge of the clearing, unable to bring himself to again endure the horror of the previous afternoon. The stench from the rotting, mutilated flesh was now almost overpowering. Dingoes had dragged some of the body parts from the pile, and an even larger number of birds of prey than the day before circled overhead. Thomas Foster approached the gruesome scene with reluctance. He stopped about fifteen yards away, holding his hand to his face. He hesitated, before moving several steps closer and stopping again. He retched. The taste of stomach acid burnt his throat as he turned away and rejoined Hobbs at the edge of the clearing.

He leant briefly against his horse's saddle before composing himself and nodding to Hobbs. 'I agree, it must be reported.'

'Good.' Hobbs placed his hand on Foster's shoulder. 'No-one should be allowed to get away with that sort of thing. I'll report it to Mr Dangar immediately, and then we'll ask Mr Foot to report it directly to the authorities.'

Foster mounted his horse and rode off toward his own property, eager to put as much space between himself and the massacre site as possible.

Hobbs wandered back down the side of the ridge, toward the huts, retracing the same Weraerai tracks he had followed with Davey the previous afternoon. As he did so he couldn't help but imagine the victims' terror as they were led off to their slaughter. When he reached the point where the tracks began, near the edge of the Weraerai camp, he spotted something in the long grass which he recognised instantly. It was old Joey's red and green tartan cap. He picked it up, brushed off the dust and dirt, and immediately returned to his hut, where he sent for Kilmeister.

* * *

'Ya wanted to see me, Mr Hobbs?' Kilmeister asked nervously.

'Yes, Charlie. Sit down,' Hobbs ordered abruptly. 'Charlie, I just can't believe that you stood by and let the blacks be slaughtered like that. It is the cruellest thing of which I've ever heard, and you let it happen.'

'Mr Hobbs, sir, I had no part in it, sir. I couldn't stop them, there were too many of them, sir. Honest.'

'But Charlie, the blacks were only here because you asked them to come here. And you talked me into letting them stay. It was entirely because of you that they were here, yet you did nothing to protect them.'

'Sir, there was nothin' I *could* do. I had no part in it.'

'I know that, Charlie, but how could you sanction it by just standing by and allowing them to be taken away and slaughtered like that?'

'But sir, there was nothing I could do. There were too many of them for me to stop them, sir.'

Hobbs ceased his line of questioning. 'Anyway, you should know that, as superintendent of this station, it's my duty to report this matter to the authorities, and I'm going to start by sending a letter to Mr Dangar.'

'Oh no, please don't, Mr Hobbs,' Kilmeister pleaded, panic beginning to stir within him.

'Sorry, Charlie, my mind is set. This is a most grave matter. I'm going to write to Mr Dangar – but why would you be so opposed to me doing so?'

'Sir, it might go against me, sir, and they'll put me in chains on a road gang.'

'It won't go against you, Charlie. You had nothing to do with the killings, so they won't put you in a road gang,' Hobbs assured him. 'Now get out of here while I write this letter to Mr Dangar.'

'But Mr Hobbs, sir, please don't.'

'I told you my mind is set, now get out of here,' Hobbs ordered firmly.

Kilmeister reluctantly retreated to the door, where he hesitated.

'Out,' Hobbs ordered, waving him away.

* * *

It was just after sunset and Anderson was cleaning up after supper, while Kilmeister sat on his bunk repairing his horse's bridle.

Burrowes opened the door and put his head in. 'Hobbs wants to see us in his hut, now.' Leaving the door ajar, he then made his way over to Hobbs' hut.

Kilmeister looked at Anderson, who immediately looked away, put the plate in his hand down and made for the door. Kilmeister then jumped to his feet and grabbed him. The stockman's labour-hardened fingers dug into the hutkeeper's shoulder as he pulled him close to his face.

'Ya keep yer hole shut, Anderson, or ya know what will happen to ya.'

Anderson wrenched himself free of Kilmeister's grasp and, saying nothing, marched out the door, with Kilmeister close behind him.

When they entered the superintendent's hut, Burrowes was already seated at the table.

'Sit down,' Hobbs directed.

'Sure, Mr Hobbs,' Kilmeister replied, taking the seat directly across from the superintendent.

'Now,' Hobbs continued, 'I've told you I am going to inform Mr Dangar about the slaughter of the blacks, and as you had nothing to do with it, and you say you don't know any of the parties involved, I want to read you the letter afore I send it off.'

'Oh no, Mr Hobbs,' Kilmeister whined softly.

Ignoring him, Hobbs commenced reading. 'Sixteenth of June, Eighteen-thirty-eight. Dear Mr Dangar —— '

'Oh no, Mr Hobbs, please don't report it. For the Lord Jesus Christ's sake, sir, don't report it.' A panic-stricken Charles Kilmeister thrust his hand across the table toward the hand in which Hobbs held the letter.

'Take a hold of yourself, man,' Hobbs ordered. 'And why shouldn't I report it?'

'Because, Mr Hobbs, sir, the blacks were rushin' the cattle and spearin' them,' accused Kilmeister.

'What? What are you talking about? The blacks didn't cause any trouble at all. They never rushed the cattle. They didn't even have any spears. What are you talking about, Charlie?'

'After ya went down to the lower station, Mr Hobbs, the blacks started rushin' the cattle and spearin' them, sir. They made some spears, sir, honest.'

'But they never did anything like that before, even when I have been away.'

George Anderson sat silently staring at Kilmeister, writhing and squirming like a bloodworm on a fishing hook. He knew Kilmeister's fate would be sealed with one word from him, and the deaths of Ipeta and her people avenged. He told himself he would find the courage to speak up when the time was right, but that time had not yet come. He told himself that, as it was the only way he could live with himself.

He told himself that, and he said nothing as he watched the worm wriggle off the hook.

'I know, sir, but this time they were different altogether, and they started spearin' the cattle, sir. They did, really.'

Hobbs hesitated and thought for a moment.

'They did, Mr Hobbs,' Kilmeister insisted. 'Honest, sir.'

Hobbs recalled Foster's warnings and considered the risk he was himself taking by informing Henry Dangar, when he knew Mr Dangar hated blacks. If Kilmeister persisted with this line, that the blacks were being a nuisance and upsetting the cattle, Mr Dangar was sure to be glad to be rid of them and annoyed with Hobbs for having allowed the blacks to camp on his land in the first place. He was putting his promising career, his livelihood in the colony, in jeopardy. More than that, he was putting his very life in danger.

'Charlie, are you sure they were rushing and spearing the cattle?'

'Yair, Mr Hobbs, they were, honest.'

Hobbs looked at the letter in his hand, and such was his faith in his convict stockman that he crumpled it and threw it into the fireplace.

'Thank you, Mr Hobbs, you're doin' the right thing, sir.'

'You'd better be telling me the truth, Charlie.'

'I am, Mr Hobbs, honest.'

Anderson sat staring at the flames consuming the letter that could have seen Kilmeister and his cronies brought to justice. He had assured himself that if he was ever again placed in a situation similar to that night, he would not allow it to happen without putting up some sort of a fight. Despite this assurance to himself, however, he had just sat there in silence while Kilmeister had smeared their characters in death. He sat there now and watched as the white paper turned to black ashes, his stomach knotting with regret.

Before he stood to leave the hut, Kilmeister watched the same flames but with totally different emotions. Relief was in fact his only emotion as he watched the fire completely destroy any indication of the massacre, unlike the bungled blaze he had tended up on the ridge.

CHAPTER NINETEEN

Sunday 17 June 1838.

William Hobbs tossed and turned on his bed, unable to sleep. It was well past midnight but each time slumber had begun to embrace him, haunting images of rotting, dismembered corpses jolted him back to consciousness. He kept seeing little Charley's beaming face in front of him, but his feelings of relief and joy at the sight of his young friend were quickly shattered when he'd look down to see the child's body was missing and his head was floating in the blackness that filled his hut.

He rolled onto his side again, facing the door, and thought about the evenings he had spent at the blacks' camp with the elders and Charley while the others sang and danced around them. These people hadn't deserved to die even if they did spear a few of the cattle. Had Kilmeister been telling the truth? Why hadn't he seen any of the dead cattle? Though he hadn't really looked, he had seen no sign of them while riding around the property over the past couple of days.

* * *

George Anderson knocked on the door of the superintendent's hut but there was no answer.

'Mr 'obbs, I got ya breakfast, sir.'

No answer.

'Mr 'obbs ... breakfast,' the hutkeeper called as he peered through a crack in the window shutter. Although his view of the inside of the hut was restricted, he could see Hobbs' bed was empty. Anderson turned and wandered around to the back of the huts, where he could see the area in which the horses normally grazed. The other horses were there but there was no sign of Hobbs' horse. He returned to the convicts' hut, where Kilmeister and Burrowes were sitting at the table eating breakfast.

'Andy, do ya know where 'obbs is?'

'Not in his hut, then?' Burrowes replied casually.

'Nah, he's not; and I can't see his horse round, neither.'

'Well, he can't be too far away. He wouldn't be goin' off without telling us, now would he?'

'Yair, I suppose not, but it is strange for him to have left without having his breakfast.'

'Aye, to be sure; he'll be back soon, then.'

* * *

William Hobbs did not return, however, until just after sunset, when the three convicts were again in their hut. Kilmeister and Burrowes were sitting at the table, while Anderson, who refused to eat with Kilmeister, was sitting on his bed. Hobbs drew his exhausted mare to a halt outside the convicts' hut, leapt from the saddle and burst in the door.

'I can't find any, Kilmeister,' he thundered at the stunned stockmen.

'Sorry, sir, pardon?'

'I said, I can't find any.'

'Any what, sir?'

'Any speared cattle, that's what, Kilmeister. I've been riding around this property since afore sunrise this morning and I can't find any sign whatever of a single one having been speared. Not one, Charlie, not one.'

Kilmeister swallowed hard while searching for an answer. 'Yair, Mr Hobbs, we was wonderin' where ya were. We was worried about ya, sir.'

'Never mind about that,' Hobbs hissed. 'Where are the cattle you told me the blacks had speared?' he snapped at the convict.

'I-I'm sorry, Mr Hobbs, didn't ya see any?' He then quickly added, 'Sir, they are out there, honest. Unless they took them away.'

'Listen, Charlie, they're not out there. And unless *who* took them away? The blacks? They're dead, remember? And you know as well as I do, no-one carries away a whole steer carcass.'

'No, sir,' Kilmeister mumbled.

'Anyway, you say they're out there, so you find them. That's your job tomorrow; and you'd better find them, or else have a damned good explanation.' With that, William Hobbs strode out of the hut.

Anderson had watched the whole exchange, delighting in Kilmeister's distress. He wanted so much to say 'Good luck finding those cattle, Kilmeister', but he bit his tongue, determined not to break his icy silence against Ipeta's killer.

CHAPTER TWENTY

Tuesday 19 June 1838.

Hobbs emerged from his hut straight after breakfast and walked over to his horse, which Burrowes had saddled for him and now held.

'Where's Kilmeister?' the superintendent asked, taking the reins from the convict.

'In the hut, Mr Hobbs.'

'Get him for me, would you?'

'Aye, sir.' Burrowes hastened to the convicts' hut, from which Kilmeister emerged moments later.

'Listen, Charlie, you keep looking for those speared cattle; and you'd better have more luck than you did yesterday, all right?'

'Yes, Mr Hobbs, sir.'

'When I get back in a couple of days, I'll want you to show them to me, all right?' Hobbs was now certain Kilmeister was lying to him, and his feelings of betrayal and frustration were such that he wanted to punish the stockman. At this point, however, Hobbs believed Kilmeister was only lying to protect his peers, and to justify his own failure in preventing the massacre. The thought that Kilmeister could be involved in the murders had not even entered his mind.

Satisfied he'd made himself clear, he mounted his horse and turned it to head downriver.

'Yes, Mr Hobbs. Bye, sir. I hope everything's goin' all right downriver, sir,' Kilmeister called after him.

Hobbs guided his mare onto the main track leading north to the lower station. It was a long and solitary ride across creeks, along the river bank, over undulating hills, across open country and along a track which wound between scattered clumps of eucalypts. He was pleased for the time and solitude that enabled his mind to wander. Away from the images of horror that haunted his hut at night, he was able to think more rationally about the situation in which he found himself. If he reported the massacre, he ran the risk of upsetting Mr Dangar. He reasoned, however, that Dangar was a fair man, and with everything going so well on the properties that Hobbs managed for him, he should accept that Hobbs had a moral responsibility to report it. His other concern was for his own safety. He spent a lot of time travelling through very isolated countryside. If someone wanted to kill him, to keep him quiet, it wouldn't be hard for them to find the opportunity.

Hobbs' mare, a fine, black-tipped bay with a flick of white on her nose, slowed to a walk as her rider weighed his options. The more he thought about it, though, the more he believed he only had one option. He had to report it. These men were riding around the district killing innocent people. Enough was enough. It really was that simple – someone had to do something to stop them. Besides, he was sure his little mate Charley wouldn't let him get a decent night's sleep until he had reported it.

Hobbs gave his mare a gentle kick. 'Come on, girl, let's go,' he urged.

He would make his visit to the lower station a very brief one, and on the way back to Myall Creek he would drop in to see Foster, to ensure Mr Frederick Foot made that trip to the authorities in Muswellbrook.

CHAPTER TWENTY ONE

Government House, Sydney – Friday 6 July 1838.

T he Colonial Secretary, Edward Deas Thomson, entered the office of the Governor, Sir George Gipps, somewhat more hesitantly than was his practice. He stood in silence, waiting while Gipps read a document placed on the large mahogany desk behind which he sat. In front of the desk were two finely crafted chairs with dark green and white velvet upholstery and finely carved timber framings. The wall behind Gipps was layered with shelf upon shelf of beautifully bound books. To Gipps' left was a large window overlooking the gardens.

Gipps continued reading while Thomson waited patiently, adjusting his black silk cravat with his milky white hands. Rather bookish looking, Thomson was an ambitious young man from a Tory background. He had arrived in the colony in 1829, at the age of twenty-eight, and started his bureaucratic career as Clerk of the Executive and Legislative Councils. In 1833 he married the daughter of the then Governor, Sir Richard Bourke, and in 1837 Bourke had appointed him Colonial Secretary. Bourke had resigned just a few weeks later, replaced by Lt-Colonel Kenneth Snodgrass as acting Governor until such time as a new Governor could be appointed and sent out from England. That new Governor, who had arrived in February 1838, was Gipps, who now looked up from his reading.

'Good morning, Mr Thomson.'

'Good morning, Excellency.'

'You seem rather sombre this morning. Whatever is the matter?' asked the governor.

'It seems there has been another problem with the Aborigines, sir. Seems like a quite awful incident up on the northern frontier. I've just received this letter from a Mr Frederick Foot, one of the local squatters, who travelled down here to report it, sir.'

'What's happened this time?' Deep anxiety immediately clouded the Governor's face as Thomson handed him the letter, which he read.

Sir,

It having been reported to me by Mr Foster, Doctor Newton's overseer, that about the commencement of last month, several stockmen assembled at one of the stations in the Big River district and, having mounted their master's horses, being armed with guns, pistols and other offensive weapons, went in pursuit of blacks.

Having come to Mr Dangar's cattle station, they ascertained that a considerable number of blacks were over there, who had come some time previous, on the promise that they would be protected, and had remained peaceably about the place. The stockmen finding that Mr Hobbs, the superintendent, was absent, bound (as I am informed) twenty-eight blacks, principally women and children, whom they took away to a short distance from the place and murdered them, afterwards burning their bodies: they would have taken more, but they were rescued by the hutkeeper, who hid them under the bed. After this diabolical act, then rode to Doctor Newton's station, where they understood there were more blacks, and riding up to the huts in a most hostile attitude, with their firearms presented, demanded where the blacks were concealed, but Mr

Foster, having heard the stockmen were in pursuit of the aboriginals, sent them away previous to their arrival, by which means the lives of ten or eleven of their intended victims were saved.

Mr Foster, who visited the scene of blood two days after in company with Mr Hobbs, describes the spectacle as most horrible. The fire was still burning, the head of one and part of the body of one, the head of another, besides several skulls and bones still remained unconsumed.

As I reside in the neighbourhood where this flagrant violation of the law took place, I consider it a duty incumbent on me to submit this statement for the information of the Governor in order that His Excellency may cause such enquiry as to be made, as His E. may deem fit, for the peace and safety of all Her Majesty's subjects in that part of the Colony.

The following, I am informed, are the names of the stockmen concerned:

'Hall's Jemmy', assigned to Mr Hall, at Hall's Creek, Big River.

Hawkins, stockman to Mr Lethbridge.

'Black Johnstone', at Mr Cox's station.

Lambert and Fleming, at Mr Cobb's station.

Mr Glennie's stockmen and one of Mr Dangar's men.

I have the honour to be,

Sir,

Your Most Obedient Servant

Frederick I Foot

Gipps put the letter down and looked up at Thomson, who remained standing in front of the Governor's desk. He shook his head slowly, looking down again at the letter which he now let fall from his hands and onto the desk in front of him.

'This is most tragic. We're going to put a stop to this sort of thing in this colony.'

'Yes, sir.' Thomson nodded. 'It certainly sounds like a most shocking case.'

'This Big River district, that's the area where Major Nunn killed the Aborigines, isn't it?'

'Yes, it's the same area, sir.'

Thomson had in fact been involved with Snodgrass's decision to dispatch Major Nunn on his foray into the Big River district. He was a political chameleon, however, and perfectly capable of changing his expressed views to fall more closely in line with his new political master.

'Well, this lot are going to feel the full weight of British law come down upon them; and as I said when I arrived, the natives of this colony are going to have British law to protect them.'

'Yes, sir. We're obviously going to have to have the matter investigated, to determine the full facts of the incident —— '

'Certainly,' Gipps cut him short. 'Well, and who is the best person to do that?'

'Probably Edward Day, at Muswellbrook, Excellency.'

'But we've got him standing by to investigate the Nunn matter, haven't we?'

'Yes, Excellency,' Thomson conceded, 'but he is the logical person for the job, being the closest police magistrate; and he is a fine policeman.'

Gipps stood up from behind his desk and paced over to the window before replying. 'Well, perhaps we shall have to delay the Nunn Inquiry for a short while, Mr Thomson, because Mr Day is just going to have to investigate this incident with the utmost urgency.'

It was the answer Thomson wanted to hear. Given Gipps' attitude to protecting the Aborigines, the last thing Thomson wanted was an inquiry which may reveal his own role in despatching Nunn on his campaign against them.

'Yes, Excellency,' he replied with a nod.

'Right, and can you have the convict assignment records checked to ascertain if we can identify any of the names mentioned in this letter?'

'Yes, sir, certainly. Excellency, I agree with you that this seems a most dreadful crime and it must be investigated thoroughly; but sir, you should be aware that doing so may enrage the squatters.'

'Don't you think I know that, Mr Thomson?'

'Yes, of course, Excellency.'

'Well, damn the squatters. I will protect the Aborigines, Mr Thomson, and that's the end of it.'

'Yes, sir,' Thomson agreed dutifully before turning to leave.

'Mr Thomson, I will put the matter before you and your colleagues at our Executive Council meeting tomorrow, but I won't be deviating from this course of action. Understood?'

'Yes, sir, I agree with that course of action.' Opening the door to leave, however, Thomson hesitated. 'Excellency, I want you to understand that I do agree with you that Mr Day has to investigate this matter, it's just that I desire you to be aware of the likely reaction from the squatters and the newspapers.'

'Mr Thomson, I'm fully aware of that and I thank you for your concern.'

'Thank you, Excellency. Good day, sir.'

'Good day, Mr Thomson.'

Sir George Gipps stood looking out the window at the sweeping gardens of Government House which rolled away from below the window where he stood and down to the waters of the harbour. As he stood there deep in thought, mulling over the contents of Foot's letter, he remained oblivious to both the spectacular beauty of the view and the fact he had just made the decision which would start a seven year war with the wealthy squatters of the colony – a war in which there could be only one winner.

CHAPTER TWENTY TWO

P olice Magistrate Edward Denny Day set out from Muswellbrook on Thursday 19 July with a party of eight troopers supplied by Major James Winniett Nunn, Commandant of the Mounted Police in New South Wales, and headed by Lieutenant George Pack. When first informed of the incident at Myall Creek, Day had not shown any interest in investigating the matter. He had been advised when Frederick Foot was passing through his district but hadn't contacted him. Now, however, he had been directed by the Governor himself to investigate the incident. In his saddle bags he carried his instructions from the Colonial Secretary, a copy of the letter from Frederick Foot and a letter from William Hobbs sent to him on 9 July, the same day Hobbs had finally written to inform Henry Dangar of the massacre at his Myall Creek station.

By Monday 23 July, Day, Pack and the troopers had travelled the two hundred miles to the Big River. They arrived at Dr Newton's property in the early afternoon, where they were greeted by Thomas Foster. News of their arrival rapidly spread throughout the district. Some of the locals were surprised that a party of mounted troopers had arrived in the district to investigate the murder of some blacks, because the last time mounted troopers had been in the district they themselves had been murdering the blacks.

Having heard of their arrival, William Hobbs rode over to meet them. He was met at the door of the superintendent's hut by his friend Thomas Foster.

'Good day, Bill.'

'Morning, Tom,' replied Hobbs, dismounting and handing the reins to young Johnny Murphy. 'They've finally arrived, eh Tom?'

'They certainly have. Come in and meet Mr Day,' invited Foster, stepping into the hut, with Hobbs following.

Day sat at the table in the middle of the room, looking up as Foster and Hobbs entered. Born in County Kerry, Ireland, Edward Denny Day was thirty-seven years old, from a military background, and known for his firmness and determination. He stood and shook Hobbs' hand. 'Mr Hobbs, I received yer letter. It be a terrible business, this.'

'Yes, Mr Day, a shocking business. I am pleased, though, that the Governor has decided to follow it up. You're very welcome here, sir.'

'Thank you, Mr Hobbs. Aye, our new Governor is very determined to protect the natives and ensure that law and order is maintained throughout these frontier districts. I just hope that I can do my part to ensure that justice is served in this particular case.'

'I'm sure you will, Mr Day. I'm pleased to see you've brought so many troopers with you.'

'Aye, just to help with rounding up the culprits.'

Hobbs, Foster and Day sat down at the table while the hut-keeper,

Robert Sexton, prepared a cup of tea for the new arrival.

'Now, Mr Hobbs, I've decided that I'm going to base myself here at Dr Newton's, as it seems that it be more central than yer station out at Myall Creek; and Mr Foster also tells me there are more huts here for my troopers.'

'Oh ... right, yes ... well, that's right. And I suppose you're closer here to the stations downriver where some of these stockmen come from,' Hobbs conceded.

'What's the matter, Mr Hobbs?' Day inquired. 'You seem somewhat disappointed.'

'Yes, well, I suppose I am, a little. I think I was probably looking forward to the safety of having you and your troopers up at Myall Creek.'

'I see, aye. Well, I can assure you, Mr Hobbs, I'll not be expecting to take long here at all. We'll be up at your station directly. There are just a few matters I must be attending to down here first.'

'Yes, Mr Day, I can understand that.'

'Good. Well, what I'll be doing firstly is sorting through with yerself, Mr Foster and some of the other witnesses, the names and stations of the suspects, and then I'll be sending Lieutenant Pack and a few of his troopers out to bring them in for questioning.'

'That's fine, sir.' Hobbs nodded as Sexton placed a mug of tea in front of him. As soon as Sexton had done so, Foster waved him toward the door, upon which the convict left the two superintendents and the magistrate in private.

The bearded Day paused while Sexton closed the door behind himself. 'Now, to start with, Mr Hobbs, according to the letter that was sent to the Governor by a Mr Frederick Foot, it seems that one of yer men was involved.'

Hobbs looked at the magistrate incredulously. 'One of my men? Oh no, sir, none of my men were involved at all. Admittedly, my men stood by and let it happen, and I have rebuked them for not stopping it, but they certainly took no part in killing the blacks.'

'Oh, I'm sorry. I had been given to understand one was involved. Mr Foot must have been mistaken, or I must have misunderstood. Didn't ye say, Mr Foster, that one of Mr Dangar's men was with the party of stockmen when they called at yer station the next day looking for more blacks?'

'Yes, Mr Day, Charlie Kilmeister was with them.'

'Yes, I know Kilmeister was riding with them the next day,' Hobbs quickly rejoined, 'but he didn't take part in the killings.' Hobbs paused as Day looked at him doubtingly. 'Mr Day, Kilmeister has worked with me for two years now, and he is a very good servant. He was the one who asked the blacks to come to our station in the first place. He was friends with many of them, as was I.' Day remained silent, merely nodding as Hobbs continued. 'Look, Mr Day, I know Kilmeister should have done more to stop it, and I also know he's been lying to me about the blacks spearing our cattle and about him not knowing any of the stockmen. But, Mr Day, he's only doing that to protect the others. You know what these convicts are like – they stick together.'

Hobbs' natural reaction had been to defend his servant, but he was unsure whether he had convinced Day, or even his own subconscious.

'All right, Mr Hobbs, I accept what you be saying for now; but I be sure, as I go through the investigation, the truth of the matter, whatever it may be, will come out,' Day responded.

Foster chose to keep his thoughts to himself, staring down at the mug of tea in front of him while Hobbs replied.

'I certainly hope it does, Mr Day, because this whole thing is a tragic business. I assume you realise, though, that the fact these convicts do stick together is going to make it very difficult to get reliable statements from the witnesses.'

'Aye, I realise that may be difficult.'

'And the problem in this case is that, apart from some just sticking together, others may well be too scared to say anything.'

Day nodded as Foster joined in to support his friend. 'Bill's right there, Mr Day. There is the feeling around the district that anyone who says anything about it really is putting their life at risk.'

'Well, that's perfectly understandable, but I'm very hopeful that I'll be able to lean on the witnesses enough to get them to make complete statements. And I'm hopeful that, with yer help, I can have most of the murderers identified and arrested before I have to start questioning too many of the convict witnesses.'

'That may be helpful, definitely,' Hobbs agreed.

'And you'd best be a wee bit careful yerselves. Yer'd be putting yerselves at risk as well, ye know ?'

'Yes, well, we're aware of that, but something just has to be done about this whole business. I also like to think we'd be safer than any convict who speaks out. They'd be less likely to attack us than one of their own.' Hobbs looked at Foster, who, Day observed, seemed uncomfortable with the whole discussion. 'Well,' Hobbs added, 'we hope we're safer.'

'Aye, but just be extra careful while I be getting this lot rounded up. I don't want anything to be happening to my main witnesses.'

'Certainly, Mr Day,' agreed Hobbs.

'Now, what I'll be doing,' said the magistrate, returning to the business at hand, 'is taking statements from you, Mr Hobbs; Mr Foster; Sexton; and the young lad.'

'Johnny Murphy,' Foster volunteered.

'Aye, Johnny Murphy; and then, Mr Foster, yer've suggested I go across the river here to another station where there be a couple of other witnesses who saw the stockmen riding around the district. It is quite close by, as I understand.'

'Yes, it is. That's Dight's station, where Bates and Mace are. The stockmen called into that station after they killed the blacks, when they were looking for more,' Foster explained.

'Right, well, they should be able to provide me with some extra names. Then I'll be heading out to Myall Creek to see yer lot, Mr Hobbs, and to take statements – and, of course, to inspect the site of the killings and collect evidence from there.'

'Well, you can have it from me, Mr Day, that will certainly be a most unpleasant task. It is just terrible what they did to those people – women and children mainly, you know?'

'Aye, so I understand – a devil of a business. Be assured, though, I'll be doing all I can to see that the men responsible are brought to justice.'

'I'm sure you will, Mr Day.' Hobbs gave the magistrate a half smile. 'Well, sir, if you don't need me any further for now, I'll head back to Myall Creek. I've got a station to run and a couple of very edgy servants over there.'

'Aye, to be sure, Mr Hobbs. Thank you for yer help. I'll be seeing you in a couple of days.'

Foster rose and escorted Hobbs from the hut while Day remained at the table taking notes. The two overseers stood outside the door exchanging reassurances while young Johnny Murphy retrieved Hobbs' mare. Hobbs then mounted his horse and rode off alone toward Myall Creek.

CHAPTER TWENTY THREE

Saturday 28 July 1838.

I t was late in the afternoon, exactly seven weeks after Fleming's gang had come to the Myall Creek station, when another large party of horsemen appeared at the top of the ridge to the west of the station huts. Like their predecessors, they were heavily armed. Like their predecessors, they paused briefly at the peak of the ridge, with the setting sun at their backs. Like their predecessors, they galloped down the slope toward the huts, and the sound of the ground rumbling beneath their horses' hooves caused panic at Myall Creek. This time, though, the panic did not strike the hearts of a whole clan of Weraerai – it struck just one heart.

Charles Kilmeister was repairing a broken rail at the stockyard on the western side of the huts when he heard the sound of the approaching troopers led by Edward Denny Day. He immediately looked to his companion, with whom he had been working in virtual silence. Anderson glanced back at him, and for the first time in weeks their eyes met briefly.

Anderson saw the panic in Kilmeister's eyes as he blurted, 'For

God's sake, mind what ya say; and don't say I went with 'em, but a quarter of an hour later.'

Anderson ignored the plea as he put down the end of the railing he was holding and walked a few yards away, in the direction of the approaching horsemen. His reaction had only caused Kilmeister to panic even more. In the period since the massacre, in the isolation of the station and with his fellow murderers on the surrounding stations, Kilmeister had felt very confident in threatening Anderson's life should he ever say anything about anyone involved. Now the odds had suddenly swung around.

'Anderson ... ' he called after the hutkeeper. 'George.'

No response.

Kilmeister hurried after him, but Anderson continued to ignore him, his eyes fixed on the approaching troopers. This was the moment George Anderson had been waiting for since one morning about three weeks before. It was shortly after Hobbs told them that Foot had left to report the massacre. Anderson had been down the creek, checking on the Weraerai's fish traps after the previous night's rain. On his way back it started raining heavily again. At first he had started hurrying toward the shelter of the huts, but as he got more and more drenched, he remembered the last time he had been soaked by pouring rain. On that occasion he had not run from it, but had instead stood and revelled in it. He remembered the feeling of joy which had swept through him as he stood in the bitter winter rain while a smiling Ipeta watched from the doorway of his hut. He had remembered, and then he had made a decision.

'Anderson, mind what ya say, for God's sake,' Kilmeister pleaded.

Anderson turned and again observed the fear in Kilmeister's eyes; it reminded him of the terror he had seen in the eyes of every one of the Weraerai that evening. He felt Kilmeister grip his forearm in desperation. The hutkeeper locked his grey-blue eyes on the stockman. 'Ya killed Ipeta.' He then wrenched his arm free and continued walking toward the troopers.

The sound of their approach had also stirred Hobbs from his

hut, and he came out to greet them. As he walked passed Kilmeister, he saw the colour had drained from his face and he appeared to be trembling. Hobbs stopped before him. 'Why are you so frightened, Charlie? You say you're innocent.'

'Th-They're enough to make anyone frightened,' he stammered in reply.

Hobbs shook his head and walked to where Anderson stood, as Day and his troopers reined to a halt in front of them.

'Good day, Mr Hobbs.'

'And to you, Mr Day. Pleased to see you, at last.'

'Aye, sorry. It's taken rather longer than we thought to get out here. You got my message, though?'

'Yes indeed. Thanks for letting me know. I would have been rather worried by now if you hadn't sent word you'd be late. How is your investigation going, anyway?'

'All things considered, we've done pretty well. We have two in custody already.'

'Really? Already? Well, come into the hut and tell me all about it. My men will look after your horses.'

'Thank you, Mr Hobbs, but I'd rather be going to have a look at the site where these murders actually happened, afore it gets dark. Could you be showing us where it is?'

'Yes, certainly, Mr Day. It's just back on that ridge you've just come over,' Hobbs replied, pointing behind the troopers. 'I'll just get my horse.'

'No need for that. Trooper, give Mr Hobbs yer horse, would you?' Day instructed the nearest trooper, who obligingly dismounted and held his horse's head while Hobbs mounted. 'Corporal McKnight, stay here and get the men settled in. Lieutenant Pack and I will be back shortly,' Day advised as he turned his horse to follow Hobbs.

'So, you've got two in custody, Mr Day. Who are they?' Hobbs inquired as the police magistrate drew alongside him.

'William Hawkins and 'Black' Johnstone.'

'Oh.'

'Aye, it was quite strange, really. Corporal McKnight and a few troopers went over to Bell's Noogera Creek station to get George Palliser, but he wasn't there. Instead they found Hawkins. Then a few hours later, while they were still over there, Johnstone came riding in and gave himself up. He said he'd heard we were looking for him so had decided to just come straight in. Strange to get such cooperation from one of the culprits, when no-one else wants to cooperate at all.'

'So you're generally being met by silence, are you?' Hobbs asked.

'Aye, to be sure. Mr Foster and yerself were certainly right about that, but I didn't really expect it to be any different. Some are cooperative, though, like the young feller at Foster's, Johnny Murphy. He was helpful. But the convicts are very difficult to get anything out of. Mace and Bates, across the river, couldn't remember much at all about the gang of horsemen. Although they went to their station, they claimed they didn't know any of them. "Never seen them before" – that sort of response.'

'That's a shame, because Bates really is a decent sort of chap.'

'Aye, I thought he seemed to be. Obviously he's scared; but I must admit, his memory improved a wee bit when I put some pressure on him. He then became more cooperative.'

'I'm pleased to hear that.'

'But Mace remained very difficult. You'd think a ticket-of-leave man would have a better attitude and would be trying to better himself.'

Hobbs nodded as he turned his horse to the right and returned to the matter at hand. 'This way, Mr Day, just over there, it is. I must warn you, though, sir, it really is a terrible sight – or it was when I saw it, and I imagine after all these weeks it will probably be even worse.'

'I expect it is, Mr Hobbs, I expect it is. Mr Foster has already described it to me in some detail.'

As they rode over a dip in the ridge and into a clearing, Day noticed a mixture of shock, confusion and disbelief cloud Hobbs' face.

'What's the matter, Mr Hobbs?'

'That's the spot just there, but ... but it's all gone. *They're* all gone!'

'What do you mean?'

'The bodies, the fire, the logs – it's all gone.' Hobbs hurried his mount over to the middle of the clearing where there was a large burnt area in the grass. Day and Pack followed.

'It's quite obvious from the fire, Mr Day, that this is the right spot.' Hobbs turned his mount in a tight circle as his eyes combed the grass around the horse's hooves.

'Aye, well, there certainly has been a large fire here, but we need more than that.'

Hobbs dismounted and started walking around the burnt patch where the once long grass had been trampled and charred. In some sections only blackened dirt remained.

'Look, Mr Day, you can see that this whole area here has been swept clean with branches or something.'

Day dismounted and joined Hobbs. 'Aye, it's quite apparent that someone has done a pretty thorough job of getting rid of the evidence, if yer sure this is the right spot.'

'Absolutely positive. No doubt at all,' Hobbs assured the magistrate.

Day turned to his assistant. 'Lieutenant Pack, could you be having a look around the area while I stay here with Mr Hobbs to see if we can find anything?'

'Certainly, sir.' Pack nodded before riding off into the surrounding bush.

'Well, we —— '

'Look, Mr Day,' Hobbs interrupted, hurriedly bending down and picking up something from the charred earth. He held it up to Day.

'A piece of bone ... perhaps a jawbone, by the look of it,' Day observed, examining it closely. 'Well, that'll be a start. Let's see what else we can find.'

Holding onto the reins of their horses in one hand, the two men crouched and began a closer search of the area.

Hobbs soon found another piece of bone. 'This looks like a section of rib. What do you think, Mr Day?'

'Aye, to be sure. Tragically, though, it's clearly from a wee one, judging by the size of it.'

'That's what I thought.'

After a brief inspection of the bone fragment, Day's eyes returned to the ground at his feet, and in silence he and his companion continued looking. After a few minutes, Day called Hobbs' attention to something in his hand.

'Here are some teeth, Mr Hobbs, and some more bone fragments as well.'

The pair continued their search until Pack returned a short time later.

'How did you go, Lieutenant?'

'Can't find a thing, sir. No bodies, no burnt logs, nothing.'

'All right. Well, we've managed to find some bones and teeth, but it's getting too dark, so that will have to do for now. Are you ready to head back, Mr Hobbs?'

'Yes, certainly, if you think that's enough?'

'Hopefully. Someone has certainly done a good job of getting rid of the evidence and cleaning the area up. You don't know who could have done that, do you, Mr Hobbs? After all, it is very close to yer huts.'

'I have no idea. I'm not here all the time. I spend a fair amount of time at the other stations, and I've been away a few times since the blacks were killed.'

'I see, aye. Well, I'd certainly be very interested in getting to the bottom of that little mystery, because it would have taken quite a major effort to get rid of all the bodies and logs that Mr Foster and yerself have described.'

'Yes, it was a very large pile, I assure you, Mr Day.'

'Well, it would obviously have involved several men and taken some time. You'd think someone on yer station must have seen something.'

'Perhaps they did, Mr Day, but they certainly haven't told me about it.'

Hobbs and Day mounted their horses and, along with Pack, began to ride back down the slope toward the huts.

'When we get back I think I should take this Kilmeister of yers into custody, at least until I've finished questioning everyone else here at yer station. I've certainly been given to understand he was involved, and I have a considerable amount of evidence against him already.'

'Well, yes, Mr Day, you have to do whatever you think best for your investigation, but he assures me he's innocent and I have to believe him. He's an excellent servant, and ... well, I just think ... ' The superintendent paused in his defence of his man.

'Aye, I understand that, Mr Hobbs, but he appeared very nervous when we rode up, and the last thing I want is him making a bolt for the bush.'

'Yes, yes.' Hobbs nodded, his brow furrowing. 'Mr Day, how did you know which one of my men was Kilmeister?'

'Oh, that was very obvious, Mr Hobbs, very obvious indeed.'

As soon as they returned, Pack took one of the troopers into the stockmen's hut. Before he had a chance to protest, Charles Kilmeister was in handcuffs and manacled to the trooper.

Hobbs stood at the door of the hut as Kilmeister looked up at him with the expression of a scolded mongrel. 'Mr Hobbs ... ' he protested.

Hobbs looked at him briefly before lowering his eyes and slowly shaking his head. 'There's nothing I can do, Charlie,' he muttered. 'I'm sorry.'

* * *

After hurriedly consuming the supper provided by Anderson, Edward Denny Day set himself up at the table in Hobbs' hut and began formally questioning the witnesses, starting with the superintendent. Hobbs explained that he was away at the lower station at the time of the massacre but that he had first heard about it when he stopped at Dight's station on the way back. There, John Bates had informed him that a party of stockmen had been up to Myall Creek and killed all the blacks except for a gin whom they had kept, and whom Bates had subsequently released. He then outlined to the police magistrate his discussions with Foster before he returned to Myall Creek and questioned Anderson and Kilmeister. He explained that Davey had taken him out to the site, where he had seen the terrible aftermath of the massacre. Day interrupted him at this point.

'This Davey is another native black, though?'

'Oh yes, he's a native black, but he's not part of this local mob. He and his brother, Billy, are from the Peel River district, though they've been working as stockmen with us for years now. Davey actually followed them when they took the blacks away. He saw much of the killings and saw them hacking up the bodies.'

'Really? This hasn't been mentioned to me afore. He could be a very helpful witness; but I don't be imagining he's a Christian, is he?'

'No, Mr Day, he's not; but why do you ask?'

'If he's not a Christian, he can't swear on the Bible, so he can't give evidence. He be therefore virtually useless as a witness.'

'Oh, I see.'

'Aye, this be a fairly typical situation with these killings of blacks; the only witnesses are blacks, and they can't give evidence.'

'Hence these men just ride around killing as they like,' muttered Hobbs.

Hobbs' comment failed to elicit a response from Day, whose mind seemed to be elsewhere. 'Hmmm,' he murmured, 'this investigation isn't going as smoothly as I would have liked, Mr Hobbs. Firstly, the bodies have been disposed of, and then we have an eyewitness who can't give evidence. Where would this Davey be now, anyway?'

'He and Billy are down at Arndell's, at Barraba. I thought they'd be safer down there on account of everything that has been happening around here.'

'Aye, safer, to be sure.' Day sat back and rubbed his eyes to relieve the strain of writing his notes in the dim light of the hut. A moment later he resumed his questioning. 'All right. Now then, so up on the ridge, what exactly did you see?'

* * *

In the stockmen's hut next door, George Anderson, Andrew Burrowes and Charles Kilmeister waited anxiously, unsure whether Day would call them that night or wait until tomorrow. Kilmeister remained manacled to the trooper, while Anderson and Burrowes lay on their respective bunks. Anderson was experiencing a mixture of emotions. He was delighted the wait for the law was over, but now that it was here he was nervous and a little frightened. British law had never been kind to him. His own experience at the Old Bailey had educated him on the random nature of the justice system, and he felt he would be foolish to place too much faith in it now.

It was getting late, and as he lay there half dozing, rehearsing his answers, he was roused by the gravelly voice of Corporal McKnight. 'Come on, Anderson, it's your turn. Mr Day wants to see ya.'

He sat up and pulled on his boots. As he started to follow McKnight to the door, the manacled Kilmeister looked up at him and tried to grab at his arm as he passed, but the chains jerked tight, preventing him. Anderson glanced down.

'George! George! You stick to me, now.' It was part plea, part order. The hutkeeper kept walking, saying nothing, and closed the door behind him. 'George … '

Inside Hobbs' hut, Anderson stood in silence beside Corporal

McKnight. Day sat on the far side of the table, with a small pile of papers and a Bible in front of him, while Hobbs sat at the end.

After stating his name and swearing to tell the truth, George Anderson was instructed to sit on the chair opposite Day. He sat down as the magistrate dipped his quill into an ink bottle and scrawled the date and Anderson's name at the top of a piece of paper. The scratching of the quill on the coarse paper and the crackling of the fire were the only sounds in the room. Day again dipped the quill into the ink and then looked up at Anderson. This was the moment.

'Now, can you be telling me, George, what happened to the blacks?'

Anderson hesitated only briefly before answering. 'Well, sir, they was camped here for a few weeks – since about the middle of May, I think. They was peaceful and didn't do no harm. Then Mr 'obbs went away to the lower station for a few days, and … ' Anderson's voice trailed off as he began to lose nerve.

'And? What happened when Mr Hobbs went away?'

Anderson peered into the inscrutable eyes of the Irishman and shifted in his seat before continuing. 'Well, sir, this party of stockmen come ridin' up fast into their camp —— '

'Were these stockmen armed?'

'Yes, sir.'

'What with?'

'Swords and guns and pistols.'

'Go on.'

'Well, they came ridin' up and all the blacks come runnin' into the hut to get away from them.'

'What happened then?'

'Well, some of the stockmen followed them into the hut and trussed
them to a tether rope then took them away.'

'They tied them all up and took them away?'

'Yes, sir, except for a few of them. There was two young boys who hid in the creek when they rode up, and a little girl that I hid from them … and … '

'And who else?'

'And two gins they left with me and Davey, sir.'

'That's all?'

'Yes, sir.'

'And what did these stockmen do with the rest of them then?'

'They took them away, over to the ridge, sir.' Anderson paused again.

'Then what happened?'

'A few minutes later I heard a couple of shots. Then it went quiet.'

'What happened next?' Day asked again, without looking up from the notes he was taking.

'Well, Davey followed them over to the ridge, and he come back later and told me they killed all the blacks.'

Day now looked up from his notes and looked Anderson directly in the eye. 'All right, then – these stockmen, who were they?'

'I dunno, sir,' Anderson replied, lowering his eyes. His back was itchy again. He rubbed it as well as he could on the back of the chair.

'Look here, Anderson,' the magistrate demanded, 'you must know *some* of them.'

The convict slowly looked up at those eyes again. This time they were staring straight through him. 'I dunno, sir,' he repeated. 'I did hear a couple of names but I don't know them. Mr 'obbs can tell ya, I'm only new in this district and I don't get round to the other stations —— '

'The names,' Day cut him off. 'Who were they?'

'Fleming and Russell, sir … but I don't know if I'd recognise any of them again if I saw them.'

'Fleming and Russell?' Day hastily recorded the names.

'Yes, sir, but I've never seen them before.'

'All right, Anderson. What about Kilmeister?'

The light in the hut was becoming increasingly dim as the fire, which had earlier burnt quite strongly, was now reduced to glowing embers. An oil lamp sat on the shelf behind Hobbs, casting the superintendent's shadow part of the way along the table until it was washed out by the light of the candle, which sat in the middle of the table, providing the only other light in the room.

The candle flickered. Anderson could feel his boss's eyes upon him as he spoke slowly, deliberately. 'When the stockmen rode up, Kilmeister went outside and shook hands with some of 'em and started talking to 'em. I didn't 'ear what they said, sir, but Kilmeister got his pistol, saddled his 'orse and went with 'em when they took the blacks away.'

William Hobbs moaned as he raised his hands to his face and slowly shook his head. Anderson could not bring himself to look at Hobbs, and Day glanced only briefly at him before returning his gaze to the convict and continuing.

'Did Kilmeister help them tie up the blacks?'

'No, sir, he was off saddling his 'orse.'

'Did Kilmeister assist with forcing the blacks away?'

'No, sir, he just rode off with them, with the stockmen and the blacks.'

'When did he return?'

'Not till the next evenin', just before sundown, when they all came back.'

'And did you be asking where he had been?'

'No, sir, I had no conversation with him at all – except I said it was a very cruel thing that the blacks had been killed. But he made no reply, sir.'

'All right. When the stockmen returned, what did they be doing?'

'Don't rightly recollect, sir.'

'Well, think, Anderson.'

'I dunno, sir.'

'How long did they stay?'

'I don't recollect, sir.'

'A day? A week? How long?'

'I don't recollect, sir.'

'When did they leave?'

'Dunno, sir.'

'What about the fire on the ridge? What can you tell me about it?'

'Nothing, sir. I don't recollect anything about it.'

'Anderson, there was a pile of dead bodies on that ridge, now they be gone. How did that happen?'

'I dunno, sir.'

'Listen, Anderson, I'll be making you think and I'll be making you remember.' The Irish magistrate leant across the table, his face close to Anderson's, whose eyes remained downcast. 'Yer under oath, and I'll be having you committed for trial for not thinking. Do you be knowing what perjury is, Anderson?'

'Yes, sir.' The hutkeeper nodded.

Day slumped back in his chair. It was late. George Anderson had said all he was going to say for now. He had named Fleming and Russell and told of Kilmeister's involvement – that was enough.

'Can you remember anything else, Anderson?' Day asked calmly.

'No, sir.'

Day looked down at his papers before glancing at Hobbs. The overseer shrugged. 'All right, that will have to be the end for now; but don't be thinking I won't be questioning you again, and yer memory had better improve.'

'Yes, sir.' Anderson nodded.

Day turned the pages he had been writing on around to face Anderson. 'This be a record of what you've just told me. Can you be reading it?'

'No, sir.'

'Can you be writing yer name?'

'No, sir.'

'Well, make yer mark at the bottom there, then.'

The illiterate convict hutkeeper did as requested. 'Will that be all, sir?'

'Aye, now get out of here.'

'Thank you, sir.' As he got to his feet, Anderson looked at Hobbs, but his overseer's head was bowed again. 'Good night, Mr 'obbs.'

Hobbs looked up. 'Good night, George.'

Anderson and McKnight left the hut, pulling the door closed behind them.

Day and Hobbs remained seated at the table in silence as Day continued scrawling notes. The scratching of his quill was now the only sound in the room, as the embers of the fire had long since ceased crackling.

Day finally stopped writing and looked at Hobbs, though he avoided the issue which was obviously on the superintendent's mind. 'I hope we can be relying on Anderson, Mr Hobbs, because we don't really have much of a case without him.'

Hobbs quickly roused himself from his thoughts. 'You don't think so, Mr Day?'

'Well, we don't have any bodies, only a few bone fragments and teeth. Davey can't be giving evidence; and basically, all the other witnesses' evidence relates to this party of stockmen riding around the countryside looking for blacks. The only one that can give evidence that they came here, found some and took them away, is Anderson. Without him, our case be very weak indeed.' Day paused before adding, 'He seems a rather stubborn sort of a chap, though.'

'That he is, Mr Day. Very stubborn.'

'Good,' Day murmured.

'Why do you say that?' asked Hobbs.

'Well, Mr Hobbs, I'd much rather have a stubborn, strong-willed chap as my key witness, than some feeble-minded sop who is going to change his story at the last minute,' Day explained, raising his rather bushy eyebrows.

'Yes, I suppose you're right; but though he's stubborn, I've never really regarded him as a strong character at all. On the contrary, the other men regard him as somewhat cowardly.'

'Aye, I can be understanding that, but there is a difference between being brave and being stubborn. Look, tonight his behaviour was, I would consider, quite strange. After naming Fleming, Russell and Kilmeister as being involved, he then refused to tell anything more about minor, rather unimportant details like when the horsemen returned or how long they be staying. The only explanation I can see for that sort of behaviour is just blind, pig-headed stubbornness.' Day slowly stroked his long, dark beard, in which the first signs of grey were beginning to appear, as he continued. 'And stubborn is what I'm going to be needing him to be, because once I get the full story from him – and I will – I'm going to be needing him to stick to it. He's obviously very fearful about what could be happening to him if he says too much – and with good reason. I'd be saying he's probably lucky to still be alive today. I'll be having my men keep a very close eye on him.'

'Yes, well, that may be for the best. And I'm sure you're right – there is a lot more that he isn't telling us.'

Day nodded. 'Mmmm. By the way, Mr Hobbs, I am sorry about Kilmeister.'

'So am I, Mr Day. I've put so much trust in him over the past couple of years I just didn't want to believe that he could do something like that to those people, and then lie to me like that.'

'Aye, I know. I wonder what those stockmen be saying to him that made him decide to join them,' Day mused.

'I don't know, Mr Day; but whatever it was, nothing can justify what he did.'

Hobbs got to his feet, put a couple of logs onto the fire and stared at the now glowing embers as he stirred them back to a steady flame.

CHAPTER TWENTY FOUR

Monday 30 July 1838.

T he police magistrate again sat in the makeshift courtroom in the overseer's hut, with Hobbs at one end of the table. The door opened and a trooper led in a handcuffed Charles Kilmeister.

'Sit down, Kilmeister,' Day instructed.

'Yes, sir.' Kilmeister sat, while the trooper remained standing directly behind his chair.

'Now, I have here evidence regarding yer involvement in the slaughter of the blacks —— '

'But, sir, I —— '

'Quiet, Kilmeister, you'll get yer turn later. First I'll be explaining to you what the procedure is going to be.'

'Yes, Mr Day. Sorry, sir.'

'Right, now I am going to read you the evidence; and when I have, you'll have the right to question the witnesses about their evidence, all right?'

'Yes, sir.'

'First I'll read through Mr Hobbs' statement.'

'Yes, sir.'

As the police magistrate read the superintendent's statement, Kilmeister repeatedly looked toward Hobbs for some sign of support, but all he received was the icy stare of a resentful man.

Kilmeister listened anxiously as Day read but felt relieved that there really wasn't too much indicating he was with the stockmen when they slaughtered the blacks. When Day concluded and offered him his right to question his superintendent, he was quick to accept the opportunity.

'Mr Hobbs, sir, did ya ask Davey about my role in it?'

'Yes, I did, when I returned to the station.'

'What did he say, sir?'

'He said you weren't with them when they rode up to the huts – but I wouldn't expect you would have been. He didn't seem to want to talk about it; and I didn't press him on it because we both know he'd be too scared to say anything against you anyway.'

'But he didn't say I went with them, did he, sir?'

'No, he didn't.'

'Any other questions for Mr Hobbs?' Day asked.

Feeling he had just had some sort of success, Kilmeister declined.

'All right, trooper, bring Anderson in, would you?'

When Anderson entered, Day instructed him to sit at the end of the table, opposite Hobbs.

'Now, Kilmeister, we'll be going through the same procedure. I'll be reading Anderson's statement of evidence and you'll have the right to question him at the end.'

'Yes, sir.'

Kilmeister shifted nervously in his seat and glanced at Anderson, but the hutkeeper refused to make eye contact, looking instead at Day. The magistrate read the evidence, and when he came to Anderson's statement that Kilmeister had got his pistol and horse and gone with the stockmen, the colour drained from Kilmeister's face. He again turned to Anderson, muttering 'No' and shaking his head. Anderson continued to ignore him, his eyes remaining fixed on Day as he read on. When the magistrate finished, he looked up and stared at Kilmeister with such intensity that the handcuffed stockman was forced to bow his head.

'Do you have any questions for this witness?'

Kilmeister slowly looked up. 'Yes, sir.'

'Go ahead.'

'George,' he pleaded, 'surely ya remember that I went after the stockmen took the blacks away, and that I only went to look for me cattle?'

Anderson focused his steel blue eyes on Kilmeister and shook his head. 'Ya went at the same time the stockmen took the blacks away.'

Kilmeister's head fell forward onto his chest as he muttered to himself unintelligibly. Day recorded Anderson's damning words before pushing the paper toward the hutkeeper, who etched his mark upon Kilmeister's fate.

* * *

It was early in the afternoon when Andrew Burrowes' questioning at the hands of the police magistrate finally finished. He had provided Day with important evidence regarding his overnight stay at Bell's station, having told him of the stockmen's stated intentions of hunting the blacks. He had also been able to name some of those present as: Russell, 'Black' Johnstone, Foley, Hawkins, Palliser and a man of Mr Glennie's.

After Burrowes had left the hut, Hobbs leant forward toward the police magistrate. 'Mr Day, while listening to Burrowes' evidence I remembered another chap that Bates mentioned to me.'

'Ah, fine, now who would that be?'

'An assigned servant at Eaton's. Bates said he felt rather sorry for him being involved in the whole business because this young chap, Jem, had said it was a bad thing, that he didn't like it and wouldn't have a hand in such a thing again. Parry, I believe his surname is. He said he was led by the others.'

'Good, good. Thank you, Mr Hobbs. That brings my list up to ten.'

Day shuffled through the papers in front of him. 'Hawkins, Johnstone, Kilmeister – already in custody. Telluse, who I have sent Corporal McKnight to pick up. Fleming, Russell, Foley, Oates, Palliser, and now Parry. If I can get confirmation on Lamb, that will be eleven.'

'Well, you're making good progress, Mr Day.' Hobbs smiled.

'Mmm. I should start bringing the rest of them in; but afore I be doing that, I want to be confronting the ones I already have in custody with the evidence I've collected so far; see if I can get any admissions from them, or perhaps some more names.'

'Well, I hope you can, Mr Day.'

'I think I may be able to. Anyway, I'll be getting the men organised to head back down to Foster's as soon as we can. I'd appreciate it greatly if you'd accompany us, Mr Hobbs.'

'Yes, certainly.'

'But before we be heading off, I think we should have a thorough search around the area to see if we can find what happened to those remains that disappeared from up there. You might care to assist us there, too, Mr Hobbs.'

'Of course, Mr Day.'

Day nodded his thanks and continued. 'Now, as for Anderson, I originally planned to keep him with us, but I think I might be leaving him here to stew for a few days. Might help his memory a little.'

'Do you think he'll be safe?'

'Aye, I think so. In fact I be counting on it. I'll be trusting that my men will be able to bring the culprits in over the next couple of days so they won't be having the opportunity to get up here to hurt Anderson even if that be their inclination.'

'Certainly, Mr Day, but the problem is that they have plenty of sympathisers in this district who might just take it upon themselves to silence Anderson.'

'Well, that's a risk I'm going to have to take, because, as we both agree, he knows a lot more than he's saying, and I need him to talk; and the more nervous he is, the more likely he is to talk. We need him to be worrying a wee bit so that his stubbornness works *for* us rather than *against* us, because, as I've said, I'll be betting that once he tells us the full story, he won't be changing it.'

CHAPTER TWENTY FIVE

Wednesday 1 August 1838.

E dward Denny Day, William Hobbs, Thomas Foster and Lieutenant Pack sat at the table in Foster's hut, eating the breakfast
provided by the hutkeeper, Robert Sexton. The magistrate had spent
the previous day taking further evidence from Hobbs, Foster, Bates
and Sexton, and questioning his prisoners – but the convicts had maintained their silence and admitted nothing. Day could delay no longer,
though, and was now ready to go and round up their accomplices.

'How long do you think you'll be away, Mr Day?' Foster asked.

'Don't really know exactly. Depends how much luck I have finding
them. But from what Mr Hobbs and yerself tell me, I have considerable territory to cover. I'll be moving as fast as I can, though. You
know, get to them afore they know we be coming.'

'Well, that's certainly going to be pretty difficult, Mr Day. Word
spreads very quickly round this district,' Hobbs advised.

'Aye, I'm finding that out. The first place I'm going to be heading, though, is up to Mungie Bundie to get Fleming. I hope what
you've been informed about him fleeing the district isn't correct, Mr

Foster, because the evidence I've gathered so far clearly indicates he be the leader.'

'Oh, he was certainly the leader,' Foster confirmed. 'He was the only squatter. I hope he hasn't fled, too, but that's the word around the district. It seems he may have headed down to the family property on the Hawkesbury.'

'Aye. Anyway, gentlemen, the sooner I get moving, the more likely I am to catch him – and the others, for that matter. Thanks for that breakfast, Robert.'

'No trouble, Mr Day,' Sexton replied with a nod.

Day and Pack got to their feet and put on their coats.

'Now, Mr Hobbs, will you be going back to Myall Creek?'

'Yes, Mr Day, I'll head up there right away. There's rather a lot to be done up there.'

'Good. Keep a close eye on Anderson. I'll be sending a trooper up to see you when I get back, and I'll be leaving two troopers here to guard the prisoners. So if you have any problems, they'll be here to assist you.'

'Thanks, Mr Day, but hopefully everything should be all right.' Hobbs rose from the table and walked to the door of the hut, together with Foster, Day and Pack. 'I certainly hope everything goes well for you and you manage to catch these animals.'

'Well, you know, Mr Hobbs, these convicts be brutalised men. Violence and cruelty be part of their lives,' Day replied.

'Yes, I realise that, Mr Day. And Fleming – what of his motives?'

'Fear, revenge, greed, bloodlust. Any or all, I would be guessing, Mr Hobbs. Take yer pick.' Day mounted his horse. 'Thanks for yer hospitality, Mr Foster.'

'See you when you get back, Mr Day,' Foster called as the magistrate wheeled his horse around before kicking it into a canter and riding away in company with Pack, McKnight and five troopers.

* * *

Day and his men rode hard throughout the day and on past sunset before camping under the splendour of the Milky Way, ready for an early morning drive to Mungie Bundie, residence of John Fleming.

* * *

It was just after sunrise, the dew was thick on the ground and the huts were silent when eight armed horsemen galloped up, breaking the morning tranquillity of Mungie Bundie. Edward Denny Day leapt from his horse and bashed on the door of the squatter's hut, while twenty yards away Lieutenant Pack did likewise at the stockmen's hut. Two troopers rode to the rear of the buildings.

Day tried the door again, with no response. 'John Fleming,' he yelled. 'John Fleming, Police Magistrate Day here. Open the door.'

No response.

'Mr Day,' Pack called from the door of the stockmen's hut, 'there's someone here, sir.'

The door opened just enough for an eye of a drowsy looking hut-keeper, Thomas Berryman, to peer through. Pack pushed the door completely open, striking Berryman on the forehead. 'Oww!' he whined.

'I'm Lieutenant Pack; what's ya name?'

'That hurt,' Berryman complained, rubbing his head.

'What's ya name?' Pack demanded.

'Berryman, sir. Thomas Berryman.'

'All right, Berryman, we're looking for John Fleming. Is he here?'

'No, sir.'

Day hurried over from the squatter's hut.

Pack turned to the magistrate as he approached. 'He says Fleming's not here, Mr Day.'

'Thanks, Lieutenant. I'll be questioning him, if you and the troopers have a look around to see if there's anyone else about the place. There be no sign of anyone at the main hut.'

'Yes, sir.'

'Corporal McKnight, you can stay with me.' The magistrate turned to the hutkeeper. 'All right, you, inside.'

Lieutenant Pack walked over to the squatter's hut, while Day and McKnight entered the stockmen's hut with Berryman.

'Now, sit down,' Day ordered Berryman once they were inside. 'Corporal, can you be having one of the men bring my papers from my saddle bags?'

McKnight nodded and immediately went to the door, where he called for a trooper to bring Day's saddle bags from his horse. A minute later, Day had his papers on the table in front of him and was ready to proceed.

'I be Edward Denny Day, Police Magistrate from Muswellbrook. Under orders from the Governor, Sir George Gipps, I be conducting an inquiry into the murder of a group of natives at the Myall Creek station in June. Now, what's yer name?'

'I already told the lieutenant that.'

Day looked up suddenly from his papers. 'Oh, yer going to be like that, are you?' From between gritted teeth, he then added, 'I don't be caring if you've already told the King, tell me.'

'Yes, sir. Thomas Berryman.'

'And what'd yer job be here, Berryman?'

'I'm the hutkeeper.'

'And yer master's name is John Fleming?'

'Yes, sir.'

'And where would Mr Fleming be?'

'Not here, sir,' Berryman answered, pulling his fingers through his wispy, mousey-coloured hair and fidgeting in his seat.

'I can see that,' Day responded impatiently, 'but *where* is he?'

'Sir, excuse me, but I've got a call of nature, sir.'

'What?'

'A call of nature, sir,'

'Go on, get out of here.' Day was already frustrated that his lightning fast dash downriver to Mungie Bundie had not netted his prize catch, John Fleming, so he had little patience for someone he could tell was going to be yet another uncooperative witness. 'Corporal, go with him, would you? Make sure he doesn't take off anywhere.'

Berryman jumped to his feet and hurried out the door, with Corporal McKnight following close behind.

Day took the opportunity to have a look around the small stockmen's hut for anything that might be of interest to his inquiry, but found nothing in the few minutes before McKnight and the reluctant Berryman returned.

'All right now, Berryman, sit down and we'll continue without interruption.'

'Can I just put me coat on? It were very cold out there, sir.'

'Hurry up.'

Berryman pulled his coat off a hook near the door. 'Would ya like me to light the fire, sir? It's pretty cold in here too, sir.'

'No, I wouldn't, now sit down,' the magistrate said firmly, looking at Corporal McKnight, who was moving toward Berryman. The corporal was a large, powerfully built man, with a mangled nose, misshapened teeth and a stated preference for physical force over the more subtle means of questioning.

Day shook his head at him and McKnight stopped moving. Berryman quickly took his seat opposite Day.

'All right, Berryman, where is Mr Fleming?'

'Dunno, sir.'

'When did he leave?'

'Don't rightly know, sir. A few days ago, I think.'

'Does he normally go away for days at a time, Berryman?'

'Yair, sir, a bit, I suppose.'

'What about in June, about the tenth, was he away for a few days then?'

'Dunno, sir, can't rightly remember.'

'You don't remember?'

'No, sir. One day's pretty much the same as another round here, sir.'

'Do you remember a couple of Mr Dangar's men – Burrowes and Reid – coming here?'

'Yes, sir.'

'Ah, good. Well, Mr Fleming wasn't here that night, was he?'

'No, sir, but he'd definitely slept in his hut the night before.'

'Oh, you can remember that, eh?'

'Yair, sir.'

'Remarkable. But what about after that? Was he away for a few days after Burrowes and Reid were here?'

'No, sir, not at all. He went lookin' for some cattle, but that was only for two days. Then he came back and stayed for three or four days.'

'When he left, did he take any weapons with him?'

'No sir, I didn't see any.'

'Well, he must be the only man who rides around this district with no weapons at all.'

Berryman made no reply.

The magistrate paused for a moment and looked Berryman in the eye, but the hutkeeper immediately looked down and fidgeted with a loose strand on his coat.

'Now, he didn't go looking for cattle, did he? He went looking for blacks.'

'No, sir.' Berryman looked up, but upon meeting the gaze of the police magistrate immediately dropped his eyes again and continued fidgeting. 'He never said nothing about goin' out after no blacks, sir.'

Day paused again before continuing. 'What about Ned Foley? Did he go with Fleming?'

'No, sir.'

'Was he away at the same time?'

'He might have been, sir. Don't rightly remember.'

'Did Foley go away at all around the time that Burrowes and Reid were here?'

'Yes, sir, I think he probably did, but only for a couple of days.'

'Did he take any weapons with him?'

'Oh, no, sir, I didn't see him take any, sir.'

'Yer not much help at all, are you, Berryman? You either "don't remember" or you "didn't see".'

Berryman didn't answer but continued looking down as he twisted the loose strand around his fingers.

'Well, Berryman?' Day snapped.

'Sorry I can't help ya more, sir.'

Corporal McKnight began to move around the table toward Berryman, but once again Day looked at him and shook his head. McKnight stopped, disappointed. Day got to his feet, collected his papers together and leant across the table. The magistrate clamped his right hand around the fidgeting fingers of the convict and said quietly, 'Don't worry, Berryman, if I need you to talk, you'll talk.'

The rather startled convict looked up, but Day immediately released his grip and walked out.

McKnight hurried out after the magistrate and quickly drew alongside him. 'Ya went pretty easy on him, sir. Why didn't ya let me make him talk?' the corporal inquired.

'He's not important. I don't be needing evidence from him about where Fleming and Foley were when I've got plenty of witnesses that say they were up river at Myall Creek. I wouldn't be giving a wee weasel like that the satisfaction of thinking anything he had to say was important.'

The magistrate threw his saddle bags across the back of his horse as Lieutenant Pack and the other troopers rode up.

'No sign of anyone else around the place at all, Mr Day; and there's no-one been in the squatter's hut, sir.'

'All right, Lieutenant, let's move on then; we've got a lot of miles to cover today.'

* * *

After a flying visit to Eaton's station, where they arrested James Parry, it was late in the afternoon when Day and his troopers galloped up to the huts at Cobb's station. James Lamb had just returned from yarding some cattle and was sitting at the table in the stockmen's hut when he heard the galloping horses warn of their approach. He got to his feet as his colleague Henry Preece opened the door and announced, 'Troopers'.

Lamb thought about climbing out the back window. He pushed the shutter open, hesitating before changing his mind and heading for the front door. He then heard his name called out and looked out to see Corporal McKnight bounding toward the doorway. There was a brief struggle but McKnight quickly had his powerful forearm locked against Lamb's throat. The stockman was soon manacled, handcuffed to a trooper and pushed onto a seat.

Edward Denny Day introduced himself to the station superintendent, John McGeachie, as he emerged from his hut adjacent to the stockmen's. After explaining the purpose of his visit to the stunned McGeachie, Day quickly set up his travelling courtroom in the superintendent's hut and sent for Lamb and Parry.

As the enchained Lamb was led out of the stockmen's hut, he looked at the trooper to whom he was handcuffed. 'I know you, don't I, trooper?'

The trooper kept looking straight ahead as he led his prisoner toward

McGeachie's hut. 'I don't think so.'

Lamb persisted. 'Yair I do. Ya name's Joe, ain't it?'

The trooper ignored him and kept walking.

'Ya name's Joe and you were with Major Nunn when we all went huntin' blacks together, weren't ya? Bleedin' joke, this is. You arrestin' me for killin' blacks. You've killed just as many of them as I have, haven't ya, eh?'

The trooper stopped abruptly beside the closed door of McGeachie's hut and slammed Lamb up against the wall, his hand gripping the convict's throat. 'Shut ya bleedin' hole, Lamb, right?' The trooper brought his face within a couple of inches of the convict's. 'Shut it or I'll shut it for ya – permanently.'

James Lamb was then shoved through the doorway by a fellow mass murderer, to face Edward Denny Day's court.

'What's the matter, trooper?' Day asked, noting the manner of his arrival with the prisoner.

'Nothing, sir,' the trooper replied, quickly regaining his composure. 'The prisoner just has a rather big mouth, that's all, sir.'

'Oh good. That's just what I be needing, a prisoner with a big mouth. The others don't seem to have any mouths at all. Just you be sitting him down with Parry there, trooper, and we'll be getting on with this.'

The trooper pushed Lamb down onto a chair beside Parry, at the end of the table, and remained standing beside him while Day questioned firstly McGeachie, then Henry Preece.

* * *

Nearly two hours later Day was just finishing up a relatively futile session when Lieutenant Pack and two troopers rode up to the huts. With them was John Deady, the hutkeeper at Bell's station, where the resident stockman, John Russell, had assembled his gang when Andrew Burrowes and Charles Reid had dropped in on June 7. Day had sent Pack off earlier to pick Deady up and bring him over for questioning about that crucial evening.

Day immediately sat Deady down and, after completing the preliminaries, began his questioning. 'Now, on the seventh of June last, do you remember two of Mr Dangar's men, Andrew Burrowes and Charles Reid, staying overnight at yer station?'

'Lots of stockmen drop into our station, sir. I don't rightly recollect that night.'

'Now don't you be getting all forgetful on me, too. Have Burrowes and Reid ever stayed at yer station?'

'Yair, I suppose they have,' Deady mumbled.

'Well, you should be able to remember this particular night because there were six to eight other men staying there as well.'

'Like I said, sir, a lot of stockmen drop into our station.'

'Surely not eight or ten at a time.'

'Well, maybe not, but a lot do.'

'All right, so they do, but on this particular night there was a large group there when Burrowes and Reid stayed.'

'I suppose so, sir,' Deady conceded.

'Right. Now then, who were they?'

'Dunno, sir. It's slipped me memory.'

'Come on, man, it be only seven weeks ago,' Day demanded.

'It may be, sir, but it's slipped me memory,' Deady insisted.

'Listen, Deady, Corporal McKnight here will be making you remember if we have to, right?'

McKnight placed his giant paw on the back of Deady's neck and slowly tightened his grip. His eyes were fixed on Day, waiting for the magistrate to give him the go ahead to have a little fun with the insipid hutkeeper, but Day did not move his eyes from Deady, who quickly relented.

'Yes, sir.'

'So, it's the seventh of June, there be a crowd of eight to ten stockmen in yer hut. Who were they? Give me some names.'

'The only one I can really remember is George Palliser, sir.'

'Good, that's one. The stockman at yer station, John Russell, was obviously there too, wasn't he?' prompted the magistrate.

'Yes, sir.'

McKnight eased his grip on Deady's neck but left his hand resting there.

'Good, let's keep going. Who else?'

'Well, maybe Telluse and Hawkins might have been there.'

'Good, and what about Ned Foley?'

Deady reacted as though he'd been stung by an insect. 'No,' he blurted, shaking his head. 'No, he weren't there that night.'

Day was somewhat surprised by the strength of Deady's denial. 'You sure he wasn't there? I've got other witnesses who say he was there.'

'Yes, sir, I'm sure Foley weren't there.'

Day pursued the matter. 'I'll be reminding you yer under oath, Deady, so I'll be asking you one more time. Was John Fleming's stockman, Edward Foley, at yer station on the night of the seventh of June last?'

Deady looked down at the table in front of him but without hesitation shook his head and replied, 'No, sir, he weren't there. He drops in sometimes but he weren't there that night.'

'All right, what about the two prisoners here?' Day asked, motioning toward Lamb and Parry.

'Dunno, sir. I don't think so, sir.'

'You don't really know much or remember much at all, do you?'

'Look, sir, I swear to ya, sir, I'm not lyin'. I don't know if Parry was there, on account of him being about the place a bit. I don't remember if he were there that night, but I'm pretty sure Lamb weren't there.'

'All right, Deady, I've got Palliser, Telluse and Hawkins – and Russell, of course. Did they have weapons with them?'

'They might have, sir; I dunno, really.'

'Deady, are you telling me yer blind? You must have seen whether they had weapons with them.'

'I suppose they did, sir; but that's normal around here, sir.'

'All right. The next morning, when they left, I assume they took their weapons with them?'

'Maybe. I dunno, sir.'

'I remind you again, Deady, yer under oath. Did they take their weapons with them the next morning?'

'Yes, sir, I suppose so.'

'All right. What weapons did Russell take with him?'

'A carbine and a cutlass, sir; but that wasn't unusual, sir. He was in the habit of taking them with him wherever he went.'

'A cutlass? He took a cutlass wherever he went? Whatever for?'

'Dunno, sir.'

'No, you wouldn't know, would you?' Day muttered.

'What, sir?'

Looking at Deady with a mixture of contempt and frustration, Day ignored the hutkeeper's question and continued. 'Did any of the other men have cutlasses?'

'I dunno, sir, I didn't notice.'

'Why am I not surprised?' cried an exasperated Day. He then looked up at Pack. 'Are you surprised, Lieutenant, that Deady here doesn't know and didn't notice?'

Pack smiled. 'No, sir; but perhaps Corporal McKnight can help him know.'

McKnight again looked at Day, eager to put his persuasive abilities to use; but it was late, and Day was tired of trying to drag information out of reluctant witnesses, especially after having spent all day in the saddle.

'Ah, that won't be necessary just yet, Lieutenant. Listen, Deady, perhaps you'd like to be having a have a chat to Corporal McKnight tomorrow morning? And you should be knowing that our Corporal McKnight is not a man known for his patience. Now, you be having a good night's sleep, son.'

Deady nodded but said nothing.

'All right, that will do for now, Deady; but if you be thinking I've finished with you, you can be sure, I haven't.'

Edward Denny Day finally retired for the night, in preparation for another early start for his investigation and ongoing sweep through the Big River district.

CHAPTER TWENTY SIX

Sunday 5 August 1838.

A lone trooper cantered his mount up to the huts on the Myall Creek station. As he dismounted in front of Hobbs' hut, the station superintendent emerged to greet him, while Anderson peered out from the partly opened door of the stockmen's hut.

'Who would that be, then?' Andrew Burrowes asked Anderson.

'A trooper.'

'I wonder what news he's got,' Burrowes mused.

'Well, I just 'ope there's some good news.' There were traces of both anxiety and excitement in Anderson's voice. 'I just 'ope they've caught them all.'

'Aye, I can understand that, George,' Burrowes replied.

Burrowes and Anderson were now alone together in the hut, with Kilmeister having been arrested and Davey and Billy sent away prior to that.

During the long, cold winter nights in the drafty stockmen's hut they had the opportunity to talk more than they had ever done previously. Anderson's regrets prevented him from saying too much about the massacre, but he had revealed enough about it for Burrowes to have gained some understanding of the horror of that night.

'I won't be able to sleep until Day's got every last one of them bastards, and I'm not even sure I'll sleep then.'

'Aye, well, let's hope he's got them.'

Anderson nodded. 'Yair.'

The hutkeeper walked from the door and continued preparing supper. After a brief silence, Burrowes spoke, as much to himself as to his colleague. 'I still don't know what made Charlie do it.'

'Because he's a bastard,' Anderson muttered while cooking, his back to Burrowes.

'Aye, I know yer've always thought that, George, and I can't really blame you, the way he treated you at times.' Although Burrowes understood Anderson's attitude to the stockman, Kilmeister had been a friend of Burrowes. As a convict, he had little choice of friends. He was either friends with those he was assigned with or he had no friends, and his initial reaction after the massacre had been to follow the convict code of loyalty, of 'sticking to each other'. His attitude had changed somewhat, though, as he came to understand the full details of the massacre from Anderson and Davey, as well as stumbling across the massacre site himself.

Anderson glanced over his shoulder at Burrowes before turning back to his task. 'It's not how he treated me, it's what he did to them.'

'Aye.' There was another moment of silence before Burrowes continued. 'But Charlie never explained to me why he did it. All he said was that I wouldn't ask if I knew what 'they' had threatened to do to him. I never got a chance to find out if the "they" he meant were the blacks or Fleming's mob.'

'Doesn't matter why, does it? The bastard killed them, didn't he?' Anderson muttered, still with his back turned.

'Aye, and it is unforgivable. They weren't just wild blacks, this mob were our friends. It must have been just terrible, George.'

'Yair.'

Moments later they heard the trooper ride away, then William Hobbs entered their hut. 'Day's back; he's at Foster's,' Hobbs announced with a smile, 'and he's got another six of them in custody. So that makes ten altogether.'

George Anderson looked at his overseer. 'That's good to hear, Mr 'obbs. Has he got Fleming and Russell?'

'No, apparently not.'

Anderson's heart sank.

Observing his reaction, Hobbs tried to reassure him. 'But he's still pursuing them, George, and hopes to get them soon.'

Anderson nodded.

'Now he wants me to go down to Foster's, first thing tomorrow morning, to give some more evidence.'

'And me, sir?' Anderson inquired.

'You're to remain here for the present – but you'll have Andy with you,' Hobbs added, looking at Burrowes, who nodded. 'And I have it that Day will send for you in a couple of days.'

'Yes, sir. Does he know where Fleming and Russell are?' Anderson asked.

'No, not yet, but I'm sure he'll find them, George, don't worry about that.'

'What about Lamb?'

'Who?' Hobbs asked, somewhat surprised at Anderson inquiring about a name he had not mentioned previously.

'Jem Lamb.'

'Yes, George, it would seem that Day has got him.'

'Good, because he's a cruel bastard, Mr 'obbs.'

'Well, I'm sure he's got him, George, so that's one less to worry about. Anyway, I'll see you in the morning, before I leave. Goodnight.'

'Goodnight, Mr 'obbs.'

Hobbs closed the door and returned to his hut. Not long after, there was a knock at his door. 'Come in,' he called.

Anderson entered as Hobbs sat on his bed removing his boots. 'Ah, that's better,' he murmured, getting up to place the boots on the floor at the end of the bed. 'Now, George, what is it?' he asked gently as he sat down at the table in the middle of the hut.

'Mr 'obbs, I've got something that might be important, sir.'

'Yes, George, what do you have there?' Hobbs asked, more than a little curious.

Anderson leant forward and put the handle of a broken cutlass on the table in front of Hobbs.

'Whose is this, George?'

'It belongs to the stockmen, sir. They left it behind in the hut, after they killed the blacks.'

'Really?' Hobbs picked the handle up and examined it closely. He pulled the oil lamp that sat on the table closer, to allow for a more thorough examination of the broken weapon. 'Hmmm. There doesn't seem to be any bloodstains on it, George. Can you see any?'

'No, sir, there aren't any?'

'And what about any marks that indicate who might own it?' Hobbs inquired as he continued to scrutinise the object.

'No, Mr 'obbs, I don't think so, sir.'

'Well, it's good that you've shown it to me, George, but I can't see that it will be of great assistance. I'll tell you what, hang on to it and I'll ask Mr Day about it tomorrow.'

Anderson nodded. 'Good. Thank you, sir.'

'Thanks, George. Goodnight,' Hobbs said, handing Anderson the cutlass handle.

'Goodnight, Mr 'obbs.' Anderson took the handle but did not turn to leave. Instead he remained standing across the table from Hobbs.

Hobbs looked up. 'Was there something else, George?'

'No, sir,' Anderson replied, slowly turning to walk out.

'Hang on, George,' Hobbs instructed. 'Come back and sit down for a minute, would you?'

Anderson returned to the table and sat on the chair opposite Hobbs. The light from the fire cast elongated shadows of the convict and his overseer onto the wall and roof at the opposite end of the hut. The faces of both young men were also cast in shadow as the flickering glow danced upon their weathered skin.

'Ready to talk, are you, George?' It was a question tinged with hope and encouragement.

'Sort of, sir.'

'Worried about Fleming and Russell?'

'A little, sir. They're cruel men, Mr 'obbs. They wouldn't hesitate to kill the likes of me, just as they killed the blacks.'

'I understand your concern, George, but I'm sure you'll be safe with Mr Day in the area.'

'What about when he leaves but, Mr 'obbs? You're not around a lot of the time, and neither's Andy ... and even Davey and Billy are gone. I'll be here by meself, sir. And Mr Fleming being a squatter and all, sir, what chance have I got with the likes of 'im? Even if he doesn't kill me 'imself, he can 'ave some of his men do it for 'im.'

'Yes, I know the danger you're in, George. I don't deny that.' Hobbs thought for a moment. 'What if I have a talk to Mr Day tomorrow? What if he's prepared to undertake to give you protection? He might have to take you into custody, which won't be pleasant – but you've been in gaol before, eh, George?'

Anderson managed a half smile and nodded in reply.

'I suppose he would only keep you in custody until the trial. Assuming, of course, that Mr Day gets enough evidence and the governor wants to pursue the case. After that, George, I suppose I could ask Mr Dangar about having you transferred out of the district.'

Anderson looked down, saying nothing.

'I know you don't like Mr Dangar, but —— '

'He hates me, sir. He wouldn't do it for me.'

'You may be right there,' Hobbs conceded. 'Look, George, no-one can assure your safety. We can only do our best. It's up to you to make the decision yourself.'

'Oh, I've already made me decision, Mr 'obbs ... but can ya just ask Mr Day about the protection, sir?'

'Certainly, George, I'll be doing it as soon as I see him in the morning.'

'Thanks, Mr 'obbs. Can I go now, sir?'

'Of course, George.'

Anderson stood up and walked to the door.

'George, just one more thing before you go.' Anderson stopped at the door and turned back to Hobbs. 'There's a murmur about the place that some men were seen carrying large sacks away from the ridge, not long after I inspected the spot where the bodies were. Do you know anything about that?'

Anderson looked at Hobbs quizzically. 'No, sir, I don't,' he answered honestly.

'Had you heard about it?'

'No, sir.'

'Seems like it could be the only explanation for what happened to the remains of the blacks. Mr Day and the troopers couldn't find anything, and I've had a good look myself, but there's not a trace anywhere.'

It was a topic Anderson had no stomach for discussing. He nodded but turned to leave without comment.

Again Hobbs stopped him. 'One more thing, George.' Anderson stood at the door as Hobbs continued. 'I want you to understand that, according to Mr Day, without you as a witness his case against these men is very weak. He believes that unless you testify, these men will go free.'

Anderson bowed his head for just a moment, then he looked back up at Hobbs. 'Can't 'ave that, can we, sir?'

'No, George, we can't. Good night, George.'

'Good night, Mr 'obbs.'

CHAPTER TWENTY SEVEN

Wednesday 8 August 1838.

George Anderson sat in the makeshift courtroom of Thomas Foster's hut. Day was across the table from him, diligently making notes, while Lieutenant Pack stood behind Anderson, with Hobbs and Foster sitting silently at the end of the table. The magistrate was so absorbed in his notes that he was oblivious to the fact that, once again, the scratching of his quill on the paper was the only sound in the room, and that all its occupants had their eyes fixed firmly on him.

Anderson coughed nervously as Day continued writing. Finally the magistrate looked up at the hutkeeper. 'Are you ready, George?'

Anderson felt the need to urinate but nodded anyway. 'Yes, sir.'

'All right, Corporal, bring in the prisoners,' Day instructed McKnight, who was standing at the door.

'Yes, sir.'

Anderson sat with his back to the door as the ten accused convicts filed through. He was surprised at the familiarity of the sound of their clanking chains, a sound he had not heard for some time.

McKnight led them around to Anderson's right, where they stood against the wall. The clanking stopped and the room fell strangely silent, leaving a void into which Anderson stared. From somewhere he found the courage to look across and meet the united gaze of the ten accused, who all had their eyes locked on him. He glanced from one to another, until he came to Charles Kilmeister. Their eyes met for a few moments, before Kilmeister lowered his head and focused on the chains around his wrists.

Day recaptured Anderson's attention by handing him a Bible and proceeding to swear him in. After completing the other preliminaries, which included reading Anderson's previous statement, Day commenced the questioning of the witness.

'Now, is there anything else yer able to add to that evidence?'

'Yes, sir. Since I was last examined I 'ave brought certain things back to me memory, sir.'

'Good. What might they be, then?'

'In the afternoon, the day after the horsemen took the blacks away, they all come back to the station, sir. They all come back together, sir, except for Kilmeister. His 'orse went lame down the creek so he had to walk back and he got there a little later, sir.'

'How much later?'

'About twenty minutes, sir.'

'Go on.'

'Well, they all stayed the night, sir, and I had to cook them all supper. I didn't want to, though, sir, but I did. They was all sittin' around talkin' about the blacks and about what they'd done to the gin they'd kept with them, sir.'

'How many of them were there, Anderson?' Day inquired.

'Ten, maybe eleven, sir, and Kilmeister.'

'Aye, so eleven, maybe twelve, altogether?'

'Yes, sir.'

'Are you sure there weren't thirteen?'

'Positive, sir. There was probably twelve includin' Kilmeister, but there weren't thirteen.'

'All right, continue.'

'Well, they all slept the night, and in the morning, after breakfast, Kilmeister told me to get a leg rope for them. When I come back with it, Fleming, Russell and Kilmeister took some burnin' brands out of the fire, then they all went off in the same way they took the blacks, over to the ridge, sir. They all went, except one they left to guard me. After they went, the one they left behind pulled a sword out of its scabbard and showed me that it was all covered with blood.' Anderson hesitated. Although pleased at the opportunity to further incriminate Kilmeister, his palms were sweating and his back was itchy again. He no longer dared to even glance at the prisoners

'Aye, continue.'

'They all came back about an hour later and got their 'orses. Then they went to Mr 'obbs hut and got Billy, the blackfella, and told him to take them to McIntyre's. They told him they wouldn't hurt him if he showed them the way. They went down there, and Billy told me they killed some more blacks there, and up at Keera Creek they killed another mob of blacks.'

This last statement of Anderson's set off a muttering among the prisoners, which McKnight quickly silenced. 'Shut ya holes, you lot.'

Anderson glanced at the corporal but not at the prisoners.

Day ignored the exchange completely and continued. 'All right, George, but we won't be worrying about what Billy told you. Just you be sticking to what you saw yerself, all right?'

'Yes, sir. Well, before they rode away with Billy, Fleming told Kilmeister to go up to the ridge, put the logs together and "make sure it's all consumed", he said.'

'Fleming told Kilmeister this, did he?'

'Yes, sir, they was the words he used – "make sure it's all consumed".'

'Aye, fine. Anything else?'

'Then they rode away to McIntyre's.'

'All right, George, now to the matter of identification.'

The clanking of chains was the only sound in the room as the prisoners shifted their stances. Their stares remained locked on Anderson, who, had he tried to intervene in the massacre of the Weraerai, would now certainly not be alive to point an accusing finger at them.

'Should've killed him when we had the chance,' James Lamb murmured to the prisoner next to him.

'Yair, should've just blamed the blacks,' George Palliser whispered in reply.

'Shut ya holes, I said,' barked McKnight.

Day looked at the line of prisoners, then back at Anderson. 'Do you see any of the men who took the blacks away amongst the prisoners?'

Anderson hesitated. His need to urinate had increased. There was now total silence, eventually broken by Day's voice.

'Well, George?'

Recalling the look in Ipeta's eyes as the men currently standing in front of him had led her away, Anderson nodded slowly. 'Yes, sir. I recognise eight of them, sir.' His words hung in the heavy atmosphere of the crowded hut. The prisoners, who had been so keen to stare at him only moments before, now dropped their eyes to avoid contact with the hutkeeper.

'Good, George.' Day had to stop himself from smiling with satisfaction. Now he had a case. 'And who do you recognise, then?' As Anderson pointed to each in turn, the magistrate stated and recorded their names. 'George Palliser ... Charles Telluse ... James Oates ... William Hawkins ... John Johnstone ... '

Anderson then pointed to one of the other convicts, a tall young man. 'He's the one they left to guard me, that showed me the sword all over with blood.' The prisoner glanced up momentarily, saw Anderson pointing at him, and immediately dropped his eyes again, the colour draining from his face.

'Edward Foley,' announced Day as his quill hurriedly scratched across the page.

Anderson now hesitated as his eyes fell upon the next in line.

Three of the murderers really scared him, and this was the only one of those three amongst the current group of prisoners. He was also the only one of the prisoners who didn't drop his eyes when Anderson looked at him. Instead he glared at the hutkeeper.

Anderson felt the weight of fear holding his sweating hand on the table in front of him as if it were under a great lump of lead. Finally he raised it briefly and pointed.

'James Lamb,' Day recorded.

Anderson then looked at the last in the line, the stockman from Myall Creek. 'And Kilmeister,' he concluded without hesitation.

'Good, George. What about the other two?'

'Well,' he began, motioning to Henry Ested, a convict stockman on Charles Smith's station, further downstream, 'he weren't with them.'

Ested sighed audibly and glanced at his colleagues beside him.

'Are you sure?' queried Day.

'Positive, sir. I never seen 'im before in me life.'

'And what about him?' Day asked, motioning to James Parry, who stood in the middle of the line of enchained convicts. Parry had deeply regretted his involvement in the whole incident and had sworn to himself long before Day had arrested him that he would never again let others lead him into participating in such a diabolical deed.

'I dunno, sir; I don't recollect 'im.'

Parry was trembling with emotion but couldn't cross his arms or turn away from the line of his murderous comrades, as the chains anchored him. His heart was pounding, and his mind, racing with regret, confused his emotions. He didn't believe he should be let off scot-free, but the possible punishment was too extreme for his minor role. He wasn't one of the leaders. He loathed everything the gang did, except for his turn with Martha. He partook eagerly in that.

'Are you sure?' Day pushed.

'I'm not sure, sir, but I don't recollect 'im,' Anderson replied.

'Aye, all right then, that'll be it for the moment.'

Day finished making some notes while all in the room looked on in silence. Anderson's back still itched but the urge to urinate had eased.

Day then asked the prisoners if they wished to exercise their right to cross examine the witness.

George Palliser was alone in taking up the opportunity. 'Yair, I would, sir.'

'Go ahead,' invited Day.

'How are ya so sure that I was there that night?' Palliser probed.

'Because I saw ya then and the next day,' Anderson explained matter-of-factly.

'Do ya even know me name? Had ya ever seen me before?' Palliser challenged.

'No, I don't know ya name, and as far as I can recollect I never seen ya before that night, but ya was with the party —— '

'Do ya realise ya under oath to tell the truth?' barked Palliser.

Anderson rose to the challenge. 'I know the nature of an oath, and I know ya was there. Ya did the same as the rest there – ya assisted in takin' the blacks away. I didn't see ya hit them as I saw some of the others do, but ya rode ya horse along at the rear of the blacks, with ya carbine in ya hand.'

Day wrote hurriedly, recording the damning evidence. Palliser quickly ceased his questioning and joined his enchained colleagues in their silence.

* * *

That evening, Hobbs, Day, Foster and Pack ate their supper around the table that served as the magistrate's bench.

'Well, you must be pleased with the way it's all going, Mr Day,' Hobbs observed.

'Aye, well, some things are progressing well, but I'm a wee bit concerned about some other matters.'

'Like what?'

'Well, I'm very concerned that there be no sign at all of Fleming or Russell, as it's very obvious they were the leaders of the whole thing. It seems to me that a couple of these chaps were just led into it thinking they were doing what their masters wanted.'

'But that Lamb's a nasty one too, sir,' Lieutenant Pack added as he dug a piece of meat from between his teeth with his thumbnail.

'Aye, to be sure,' Day agreed. 'But I'm certainly not going to be giving up on Fleming and Russell, though. I'm going to do everything I possibly can to be finding them both. If, as it appears, Fleming has left the district, I'll just have to be sending a warrant for his arrest down to the Hawkesbury district, where you say his family's property is located, Mr Foster.'

Foster nodded. 'Yes, that's right.'

'And I'll be doing all I can to get him. As you'd understand, though, gentlemen, it is of course much more difficult to find him than it is these assigned convicts who really can't be going anywhere except to bolt into the bush. As for Russell, being an ex-convict, he doesn't have Fleming's contacts across the colony, so I tend to think it's likely he'll be still in the district. Perhaps someone is harbouring him. What do you think, gentlemen?'

'Yes, quite possibly, Mr Day,' replied Hobbs.

'Very likely, I would say,' agreed Foster.

Magistrate Day thought for a moment before continuing. 'Another thing I be concerned about is, who is the twelfth member of the party? It seems apparent that it wasn't Ested. Anderson is quite sure he wasn't there, so I've had to let him go this afternoon. I'll be arresting that Deady chap, though, the hutkeeper up at Bell's, for perjury.'

'Really?' remarked Foster, a little surprised.

'Aye, he lied to me repeatedly about Ned Foley being at Bell's the night they all gathered there; you know, when Burrowes and Reid dropped in.'

'Obviously trying to protect him,' suggested Foster.

'Exactly,' Day agreed.

'What about Parry, Mr Day?' Hobbs inquired.

'No, although Anderson isn't sure about him, I have rather a lot of other evidence against him. Yer sure he was with them, aren't you, Mr Foster?'

Foster nodded. 'Quite sure.'

'And Bates was sure too, so I've got plenty against him. But if Ested wasn't there, that means I've only got eleven names, and Anderson's pretty sure there were twelve of them – and there's plenty of other evidence to support that number. The question then be, gentlemen: who was that twelfth man?'

'Can't help you there, I'm sorry, Mr Day,' Foster admitted.

'Aye, well, I'll just have to be continuing my inquiries until I find out. I'll tell you what I be pleased about, though, and that's the evidence Anderson provided today. He quite surprised me.'

'He surprised me too,' said Hobbs.

'I didn't think he'd have it in him,' added Foster.

Lieutenant Pack, who had followed the conversation in virtual silence to this point, now leant forward. 'You know, gentlemen, my old Granma used to say that sometimes people do really surprise ya. She used to say to me, "We should be tolerant of all people because we are all erring, struggling human beings and sometimes it's the very thing that we don't like in a person which makes them stand by us when we really need them to, when no-one else will".'

The other three looked at the lieutenant in stunned silence, surprised at his sudden outburst of homespun philosophy. Finally Day asked, 'How do you remember all that so well, Lieutenant?'

'Well, she used to say it rather a lot, Mr Day. I think she read it in a book. To be honest, sir, she went a bit funny in the head near the end and that was about all she ever said – over and over again. Got a bit boring, really.'

'Aye, I imagine it would,' Day agreed, smiling.

'Well, strange as it may seem, Lieutenant, I think your old Granma might have had a point,' remarked Hobbs.

'Really, Bill?' asked Foster.

'Well, have a look at Anderson. Mr Day had said to me before that he would much prefer a stubborn chap like Anderson for a witness than some weak sop.'

The magistrate nodded. 'Aye, I did indeed.'

'And I can see why, Mr Day.' Hobbs paused.

Foster sat forward in his chair. 'Go on, Bill, I'm curious,'

'Well, his stubborn, uncooperative nature is why Mr Dangar doesn't like him – hates him, in fact. And because he's like that and he's not a horseman and doesn't go along with the other men, he's not popular with them either. But I've often wondered why, when someone like Kilmeister went along with those stockmen that night, a chap like Anderson had the strength to resist the pressure to join them, and … ' Hobbs paused for a moment, crystallising the theory he was warming to as he went along.

'And?' urged Foster.

'And what is it that gives him the strength today, to sit there and give evidence in the face of all those men, his fellow convicts.'

'I think my promise of protection helped,' offered Day, despite fully appreciating Hobbs' point.

'No doubt it did, Mr Day, but we both know that you'll only protect him until the trial, if this matter gets that far, and Anderson knows that too. After that, though, he's got a life sentence to serve amongst other convicts. They'll kill him, is my guess, sooner or later; unless, of course, we can get him right out of the district – and even then he probably won't be safe around other convicts. But I think the lieutenant's old Granma was right. It's the very things that made Anderson unpopular that gave him the strength to do what he did that night and to do what he's doing now. He's stubborn, strong-willed, uncooperative and doesn't go along with the mob. You know, Lieutenant, your Granma might have been a bit funny in the head but I think she was a very wise old lady.'

CHAPTER TWENTY EIGHT

E dward Denny Day, Lieutenant Pack and five of the troopers had spent days scouring the countryside looking for Fleming, Russell and the mysterious twelfth man. Their journey had taken them all the way north along the Big River to the very limit of white occupation, without any success. They had, however, picked up Charles Reid at Dangar's lower station, to help them with their inquiries and to corroborate various evidence.

On the fifth day of their journey they had been riding since early morning, and it was mid-afternoon before Day allowed his men to take a break for lunch. They eased their horses over to the base of a slope about twenty yards from the half beaten track that formed the road in that remote district. After dismounting and tethering their horses to various branches and saplings, they scattered themselves across the slope to enjoy yet another meal of police rations. It was a pleasant afternoon and the late winter sun warmed the weary riders.

Day and Pack sat with Charles Reid, discussing the progress of the inquiry.

'So, Mr Day, you've got them all except Fleming and Russell, have ya?'

'Aye, and one other we haven't been able to identify yet. It seems he might be assigned to Mr Glennie, but I be quite sure I'll be able to ascertain that a little later. At the moment, though, I be most concerned about the other two.'

'It was certainly a fearful thing they did, sir. I only spent one night at the station while the blacks were there, but they was quiet and friendly people,' Reid observed.

'Charlie, in my time in the army with the 62nd Regiment in India, I be seeing some terrible things and mixed with men who'd served all over the world – in the Napoleonic Wars, in Africa, everywhere – and I can be assuring you, I've never seen or heard of an atrocity the like of this one. What they did to those wee babies and their mothers. Do you know Davey, the blackfella, told Mr Hobbs wee babies had their brains bashed out against trees and rocks in front of their mothers? Mothers were raped and mutilated in front of their littluns, before they be all beheaded and dismembered.'

Reid said nothing. No-one had told him the detail until now. He merely shook his head.

'This be just a devil of a crime,' Day continued, 'and so I be determined to track down these men who were the leaders.'

'Just shocking, sir,' Reid now murmured.

'Strange thing, though, when I retired early from the army and came out here to New South Wales, I thought I would be getting away from such things – war and killing. Anyway, I hope you can be helping the inquiry. I've got a lot of evidence together in the last few weeks. As I mentioned to you afore, I really just be needing you to confirm some of the statements I already have, particularly that of Andrew Burrowes, and also be confirming identification of some of the prisoners.'

As the three sat, absorbed in their discussion, a lone rider came trotting along the track. He was a very thickset man on an imposing black horse, and was at first oblivious to the presence of the troopers resting in their partly obscured location on the slope.

'I certainly hope I can help, sir. I want to … ' Reid stopped mid-sentence as his attention and that of his companions was distracted by the rider. He suddenly lunged forward, grabbing Day on the arm and pointing at the lone horseman. 'That's him, sir!'

'Who?'

'Russell. John Russell!'

At that moment the rider spotted the troopers and immediately kicked his mount in the ribs. The horse whinnied in shock as it charged off along the track at a full gallop.

Pack and Day jumped to their feet and leapt onto their horses, ripping their reins from the saplings as they did so.

'Come on, you men, that's Russell,' yelled Pack as the troopers quickly roused themselves to join the pursuit.

Russell had quickly gained a break of nearly sixty yards over Day and Pack as he rounded a bend in the road, out of their sight. By the time Day and Pack rounded the same corner there was no sign of Russell on the road ahead.

'Up there, sir,' yelled Pack, pointing to the fleeing horseman riding up the side of a hill by the road and into the trees.

'Tell two of the men to stick to the road ahead and send two back the way we came,' Day ordered as he urged his mount up the slope after Russell.

Pack followed Day up the slope, turning and yelling out Day's instructions when the troopers came into view.

Russell reached the top of the slope, riding along it for a time as Day and Pack pursued him. The fleeing former convict had just started down the other side of the hill when the two troopers who had been sent on the road ahead rode through a clump of trees and into view below. Day yelled to them, and the two turned to confront Russell as he urged his mount between the fallen logs and rocks that littered the slope.

Lieutenant Pack yanked his mount to a halt at the top of the ridge and quickly drew his carbine from the side of his saddle. He calmly raised it to his shoulder. He peered along the barrel to the sight at its tip. Beyond the tip he could see the back of John Russell. The lieutenant's eye locked onto the fleeing figure bobbing about as his horse leapt and lunged down the slope, before raising his carbine to the sky, just above the horizon, and pulling the trigger. The crack of the gunshot echoed across the valley below.

Russell glanced back over his shoulder, to see Day still pursuing close behind and Pack on top of the ridge above. He looked ahead of him again and, for the first time, saw the two troopers, pistols drawn, eighty yards ahead of him on the road.

'Russell! Halt!' yelled Edward Denny Day, desperate to capture one of his most sought after quarry before an over zealous trooper shot him.

Russell wheeled his horse sharply to the right. The imposing animal responded, its eyes flashing, nostrils flared and sweat glistening on its ebony coat. Russell wrenched its head around again to face Day, his hand reaching for the carbine at his side.

Day eased his mount to a halt and drew his pistol. The magistrate and the murderer confronted each other. 'John Russell, get off that horse.'

Russell did not move as his excited mount pranced around beneath him.

'Get off the horse, Russell,' demanded Day. 'Get off it or you be a dead man.'

Russell said nothing, but again glanced over his shoulder as the two troopers cantered their mounts up behind him. Slowly the ex-convict swung his leg from the saddle as one of the troopers pulled a set of handcuffs from his belt.

'John Russell, I'm Police Magistrate Day. You may have heard I be looking for you.'

CHAPTER TWENTY NINE

Tuesday 14 August 1838.

The news of Russell's capture had an immediate effect on George Anderson. The tension which had gripped the back of his neck and his shoulders for so many weeks he had come to believe it was normal, suddenly eased along with the queasiness in his stomach. With Russell in custody and local reports quite definite that Fleming had fled the district, Anderson felt the immediate threat to his life had been greatly reduced. He therefore managed to indulge in his first good night's sleep since the massacre, despite the fact it was on a makeshift bed on the floor of the stockmen's hut at Dr Newton's station.

By the time he awoke in the morning, though, his anxiety had returned. What if the fact Russell was now in custody only increased the urgency and determination of the gang's supporters to silence him? It was not a pleasant thought but it was a persistent one – and one of considerable validity given Russell's standing in the district. As the idea nagged at him he could feel his neck and shoulders tightening again. He sat up on the floor and rubbed the back of his neck. This morning he would have to confront and identify Russell. His stomach squelched.

* * *

Edward Denny Day had again set up his courtroom in Thomas Foster's hut and was going about building the case against Russell. His major focus was the crucial matter of identification. He started by questioning Foster.

'Now, Mr Foster, do you recognise the prisoner?'

'Yes, sir. He is the man referred to in my earlier statement as John Russell. He accompanied the party when they came here on the morning of the eleventh of June, subsequent to the blacks being killed.'

'And was he armed, Mr Foster?'

'That I couldn't swear to, sir; I really don't know.'

'Are you sure you can't remember?' pushed Day.

'Yes, Mr Day, I'm sure. I did not notice whether or not he was armed.'

'Thanks, Mr Foster. That will be all for now.'

As Foster stood to leave, Day put down his quill, put his hands to his face and gently shook his head. Foster glanced at Russell as he left the hut.

Day called his next witness, John Bates, the convict hutkeeper at Dight's.

'Now, Bates, can you be telling me if you recognise the prisoner?'

'I don't think so, sir,' Martha's liberator replied.

Day paused before continuing. 'You be telling us previously about the party of horsemen who had breakfast at your station on the eleventh of June. Was the prisoner with them?'

'I dunno, sir,' Bates mumbled.

'You be having a good look at him, Bates,' urged Day, leaning forward across the table in an attempt to catch Bates' gaze, which was shifting everywhere except toward Russell and himself. 'Was he with the party of horsemen or not?'

John Bates glanced quickly at John Russell, and when met by the stockman's glare his eyes immediately began shifting around nervously again. 'Sir, there was a man who looked a bit like him, but I've never seen this man before in my life.'

Day was incredulous. 'Are you sure?'

'Yes, sir. I've never seen him before, sir.'

Russell smiled a half smile as Day dismissed Bates and called impatiently for William Mace, the overseer at Dight's.

'Mr Mace, can you be telling me if you recognise the prisoner?'

'I'm not sure, sir.'

'Was the prisoner with the party of horsemen who had breakfast at yer station on the eleventh of June?'

'Well, there was a man there of a similar size but he had whiskers and something of a beard at the time. Now that he's shaven, it's hard to tell if it's the same man.'

'Do you be recognising the prisoner as being with the party that called at yer station that morning?'

Mace shook his head slowly as the silence of the bush closed around Russell. 'No, I'm not sure.' Day knew exactly what was happening – his case against Russell was evaporating before his eyes. Russell allowed himself a full smile this time. That smile quickly vanished from his face, however, when he heard Day call the name of the next witness.

'George Anderson, please, Corporal.'

Day asked for Anderson with feelings of hope and apprehension battling for supremacy in his mind and heart. He was hopeful Anderson would have the courage to identify Russell. If he didn't, Day would not have a case against one of the known leaders of the massacre.

Corporal McKnight pushed the door open and was followed into the room by the Myall Creek hutkeeper. Russell glared at him as a pugilist might stare at an opponent in a makeshift ring in the slums of London.

Anderson knew full well Russell would be there, but he couldn't stop his gut from twisting when he saw him. As with the others, though, he forced himself to look straight back at the enchained prisoner. He was only capable of doing so for a moment, however, before he quickly turned his attention to Day and took his seat opposite the magistrate.

As Day again swore him in, Anderson wiped the sweat from the palm of his left hand on his battered pants, rubbing his back against the chair at the same time.

Day got straight to the point. 'Anderson, do you be recognising the prisoner?'

Daring only to glance in Russell's direction, Ipeta's lover didn't hesitate. 'Yes, sir. He's the one I referred to in me statements as "Russell". He was with the party of 'orsemen that took the blacks away, and with them when they come back the next evening.'

Day sighed with relief, though he still sought clarification of Mace's earlier evidence. 'You be sure? What about his whiskers? Did he have whiskers or a beard at the time in question?'

Anderson hesitated briefly before he again looked at Russell, the intensity of whose stare made him look straight back at Day. The magistrate's and the convict's eyes met.

'No, sir,' Anderson answered quietly. 'There's no difference in his face at all, save for what might come from not shavin' for a couple of days. I'm positive that's John Russell and he was one of them.'

'Thank you, Anderson.' Day smiled as he hastily scrawled his notes.

CHAPTER THIRTY

Tuesday 28 August 1838.

I t was mid-morning when Edward Denny Day, Lieutenant Pack and four troopers rode up to Foster's hut with two new prisoners. They were John Deady – whom Day had arrested on a charge of perjury for his vain attempts to protect Edward Foley – and John Blake, assigned convict stockman at Glennie's Gineroi station, whom Day was convinced was the twelfth man of the party.

After dealing with the rather straightforward matter of assembling the perjury case against Deady, Day set about attempting to confirm his suspicions about Blake. Thomas Foster was again the first to be questioned.

'Mr Foster, can you be recognising the prisoner?'

'No, I'm sorry, Mr Day, I don't, really.'

'Was the prisoner with the party of horsemen who called at this station on the morning of the eleventh of June last?'

'I really don't know. He may have been; but as there were rather a lot of them, I really didn't have a good look at all of them.'

Foster was followed by Robert Sexton, Foster's assigned hut-keeper.

'Can you be recognising the prisoner?' asked Day.

'I'm not sure, sir. He might have been with the party, but I can't really say for sure.'

Day sat back in his chair and looked up at the roof for almost a minute. He then looked back down at Sexton and waved him away. 'Out,' he said. 'Bring in Bates.'

John Bates, the "old man" of the Big River district, entered and sat opposite Day.

'Do you be recognising the prisoner?' Day asked immediately after swearing in the witness.

'Yes, sir. He was one of the party of horsemen that came to our station that mornin', sir.'

'The morning of the eleventh of June?'

'Yes, sir.'

'You be sure?' Day asked, a smile creasing his face.

Bates nodded. 'Yes, positive, sir. He was the one that had the black gin with him, who he left with me. He came back for her later but she'd gone because I hadn't detained her.'

And so John Blake, the twenty-seven-year-old butcher who had left a wife and two children behind in Ireland when he was transported, was identified as the twelfth and final member of John Fleming's gang. Ironically enough, Blake, the only married man in the party, was only identified through his connection with Martha. Whether it was a connection borne of lust or from a desire to protect little Charley's gentle mother from further depredations at the hands of the others is unknown.

CHAPTER THIRTY ONE

Tuesday September 11 1838.

G eorge Anderson awoke as the dawn's first light drifted through the bars of the cell window. In his early morning daze, Anderson panicked momentarily upon seeing the bars, before quickly remembering why he was there. He rolled onto his back and lay staring up at the ceiling of his sandstone sanctuary.

He was immediately struck by how different it felt being in a cell as a protected witness rather than a prisoner, which he had been the last time he was in such a cell. He wasn't exactly sure what the difference was, though. He was still a convict, he still had no freedom and he still had a knot of fear in his gut, courtesy of the threats and abuse screamed down the corridor by the eleven prisoners scattered about in the other cells of the Muswellbrook police lock-up. They had arrived the previous evening after walking in chains from the Big River. Day, having successfully completed his inquiries, had brought Anderson down several days ahead of the others. Much to Anderson's relief, Day had assured him the prisoners would be leaving that morning.

They would continue their walk to Newcastle, where they would board the *Sophia Jane* to sail to Sydney.

Anderson had experienced very mixed emotions as he left Myall Creek with Day. It had been the scene of the worst moments of his life, but it had also been the scene of the happiest. Also, Hobbs had been particularly good to him in recent weeks, with the pair of them having developed a somewhat strange interdependence as they became aware of how much the whole case depended on each of them. Although they knew Anderson's evidence was far more crucial, they became aware the case would collapse if either of them recanted their evidence, leaving the other stranded without an ally. It was with some hesitation, then, that Anderson left his ally behind, trusting that he would be true to his word and follow through with his evidence.

As he lay on his prison bunk, Anderson's mind drifted back to Myall Creek and to the worst moments of his life - that evening that had changed his life and ended Ipeta's. Her face came clearly to his mind, as if she were there before him: her smooth black skin; her soft, full mouth; and that look in her eyes. That look that had contained sheer terror and which made him ache with pity for her, yet at the same time held a mirror of piercing clarity to the depths of his own soul. It was a look he would never forget and from which there was no escape. It was a look which, though it unnerved him, only reinforced his feelings for her – feelings which enabled him to confront the fear which seized him as a harsh, gravel-voiced scream suddenly echoed around the stone walls of the lock-up.

'You're a dead man, Anderson.'

CHAPTER THIRTY TWO

Tuesday 18 September 1838.

H enry Keck, the head gaoler of the George Street prison in Sydney, ushered the well-dressed gentleman into the dingy interviewing area.

'I'll just get the prisoners for ya, Mr Scott,' advised Keck.

'Good. Thank you, Mr Keck,' replied Robert Scott, Henry Dangar's friend and dinner guest. He was the first to visit the prisoners, who had arrived the evening before, after the long trip down from the Big River district.

A few minutes later, the dishevelled-looking prisoners shuffled into the other side of the interviewing area, where they were separated from their visitor by two iron doors set several feet apart. Keck stood at the end of the space between the doors as the conversation between the squatter and the prisoners started.

'Hello, men. How are you all?' Scott asked.

The prisoners muttered a variety of replies, unsure of the purpose of the visit from the finely dressed gentlemen.

James Lamb then recognised the visitor.

'Hallo, Mr Scott.'

'Hello, my man, how are you? You're ahh ... '

'Jem Lamb, Mr Scott.'

'That's right, Jem. You're Mr Cobb's man, aren't you?'

'Yes, sir.'

'Good, good; and how are you all bearing up?'

'Not too bad, sir. We're all a bit tired from the trip down. We had to walk all the way down to Newcastle, then we got the ship down yesterday.'

'Yes, I heard. That's a frightfully long walk.'

'Yair, it is; but apart from being tired, we're all right. Couple of the young blokes are a bit worried but —— '

'Yes, well, that's exactly why I'm here,' Scott interjected. He then raised his voice slightly to address all of the prisoners. 'For those of you who don't know me, my name is Robert Scott. I'm a man of considerable means and a great deal of influence in this town. I'm also a personal friend of Mr Dangar's. I have just come from a meeting with Governor Gipps at which I led a deputation of landowners to express our concern over the problems with these black savages and the government's lack of action in sorting out the problems. I've come down here to assure you men that everything will be all right if you just stick together and say nothing. We've had a meeting among the landowners and we've raised a considerable sum of money for your defence. We have in fact hired the best lawyers in the colony to defend you.'

'Pleased to hear that, Mr Scott,' Lamb replied.

'So ya think we'll be all right, then, do ya, Mr Scott?' asked Ned Foley, his face pressed against the bars of the door.

'Have no fear at all, my boy, I'm sure you'll be all right.'

'That's good, sir, 'cause ya know we was only doin' what our master's wanted us to.'

'I know that; but look, they've only got one witness of any importance, and that's Anderson,' Scott offered reassuringly.

'That little maggot will be too scared to give evidence against us in court,' Kilmeister responded.

'Well, maybe he will be; but if he does, I've organised to produce evidence of his insanity,' Scott replied.

'Oh, good, sir. He *is* crazy.' Kilmeister nodded enthusiastically.

'We should've just killed him along with his black friends,' scowled Lamb.

'Perhaps if Russell had just given him his gin when he asked —— ' James Parry began, before being cut short by Lamb.

'Stop whinging about it, Parry.' Turning to Scott, he added,' Ya know Russell escaped, do ya, Mr Scott?'

'Yes, I'd heard that. While you were going through the Hunter Valley, wasn't it?'

'Yair. Do ya know if they've caught him, sir?'

'No, I don't believe they have; but I don't know that him escaping is a good thing.' Scott hesitated for a moment before continuing. 'Anyway, it doesn't matter now. You chaps probably don't realise the uproar you being arrested over killing a few of these black pests has caused in this town.'

'Has it, sir?' asked Kilmeister.

'My word it has. People realise that if there is to be growth and prosperity in this colony, we can't have people being arrested for killing a few savages that are getting in the way and threatening the settlers in the frontier districts. Look, lads, I'm a part owner of *The Sydney Herald*, and we are making sure it is pushing for your release. The Governor is under a great deal of pressure to drop the case, and we plan to maintain that pressure. All you lads have to do is stick together, admit nothing, and no harm will come to you, all right?'

There were nods and comments of agreement from the prisoners, before Scott urged Lamb to come closer to the bars of the door. 'I hear you settled some other blacks up at Keera Creek, as well, Jem,' Scott said quietly.

'Yes, sir,' Lamb replied in a low voice, nodding discreetly.

'How many?'

'At least twenty or thirty, I'd say, sir.'

Scott smiled. 'Good, good. We've got to clear them all out of the whole district.' He then stepped back from the door and raised his voice, directing his comments to all the prisoners. 'You chaps keep your chins up. You really have done a fine job for this colony. You may have been brought out here merely as convict labourers but, well ... you've really risen up and become like ... soldiers for the Empire ... getting rid of its enemies who stand in its way.' Scott liked the concept so much he felt it bore repeating. 'That's exactly what you are – soldiers for the Empire. So keep your chins up, stick together and say nothing. Right, lads?'

'Yair, Mr Scott.'

'Thanks, Mr Scott.'

'Good. Now, have you lads got enough to eat?'

'Some meat would be good, sir,' suggested Foley. 'And maybe some eggs, sir.'

'I'll see what I can organise for you. I'll be back in a couple of days.' Scott then turned to the gaoler. 'Thank you, Mr Keck.'

Robert Scott then followed Henry Keck from the interview room, leaving the prisoners in much brighter spirits.

CHAPTER THIRTY THREE

Wednesday 10 October 1838.

William Hobbs and Andrew Burrowes were unsaddling their horses after a day's mustering when they saw two riders approaching from the west.

'Wonder who this could be, boss?'

'Don't know, Andy.' Hobbs squinted into the setting sun. 'They look well dressed. They're obviously not locals.'

'Aye,' agreed Burrowes, taking the saddle from his horse and throwing it onto the ground against the wall of the stockmen's hut. He then looked up again at the approaching riders. 'Nice horses, too, Mr Hobbs. They be squatters, to be sure.'

'Yes, in fact I think one of them is Mr Dangar.'

'Mr Dangar? What would he be doin' here?'

'Don't know, Andy. He's never been here before,' Hobbs remarked as he walked over to greet the owner of the Myall Creek station. 'Good afternoon to you, Mr Dangar,' he called as the two riders drew their mounts to a halt.

'Hello, Mr Hobbs,' Dangar replied flatly.

'And how would you be, sir?' Hobbs asked, a little anxious at his boss's unannounced appearance at his most remote station.

Dangar slid from his saddle and approached Hobbs. 'Well, I'd be a lot better if I hadn't had to ride all the way up here, wouldn't I?'

Somewhat surprised by Dangar's hostile tone, Hobbs asked, 'And what brings you up here, sir?'

'Oh, I thought you knew all about that, Bill. A little problem with the blacks, wasn't there?' Dangar remarked.

'Oh yes, certainly, sir.'

The other rider, who had now dismounted, approached Dangar and Hobbs.

'By the way, this is Mr Samuel Cook. Mr Cook is engaged to my daughter,' said the squatter, softening for a moment.

Hobbs leant forward and shook the newcomer's hand. 'Nice to meet you, Mr Cook. Welcome to Myall Creek.'

'Thank you, Mr Hobbs,' Cook replied, nodding.

'Well, let's go inside,' said Dangar. 'I'm quite exhausted from that ride.'

'Yes, of course, sir,' replied Hobbs, stepping aside and motioning toward his hut.

'And who's this, then?' asked Dangar, noticing Burrowes.

'I'm Burrowes, sir. Andrew Burrowes.'

'Ah yes, Burrowes – the only assigned man I've got left on this station. I should remember him, shouldn't I, Mr Hobbs?' Dangar observed.

'Look after the horses, would you please, Andy?' asked Hobbs as he followed his boss into the hut.

Upon entering the hut Dangar and Cook removed their coats, before sitting down at the table.

'Would you like some tea, gentlemen?'

'Yes, of course,' replied Dangar.

While Hobbs went about preparing cups of tea for his surprise guests, a rather uncomfortable silence descended upon the small hut, which the overseer quickly tried to break.

'And how was your trip up, Mr Dangar?'

'It is a damned long way, Mr Hobbs, and I shouldn't have had to come.'

Not wanting to pursue that line of conversation, Hobbs again asked Dangar about his trip. 'Did you have any trouble finding the place, sir?'

'No. James Glennie accompanied us as far as his place, then one of his men showed us the way here.'

'Ah, that's good, sir.'

The uneasy silence returned briefly, before the squatter said coldly, 'What do you think you were doing, reporting this little incident with the blacks to the authorities?'

Hobbs was totally taken aback. 'I believe it was the right thing to do, sir.'

'*The right thing to do* be damned,' Dangar scoffed. 'Listen to me, Hobbs, all it has done is cause totally unnecessary bother over a trivial matter. The squatters down in the Hunter Valley are horrified that such a thing could cause so much trouble.'

'Pardon me, sir,' Hobbs objected, 'but it is hardly a trivial matter. Twenty-eight innocent people, women and children included, were brutally butchered, sir.'

'Don't give me this "innocent people" line, Hobbs. They were black savages, nothing more than that. They're a damned nuisance, and if there is to be progress and growth in this colony, the sooner they're wiped out, the better.'

'Sir, they were peaceful people. I knew them. They had been living right outside this door for weeks. They were friendly people, sir,' Hobbs implored.

'You sound like a bleeding heart Whig, just like our fool of a governor. The point is, they shouldn't have been "right outside this door". That's precisely how this whole mess came about. If you had been doing your job, for which I have paid you most handsomely, they would not have been here.'

'But, sir, you must understand the circumstances —— '

'I don't want to hear anything about "the circumstances". Anyway, you can argue all you like, Mr Hobbs, because I've already decided to terminate your services.'

Hobbs was incredulous. 'What? I beg your pardon, sir?'

'Don't tell me your hearing is as bad as your judgement?' Dangar got to his feet and began pacing about the room. 'Your services are no longer required. You simply have not done the job for which I'm paying you. You've allowed yourself to be distracted by this whole business with the blacks. You've given me to understand that some of my cattle have strayed. That's correct, isn't it?'

'Yes, sir, but we'll get them back. That's what Burrowes and I have been doing for the past couple of weeks.'

'That's no good to me, Mr Hobbs. They shouldn't have been allowed to stray in the first place. That's what Mr Cook is here for. He's going to take over from you.'

'Sir, but we have an agreement.'

'Not any more we don't.'

'Whatever happened to "my word is my bond" – that principle of yours you said you took such pride in, sir?'

'That doesn't apply when people in my employ behave as you have behaved and neglect my business.'

'Sir, I have done the right thing. I know that in my own mind.'

'Hobbs, you are a naive fool. You think that these men are going to be convicted over this matter, don't you?'

'I don't really know, sir, but Mr Day believes he has collected very strong evidence against them.'

'Well, let me acquaint you with a few facts, Hobbs. These men will not be convicted. You have no idea of the furore this case has caused in Sydney and in the Hunter Valley. We've already organised the best lawyers in the colony to defend them, and we've collected over three hundred pounds to pay those lawyers —— '

'Three hundred pounds, sir?' Hobbs interjected.

'Yes, Hobbs, three hundred pounds. Sounds like a lot of money to you, doesn't it?'

'Yes, sir, it certainly does.'

'Well, let me tell you, it isn't, when compared to the amount of money we have invested in this colony. And we're determined to protect our investments. Apart from all the local squatters, there's millions of pounds being poured into the expansion of this colony by powerful English investors. You don't think any of us are going to stand by and watch our investments suffer because of problems with these black savages, do you?'

'They're not savages, sir,' Hobbs retorted, his cheeks quivering with suppressed indignation.

The squatter and the superintendent were now both pacing at opposite sides of the table, at which Samuel Cook sat in absolute silence.

'They *are* savages, Mr Hobbs, and the sooner this colony is rid of them, the better.'

Hobbs swung around and opened his mouth to snap back; then, thinking better of it, he merely glared at the squatter for a moment, before sitting at the table and holding his head in his hands.

'Anyway, Hobbs,' Dangar continued, 'I don't believe the case will even get to trial, because I don't believe our fool of a Governor will have the courage to stand up to the pressure we're putting on him to drop the whole matter.'

Hobbs didn't reply. He remained sitting with his head in his hands.

'You know, my good friend Robert Scott is a very influential man and a part owner of *The Sydney Herald*. Well, he is ensuring *The Herald* pushes this matter very strongly. It is portraying Gipps as the fool that he is, as well as making it clear to its readers that the blacks are just in the way of progress in this colony. *The Gazette* is taking the same line as well; and you can have it from me, there isn't a Governor born who is going to stand up to constant criticism from the newspapers.'

Hobbs still made no reply. Dangar claimed to have the law, money, public opinion and the newspapers all on his side, and it was beyond

Hobbs' capacities to argue how they could all be wrong. His heart told him they were, though.

Dangar drew a cigar from the pocket of his jacket and lit it.

Hobbs finally looked up. 'Very well, Mr Dangar, I'll get myself organised and be off the station by the end of the week.'

'Oh no you won't.'

'I beg your pardon, sir? I thought you just told me my services were terminated.'

'They are, but not until you have completed the work you are supposed to have done under our agreement. What about all these cattle that have wandered off all over the run? You have to get every last one of them back before you are free of your obligations to me.'

'But, sir, with just the two of us, that'll take over a month.'

'Well, that's how long you'll have to stay on. You're not leaving this station until you finish the job I've employed you to do.'

'Mr Dangar, you know I can't possibly stay here for a month. I have to go to Sydney for the trial. I have a subpoena from Mr Day.'

'Well, it looks like you will be unable to attend, doesn't it? You have to finish your work here.'

'I have to go down to the trial, sir, and that's —— '

'Listen, Hobbs,' Dangar interrupted sharply, 'I've already told you the case will be dropped; and even if it isn't, the men will be acquitted, so you'll just be wasting your time. Now forget about it. This business with the blacks has already caused enough disruption to my properties without you running off down to Sydney when you should be here finishing your job for me.'

'I'm going down for the trial, sir. I'm quite determined in that.'

'Hobbs, if you go off to Sydney for that trial, you won't be seeing a penny of your last four months' pay.'

'What? But you're already late in paying me that money, sir,' replied a stunned Hobbs.

'Well, that's terribly unfortunate, isn't it? But I won't be paying you a penny of it if you go to that trial instead of staying here and looking after my property; and what's more, my man, I'll make sure you don't get another job on any property in this colony.'

'You can't do that, sir.'

'I can and I will.'

Hobbs refused to be forced into pleading with the squatter or to argue anymore. He shook his head as he got to his feet. 'I'll be going to the trial.' He walked to the door of the hut, then paused after opening it, turning and glaring at the squatter, who was chewing on his cigar. Hobbs said nothing, however, and instead stepped out into the beautiful spring evening and strode across to the bank of the creek.

CHAPTER THIRTY FOUR

Friday 26 October 1838.

E dward Deas Thomson, the Colonial Secretary, and the Attorney-General, John Plunkett, entered the office of Governor Sir George Gipps. Thomson carried a collection of broadsheet newspapers under his arm.

'Good morning, Excellency.'

'Good morning, gentlemen,' returned Gipps. 'Sit down, please,' he invited, motioning to the two chairs in front of his desk.

'Thank you, sir.'

'Before we discuss this Myall Creek case, Mr Plunkett, tell me, Mr Thomson, what is in the newspapers, or don't I wish to know?'

'Well, there is quite an amount on the Myall Creek case, sir, as well as the usual debate on the Aboriginal issue in general,' replied Thomson, placing the broadsheets on the Governor's desk.

'Hmmm, still going on, are they, about "protecting our settlers and getting rid of the black savages"?'

'Yes, sir, there's plenty of that sort of thing, but you actually have a little support from certain parties, too, sir,' replied Thomson, picking up a copy of *The Sydney Herald*.

'Ah, that's a pleasing change. I'd be sure it hasn't come from *The Herald*, though.'

'Well, you're right there, sir, though you will recall that letter they published a few weeks ago from the Murrumbidgee landowner calling himself "Anti-hypocrite". He wrote to object to the waste of public money on Reverend Threlkeld's mission and other similar missions for the Aborigines, who he described as … ah, here's the quote, "the most degenerate, despicable and brutal race of beings in existence".'

'Yes, of course I do. He also accused the Aborigines of eating their own children and having less affection for them than a sow has for its litter, or some such nonsense. Ah yes, and then there was something about it being "the duty of every man to exterminate them from the face of the earth", or words to that effect. Does it sound like I remember it, Mr Thomson?' Gipps asked rhetorically.

'Yes, it certainly does, sir.'

'Yes, well, unfortunately one cannot easily forget that sort of verbal bile.' Gipps looked at Plunkett. 'One can only wonder how people get to be filled with so much hate that they make up such lies to justify their own prejudices.'

'I don't know, Excellency,' the Attorney General replied sombrely. 'The concern is, though, sir, that there are so many in this colony who are given to feelings of that nature and actually believe those lies.'

Gipps nodded. 'Well, it certainly is a concern, and I'm not really sure how we overcome it. Obviously ignorance is the greatest problem, because ignorance is the breeding ground for such sentiments.' Gipps stopped for a moment before returning his attention to the Colonial Secretary. 'Anyway, Mr Thomson, what about Mr "Anti-Hypocrite"?'

'Well, sir, they have published some replies to his letter, and although most support him, two letters are opposed to the views of "Anti-Hypocrite".'

'Good. What do they have to say?' Gipps asked, sitting forward in his chair.

'Well, one calling himself "An Australian" is horrified that, and I quote, sir, "in this enlightened age and in a Christian community anyone should air such unfeeling, inhuman and brutal sentiments in a public newspaper, and I blush to think they were written by a countryman of mine, by an Australian".'

Gipps nodded enthusiastically. 'Excellent. I'm pleased there are at least some decent people in this colony.'

Thomson continued. 'And another one, calling himself "W.I.", notes the name of the district that "Anti-Hypocrite" is from, Murrumbidgee, and how similar it sounds to "Murder-em-I-bid-ye". He goes on to say that from his own experience of the Aborigines, he knows they have normal human feelings and a deep affection for their children. He concludes by saying "It is high time the people of this colony realised the responsibility they had incurred in occupying the blacks' natural inheritance and increased the paltry expenditure on the missions and their welfare ten- or even twenty-fold to avert the wrath which the blood of this injured people may bring on the heads of this generation and on the heads of our children".'

Thomson put the paper down and looked up at the Governor, who had been sitting back in his chair while listening and now remained deep in thought. After a few moments he remarked, 'He makes a most excellent point, doesn't he, Mr Plunkett?'

'Most certainly, sir,' agreed the Attorney-General.

Gipps sat forward for a moment before wondering aloud, 'That is the inherent conflict, though, isn't it, Mr Plunkett? Occupying the Aborigines' land to expand the colony, but at the same time protecting their lives and rights. As *The Herald*'s correspondent suggests, I wonder how successful we'll be and what legacy we will leave for future generations?'

'It certainly is a most complex problem, sir. I am sure, however, Excellency, that anyone would understand you are doing everything you possibly can. And it certainly is made most difficult when at every turn you are having to fight the squatters and monied classes in this colony.'

'Hmmm. Well, the one thing I know is that protecting the Aborigines has to be my highest priority in the matter. Those it's not too late to protect, that is. You will have noted Mr Day's rather disturbing comments in his report on the Myall Creek matter.'

'Which comments in particular, sir?' asked Plunkett.

'Those in which Mr Day describes the Myall Creek murders as part of "a war of extermination against the Aborigines" in that district.'

'Yes, sir,' replied Plunket. 'I am given to understand, however, it is the same in other districts, sir; in fact, that it is the same tragic story of slaughter right across the colony's frontier districts.'

'I certainly hope that isn't true, Mr Plunkett; but if it is, it is all the more reason why we have to pursue this case as thoroughly as we possibly can. To get the message through to the landowners of this colony, and to their servants, that they cannot go around the countryside slaughtering the natives as they like. I will give them the full protection of British Law.' Gipps brought his clenched fist down on the desk in front of him.

There was a strained silence in the room for a moment, before Thomson spoke. 'Yes, of course, Excellency, I agree with you completely, sir. You should understand, however, sir, that it may take some time for that message to get through, because some of your predecessors had a somewhat different view.'

'I understand that fully, Mr Thomson, and that's still further reason why we must pursue this case. People must realise that times have changed, that those days are behind us. Anyway, before Mr Plunkett outlines the progress of the case for me, was there anything else from the newspapers I should be informed about? What has *The Herald* to say about those responses to "Anti-hypocrite"? Surely even they have to appreciate the validity of their correspondents' comments.'

'Ah, I think you give them credit for rather too much decency, sir,' remarked Plunkett. 'What does their editorial say again, Mr Thomson?'

Thomson folded back a page of the broadsheet. 'Here it is: "'An Australian' does not conclusively answer the views of 'Anti-hypo-crite'"; and I quote, sir, they "are old fashioned enough to prefer our European fellow-subjects to savage barbarians". They go on to say, sir, that the government's "first task is to secure the white settlers from violence and rapine, after which they might have leisure to devote to the hopeless task of trying to civilise the savages of New Holland".'

Gipps sat back in his chair and slowly shook his head. 'Well, what else can we expect from *The Herald*? It's just a mouthpiece for the landed gentry of the colony. Mr Scott and his friends have just too much influence down there. What does *The Colonist* have to say on the subject?'

'Well, Dr Lang is questioning the whole British Colonial system in respect of indigenous peoples, Excellency.'

'Ah, really, what does he have to say?' Gipps got to his feet and wandered over to the window.

Thomson picked up another newspaper from the desk. 'Well, sir, he quotes various sections of the Buxton Committee's Report to the House of Commons in London, notably the evidence of certain prominent missionaries.' Thomson paused while he scanned the pages. 'Yes, here, sir, he quotes the Reverend Coates' submission to the committee. "With regard to New Holland: The Aborigines have been dispossessed of their country by an act of the British Government; and not only dispossessed of it, but their condition rendered much worse than it previously was, by the introduction among them of European vices and crimes".'

'Very perceptive of him. Anything further?' asked Gipps, gazing out the window.

'Yes, sir. He then quotes Reverend Beecham, who submitted: "I regard our present system as founded on a principle of injustice and wrong. When I read some of our Acts of Parliament which relate to the formation of our colonies, I find that the lands of certain countries are sold to colonists, without any reference whatever to the aboriginal inhabitants: the very countries which, at the times when the Acts are passed, are occupied by various aboriginal tribes, are all disposed of, as though they were waste and uninhabited regions". He concludes, sir, by saying, "I have ever thought, and must still continue to think, unless eternal justice itself should change, that this is essentially and morally wrong; and that our colonisation system is thus based upon a principle of unrighteousness". Reverend Lang then says that the Aborigines "have as an incontrovertible fact an inalienable right to their own soil and that it is nothing short of usurpation and robbery to take from them, their soil and means of subsistence, without a fair and adequate compensation".'

Gipps had returned to his seat and now leant on the arm of the chair, stroking his brow. 'Hmmm. He certainly makes a strong case, and it only provides more reason for British Law to protect the Aborigines. Since the system doesn't compensate them for the loss of their land and livelihoods, the law must at least protect their lives.'

'Exactly, sir,' agreed Plunkett.

'There is a view about the place, sir,' offered Thomson, 'that they are compensated by virtue of their being civilised and Christianised, sir.'

'What?' snapped Gipps.

'It's not a view I support, sir, but it *is* widely held, sir,' Thomson quickly added.

'I would most certainly hope you wouldn't support that type of cultural arrogance, Mr Thomson.'

'Yes, sir.' Thomson then hurriedly changed the subject. 'Ah, sir, *The Gazette* also had something to say on the subject, sir.'

'Well, they would not be any better than *The Herald*.'

'You are correct, of course, sir, but they editorialise on the Myall Creek case directly, sir.'

'Oh, again! What do they say this time?'

Thomson picked up the newspaper. 'It starts, "For many months back we have never failed to use every effort to set the government in motion toward putting a stop to the aggressions of the blacks, and affording protection to the white residents of the interior. We have again and again warned His Excellency that an impression was abroad that there existed on the part of the government a strong disinclination to extend to the settlers the protection that it is their bounden duty to afford". Further on it says " … the blacks in the Liverpool Plains district have recently been very troublesome, and convict stockmen and shepherds have fallen victim to the bloodthirsty ferocity of the savages in that quarter; besides which great quantities of sheep and cattle have been destroyed". It goes on sir, " … we have no wish to prejudice the cases of the unhappy men who are under committal for murder and awaiting trial —— "'

'They don't wish to prejudice the case? Ha!' interjected Gipps. 'Why, that's their very intention. Enough, enough, Mr Thomson; I've heard enough of their attempts to pressure and intimidate me. I will not be intimidated by these people.' The Governor again got to his feet and paced over to the window. 'And to show them I won't be intimidated and that British Law will protect the Aborigines, we must proceed with this case. Them and their "protect the whites from the black savages"! There has been a handful of whites killed in that area in the last couple of years, and, according to the information Mr Day has gathered, in some cases the Aborigines have been blamed when the assigned convicts have killed each other. He further informs us that, in that time, there has been, at the very least, many hundreds, probably thousands, of Aborigines slaughtered by soldiers and stockmen. And those that haven't been killed have been driven off their land. Who needs protection from whom, I ask?'

Thomson and Plunkett sat in silence as the Governor finished his tirade and returned to his seat behind the desk.

'All right, Mr Plunkett, how is the case progressing?' Gipps asked after having composed himself. 'I am given to understand that Russell fellow has been recaptured.'

'Yes, sir. He's now safely in the gaol here with the rest of them.'

'Good. And what about John Fleming? Any information on him?'

'No, sir, not a word,' Plunkett replied regretfully.

'Our fifty pound reward hasn't helped, then?'

'Unfortunately no, it hasn't, sir. They are, as you know, a wealthy family, sir, and able to hide him very effectively.'

'Well, we must keep trying, because we really need to capture him to show these people that, whether you are a convict or free man, you cannot just go around wantonly slaughtering the natives.'

'Yes, sir. Believe me, though, Excellency, we are trying and we will continue to do so,' assured Plunkett.

'Good. But apart from the Fleming issue, how do you believe the case is progressing?'

'Quite well, sir, considering it is a very difficult case to prove.'

'Yes, yes, I know, you've explained that to me previously.'

'Well, it is, sir, unfortunately. We've got no body, no really positive identification of any of the victims, and no witness who actually saw the crime take place.'

'Yes, I understand that, but what about this Anderson fellow? From reading Mr Day's report and considering the evidence he collected, it would seem a very clear-cut case.'

'Well, logically it is a very clear-cut case, and I have no doubt about the guilt of these men. Mr Day has done a fine job, but it is quite another matter to prove the case in a court of law to an almost certainly hostile jury. Because of the difficulty with identification, sir, I have decided to charge them with the murder of an Aboriginal named Daddy and with the murder of an Aboriginal male, name unknown. I believe that's the best way to cover the identification issue.'

'Excellent. Well, I'll leave that to your legal judgement, anyway, Mr Plunkett.'

'And as for Anderson, sir, well, he finally arrived yesterday from Muswellbrook, where he has been in custody under Mr Day's protection. He's now on Goat Island. I examined him late yesterday; and yes, he is certainly the key to our whole case.'

'And how did he seem? Is he prepared to go through with it?'

'I think so, sir. He's a typical convict – in that he's an ignorant and uneducated chap – but he seems to have a certain determination about this matter, despite the fact that he undoubtedly fears for his life. Being held in custody for so long, though, is obviously a most unpleasant experience. It's a very solitary existence, being kept away from other convicts, sir, but he seems to be coping with it all quite well.'

'Well, I'm not particularly concerned about the man's social arrangements, Mr Plunkett, so long as he's prepared to go ahead with his evidence.'

'Yes, Excellency, he certainly seems prepared to, sir.'

'Good. And have you settled on a date for the trial?'

'Yes, sir, Thursday the fifteenth of November,' Plunkett replied.

'Good. Now, is there anything else we need to discuss, gentlemen?'

'No, that is all, sir,' Thomson replied as he and Plunkett got to their feet.

'Thank you, then, gentlemen. I now have plenty of other matters to attend to here.'

As Plunkett and Thomson walked to the door, Gipps called out, 'Mr Plunkett.'

'Yes, sir?'

'Do everything you can to capture that Fleming, would you?'

'Yes sir, we will.'

With that, the Attorney-General closed the door behind him.

CHAPTER THIRTY FIVE

15 November 1838.

George Anderson slowly swung his feet to the floor beside the bunk in his gaol cell on Goat Island, in the middle of Sydney Harbour. Protective custody had not been easy. He sat up and buried his head in his hands. He hadn't slept, and he felt nauseous. Today was the day, and he desperately wanted it to be over. He retched violently but nothing was expelled from his empty stomach. He stood up and paced around his cell, then lay back down on his bunk.

Since being caught in the rain that day he had not had a moment's doubt that he would go through with it. The rain had brought that feeling flooding back to him – that feeling he had experienced while standing in the cold winter rain, with the warmth of her eyes upon him. He had not had a moment's doubt since then; and now the day was here, he still had no doubt. Her image was with him always.

'Come on, Anderson, ya ready?' came a voice from beyond his cell door.

* * *

The Supreme Court on the corner of Elizabeth and King Streets was one of the more impressive buildings in bustling young Sydney Town, the population of which had grown rapidly to nearly twenty-five thousand. It was a new, double-storeyed brick building, and Sydneysiders had arrived from all directions – on foot, on horseback and in open-topped horse-drawn carriages – to attend the most important and controversial trial in the colony's fifty-year history. The courtroom was full, and those who had not arrived early enough to gain access milled around outside the doors or wandered in the park adjacent to the courthouse, determined to remain in the immediate vicinity to obtain word of the proceedings as the trial progressed.

Inside the courtroom it was standing room only – and there was little enough of that. Those who had been fortunate enough to obtain a seat stood as the Chief Justice, Sir James Dowling, entered. Robert Scott and Henry Dangar stood beside each other and immediately behind the defence team they had hired: William Foster, William a'Beckett and Richard Windeyer, the colony's finest.

The silence of the courtroom was soon disturbed by the clanking of chains as the eleven prisoners were led into the dock, where they stood in silence while the charges against them were read: nine counts for the murder of a male Aboriginal black named Daddy and a male Aboriginal black, name unknown.

'Prisoners at the bar, how do you plead?' asked the clerk of arraigns.

'Not guilty,' was the response.

Now, for the first time, Charles Kilmeister's eyes wandered from the clerk and the judge across to the body of the courtroom, where he received an approving nod from Henry Dangar. Kilmeister nodded back.

The Attorney-General, John Plunkett, whispered a few words to his assistant, Roger Therry, before standing to address the jury. 'The case, gentlemen, you are called upon to try is one of no ordinary importance to this colony. I am sure the case will receive all the attention it demands. When eleven men are placed at the bar for a capital crime, it is itself sufficient evidence of the importance of the case.

'Before going into the case I must entreat you, gentlemen, to dismiss from your minds all impressions which may have been produced by anything you may have heard or read on the present subject. Gentlemen, murder is regarded as the greatest crime in all nations, but here is a case which shows that there are graduations even in murder. The charges only show, at the utmost, the death of two men, whereas in fact on the same day and in the same hour the lives of twenty-eight individuals – men, women and children – were sacrificed, without any cause or provocation to palliate the most atrocious crime in the sight of any laws, human or divine.

'I am sincerely glad to see the prisoners defended by counsel. I am glad to see the present prisoners in that situation, but a rumour has gone that this defence has been made at the instance of an association, illegally formed, for the purpose of defending all who may be charged with crimes resulting from collisions with the natives.' Plunkett now moved his gaze from the members of the jury and glanced toward Henry Dangar and Robert Scott, seated behind the defence counsel. He paused before continuing. 'I say that if such an association exists, that if there be men who have joined together for the purpose of defending such men as these, the object of that association is to encourage bloodshed and crime of every description.'

Plunkett now returned his focus to the gentlemen of the jury. 'Gentlemen, I have too high an opinion of you, and of the public at large, to think for a moment that any bloody article appearing in a paper, or papers, will at all influence you in the verdict you are to give this day.

'Gentlemen, it has been promulgated from the bench, by the judges of the land, that the black is as amenable for his evil acts as the white man, and therefore as much entitled to protection by the laws. These crimes were committed in cold blood and arose from no dispute. It was malicious and not caused by any momentary irritation or excitement. I have endeavoured to do my duty and I will now call the witnesses.'

Thomas Foster was the first witness called. Questioned by Plunkett, he outlined what he had seen of the stockmen's activities, before detailing the macabre scene Hobbs had shown him on the side of the ridge.

William a'Beckett then rose to cross-examine the witness. 'Mr Foster, these tracks that you say you followed from the hut, where were they exactly?'

'They were in the road that leads between Mr Dangar's place and mine.'

'And did you follow these tracks all the way to the place where you say you saw these bodies?'

'No, I don't think I tracked them all the way.'

'They might therefore have been just any tracks in the road?' observed a'Beckett.

'It was wet. It was very easy to track any horses.'

A'Beckett paused and looked down at his notes before continuing. 'You say, Mr Foster, that when these men came to your station the next morning they were armed. How many of them can you say beyond doubt were armed?'

'I would only swear that two of them were armed with pistols.'

'Only two of the whole party, Mr Foster?' a'Beckett remarked smugly. 'And is it unusual to carry pistols in the bush?'

'No, it's not. It is customary to carry pistols in the bush,' admitted Foster.

'Is it then unusual for stockmen to be mounted?' a'Beckett continued.

'No, they are always mounted.'

'And, Mr Foster, can you tell the jury why it is normal to carry pistols in the bush?'

'It is in consequence of the fear of danger from the blacks.'

'Really, Mr Foster? And have you ever been attacked by the blacks?'

'I have been very fortunate. My station is a central station, and I believe that is the reason I have not been attacked. My neighbours have not been so fortunate,' volunteered Foster, who, unlike Hobbs, had managed to retain his position as superintendent.

John Plunkett shook his head as his assistant, Roger Therry, whispered to him. 'What's he think he's saying? He's supposed to be our witness.'

'I suppose that is why Mr Day put a fifty pound surety on him to attend today. Day was concerned about how scared he has been,' Plunkett replied.

Therry nodded as a'Beckett continued. 'Mr Foster, are the blacks in the district normally armed?'

'I cannot say. That was the first party of blacks I had seen.'

A'Beckett glanced at his colleagues on the defence counsel's table, then looked at some notes before asking, 'Did you see any children's skulls amongst the remains on the ridge?'

'No, I didn't see any children's skulls. I have told you all I saw.'

'And did Mr Hobbs say that anything at the scene had changed from the night before, when he had seen it?'

'No, he did not say there was any difference.'

'Thank you, Mr Foster. That is all for now,' a'Beckett concluded. As he resumed his seat, he received an approving nod from Robert Scott, seated behind him.

Sir James Dowling looked toward John Plunkett. 'Any further questions for this witness, Mr Plunkett?'

'Yes, your Honour.' Plunkett immediately got to his feet, remaining behind his table. 'Mr Foster, the road in which these tracks were made, is that a commonly used road?'

'Well, we call it a public road but it is very rarely used.'

'And therefore it would be unusual to have a large group of tracks like this on that road?'

'Yes, but it is not unusual to meet large groups of men out looking for blacks.'

'And these natives camped at Dangar's, were they quiet?'

'Yes. Well, the ten blacks who accompanied me to my station were quiet.'

'And were they armed?' Plunkett asked, still standing behind his table.

'No, they weren't.'

'And, Mr Foster, did you know this Aborigine named Daddy.'

'Yes, I had seen him.'

'Thank you, Mr Foster,' said Plunkett, resuming his seat.

Given his opportunity, a'Beckett was immediately on his feet again with further questions for the witness. 'Mr Foster, I thought you had only been to the Myall Creek station once while the blacks were there. How do you know who Daddy was?'

'Because I had seen him. He was called "Daddy".' Foster then turned to Sir James Dowling. 'He was a very big, very old man, your Honour.'

Sir James nodded but said nothing.

A'Beckett continued. 'All right, now, Mr Foster, when you took these ten blacks down to cut bark at your station, weren't they armed with tomahawks?'

'Well, they were unarmed except for two or three tomahawks for cutting the bark with,' Foster conceded.

'Thank you, Mr Foster. No more questions, your Honour.'

William Hobbs' name was then called, and the former superintendent of the Myall Creek station entered the witness box. As Hobbs was being sworn in, his eyes drifted around the courtroom, from Plunkett and Therry in front of him, to the defence counsels, and then to Henry Dangar. Dangar was looking directly at him, and as their eyes collided, without breaking his gaze Dangar immediately began whispering something to Robert Scott beside him. It made Hobbs feel even less comfortable than he already was. He shifted his eyes again, this time to the prisoners in the dock. There was Charles Kilmeister, chained and manacled. He looked drawn and exhausted. On seeing him, Hobbs was hit by a conflict of emotions. On the one hand, his instant reaction was pity at seeing his former faithful servant and companion in such a state and in such a situation. That pity quickly turned to anger, however, as he remembered why Kilmeister was there and visions of the dismembered Weraerai came back to him, as they did almost every night in the solitude of his bed.

Kilmeister looked at him with the pitiful look of a rejected dog. Hobbs looked away.

After taking him through the initial parts of his evidence, the Attorney-General focused on the more crucial aspects. 'And, Mr Hobbs, what did you find when you followed those tracks with Davey?'

'We arrived at a spot where there were a great number of dead bodies; but the stench was so great that I was not able to be accurate in counting them.'

'Did you endeavour to count them?'

'Yes, I tried to count them, but I made more of them sometimes than others. The most I made was twenty-eight. The skulls which had been burnt were easily discernible.'

'What is the least number of bodies you could absolutely swear you saw there?'

Hobbs thought for a moment before replying. 'I will undertake to swear that there were the remains of above twenty.'

'And what sort of a state were these bodies in, Mr Hobbs?'

'They were very much disfigured.'

'Now, in regard to the identity of the victims, did you know the Aboriginal black called Daddy?'

Hobbs nodded. 'Yes, very well.'

'And could you describe him for the court?'

'He was a very old man, and he was the largest man I ever saw, either black or white.'

'Now, Mr Hobbs, was Daddy's body there amongst all the dead bodies on the side of that ridge?'

'I saw a large body there but the head was missing. From the size of it, though, I think it was his.'

'You say you "think" it was Daddy's body. Can you be any more sure about it than that?'

A'Beckett immediately jumped to his feet. 'Your Honour, the Attorney-General is leading the witness.'

Justice Dowling leant forward over the bench. 'Yes, if you could rephrase that question, thank you, Mr Plunkett.'

'Certainly, your Honour.' Plunkett paused briefly before continuing. 'Mr Hobbs, how sure are you that this body you are referring to was Daddy's body?'

Hobbs again thought for a moment. 'I could not swear it was Daddy's body, but I am perfectly satisfied within my own mind that it was his.'

Plunkett nodded. 'Thank you, Mr Hobbs. Now, can you describe for the court the state of the body which you believe in your own mind to be that of Daddy?'

'Well, it was lying on its back. There was no head and the fire had destroyed nearly all of the flesh.'

'And when was the last time you had seen Daddy alive?'

Hobbs remembered the old man standing with the other elders and young Charley bidding him farewell as he left for the lower station. 'I had left him on the station when I went downriver.'

'Now, can you tell us about the other remains you saw there?'

'Well, I saw the children's heads quite distinctly.'

'How many children's heads did you see?'

'There were ten to twelve small heads ... '

A wave of murmuring rolled around the packed public gallery. Hobbs waited for it to subside as Sir James Dowling slammed his gavel. Once the courtroom was silent again, Hobbs added, ' ... and also some children's bodies.'

The muttering started again, this time becoming so loud it drifted beyond the large timber doors at the back of the courtroom and across the narrow hallway to a small anteroom where the prosecution's prize witness sat in silence next to a police guard. George Anderson's mind had been ricocheting between thoughts of Ipeta and the threats made against him by her killers. The moment when Russell had shoved his pistol in his face and threatened to come back and kill him if he ever said a word to anyone kept recurring despite the fact that Russell was now in chains in the dock. Anderson was very aware that John Fleming was still at large and quite capable of making good Russell's threat, or again having someone else assist with his sullied deeds.

The mutterings from the courtroom brought his mind back to the present, and his anxiety increased as he was struck by the reality that he would soon be called to testify. His neck was tense. His back was itchy. He looked down at the palms of his hands, wiping the sweat from them on the new trousers which Plunkett had organised for him. They, along with the new shirt he wore, were the first new clothes he had had since those he purchased with the proceeds of the robbery which had seen him transported. They may have been new but they were stiff and uncomfortable, and his battered old boots looked totally incongruous beneath them.

Inside the courtroom, John Plunkett conferred briefly with Roger Therry, while the gallery continued murmuring until again silenced by Justice Dowling.

Plunkett continued. 'Now, Mr Hobbs, can you tell us how the blacks came to be on your station?'

'They were brought there by Kilmeister,' Hobbs answered, glancing over to the dock, where Kilmeister immediately dropped his eyes as members of the public gallery again began whispering and pointing.

'And how did they behave while they were on your station?'

'They behaved well. They were not offensive in the least degree.'

'And did you speak to Kilmeister after you had seen the bodies of the blacks?'

'Yes, I had several conversations with him.'

'What about?'

'I pointed out the indecency with which the remains had been treated. He offered to go up and bury them, but I told him that, if his protestations of innocence were true, it would do him an injury to interfere in any such way when the matter was investigated.'

'And you say Kilmeister protested his innocence when you questioned him?'

'Yes.' Hobbs nodded, then again looked over to Kilmeister, who again dropped his gaze to the floor. 'He always denied knowing anything of the crime, and I always believed him innocent, until the depositions were taken by Mr Day.'

'Why did you believe him innocent, Mr Hobbs?' questioned Plunkett.

'Because he was daily singing and dancing with the blacks after his return from the run. He thought very highly of them.'

'Thank you, Mr Hobbs. I also understand you are no longer employed by Mr Dangar?'

'That's correct, though Mr Dangar has not yet settled with me; but I believe I will leave his employ as a result of this affair.'

'Thank you, Mr Hobbs. I have no more questions at this time, your Honour.'

As Plunkett resumed his seat, the three defence attorneys sat huddled in hurried consultation, before William Foster stood to take his turn at cross-examination.

'Mr Hobbs, what sort of a servant was Charles Kilmeister?'

'He has always been a good servant.' Hobbs again looked toward the dock and finally engaged the eye of the enchained Kilmeister. 'In fact, I very much doubt whether there is in New South Wales a better servant than Kilmeister. I should not have thought he would wantonly attack another.' It was a statement intoned with a considerable degree of regret, and one which Kilmeister received with extremely mixed emotions. It was a strangely commendable reference from someone who was giving evidence that could see him hang, but Kilmeister understood it was Hobbs' way of saying, 'You were a good servant. Why did you do it, you fool?'

'"An excellent servant", then!' Foster commented, glancing toward the jury. 'And Mr Hobbs, why did Kilmeister not want you to report this matter?'

'He was afraid if this case was investigated that he may be returned to government service.'

William Foster looked up toward the ceiling and gripped the front of his robes with both hands. 'Mr Hobbs, these weapons that were kept about the station, what were they for?'

'They were there for personal safety.'

'Did you carry firearms, pistols, yourself?'

'Yes, I did.'

'Do you think it is dangerous for anyone to go into the bush that far from the settlements without firearms?'

'Yes, I do,' conceded Hobbs.

'Thank you, Mr Hobbs.' Foster again paused before continuing. 'Mr Hobbs, this body that you say you believe was that of Daddy, you said there was no head on it, is that correct?'

'Yes,' agreed Hobbs.

'So, there was no head on it, and you also stated that nearly all the flesh was burnt off it. How could you even ascertain with any certainty whatsoever that it was a man and not a woman? Can you swear that it was a man?'

'No, I couldn't swear that it was a man,' conceded Hobbs, 'but it was a large frame.'

'Mr Hobbs, can you even swear that the black called Daddy is not now still in existence?'

'No, I couldn't swear that he isn't in existence.'

'Thank you, Mr Hobbs.' A triumphant William Foster smiled as he flicked his flowing black gown to the side and resumed his seat, well satisfied with his performance.

The Attorney-General sat, arms folded, staring at William Hobbs while Roger Therry whispered to him. Plunkett was soon on his feet again.

'Mr Hobbs, can you swear Daddy is dead?'

'No, I can't swear he's dead,' Hobbs answered somewhat regretfully.

'Have you seen him since this incident?'

'No, I haven't.'

'And Mr Hobbs, have you ever seen a female with as large a frame as that of the headless body you believe "in your own mind" was that of Daddy?'

'No, I haven't.'

'And since this incident, have you seen any of those Aborigines who were on your station?'

'No, sir, I haven't.'

'Thank you, Mr Hobbs. No more questions of this witness, thank you, your Honour.' John Plunkett resumed his seat.

'George Anderson … George Anderson.'

Anderson's stomach leapt. The guard seated next to him looked at him and grunted. 'Come on, that's you.'

The Myall Creek station hutkeeper stood up and, accompanied by the guard, walked out of the anteroom and across to the back door of the New South Wales Supreme Court. He looked in onto a sea of whispering, mumbling faces that stared at him as he entered the crowded courtroom. He saw Henry Dangar seated with a group of well-dressed gentlemen behind the defence attorneys. He then noticed the prisoners in the dock, but didn't focus on them as individuals. The next thing he was aware of was being in the witness box and swearing on a Bible. A few moments later the Attorney-General stood up behind his table and began questioning him.

'Mr Anderson, can you tell the court what happened when Mr Hobbs was away downriver in June last?'

Anderson hesitated for a moment, his eyes shifting around the room. In the dock he spotted Kilmeister, who, along with all his colleagues, had fixed his gaze upon the hutkeeper. Anderson looked back to Plunkett as he answered. 'Yes … On a Sunday afternoon, about ten men came on horseback, armed with muskets, swords and pistols.'

'Were they all armed?' asked Plunkett.

Anderson nodded. 'Yes.'

'And where were you when they came riding up?'

'I was sitting in the hut with Kilmeister, the stockman.'

'And what did these men do?'

'They came galloping up with their guns and pistols pointed at the blacks.'

'Can you identify the prisoners in the dock as these same men?'

A heavy silence descended upon the courtroom. All eyes were on the hutkeeper as he now looked back at the prisoners in the dock. His back itched and he was more aware than ever of just how hot and uncomfortable his new clothes were.

Plunkett waited.

Finally Anderson spoke. 'Russell, Telluse, Foley, Black Johnstone, Hawkins, Palliser, Lamb and Oates were there.' Each of the prisoners shook their heads and muttered as Anderson identified them. He then added, 'Blake and Parry I can't swear to.'

'Thank you. Now, when these men came galloping up with their pistols drawn, what did they do?'

'They spread out in a line to surround the blacks.'

'And how did the blacks react?'

'They came running into the hut.'

'And what did the horsemen do then?'

'Some of them got off their horses, and Russell took a rope from his horse's neck and began undoing it.'

'And what happened then?'

'While Russell was preparing the rope, I asked 'im what they was going to do with the blacks. He said they was going to take them over the back of the range and frighten them.'

'What did Russell do then?'

'He went into the hut with some of the others, tied the blacks and brought them out.'

'And what were the blacks doing at this time?'

Ipeta's lover hesitated as the images of that moment again came back to him. They were images he had lived with night after night, but always in the solitude of his isolated hut at Myall Creek, or alone in his police cell for the past two months. Now he had to deal with it in front of the hostile gaze of the prisoners, the squatters and the murmuring public gallery.

His senses swelled with little Charley's cries of 'Jackey-Jackey' and visions of Ipeta. Jackey-Jackey's cheek quivered momentarily as he looked at John Plunkett and answered. 'The blacks were pleading for help. The mothers and children were cryin', and the little babies who were too small to walk were all cryin'. All the blacks were all tied to the long rope and one of them was handcuffed to it.'

'And what happened then?'

'Russell brought out the end of the rope and gave it to one of the men on 'orseback, and they took all the blacks away except for two boys who had jumped into the creek when the men rode up.'

'Were there any others left behind?'

Anderson nodded hesitantly. 'They left one black gin with me and another one with Davey. And there was a little child that was in the back of the hut when they were tying the blacks. Instead of letting her go with the party I pulled her into the hut and hid her there.'

'And do you know the Aboriginal black known as "Daddy"?'

'Yes, the oldest of the lot was called "Old Daddy".'

'Can you describe him for the court?'

'He was a very old, big, tall man.'

'Thank you,' said Plunkett, hesitating while he gathered his thoughts. 'Now, what did Kilmeister do when these men came up to your hut?'

'Kilmeister went outside and talked to them for about five minutes.'

'What did they talk about?'

'I don't know; I paid no attention.'

'All right. What did Kilmeister do then?'

'While they were tying the blacks, he went and got his horse and took his pistol and went with them.'

'Were all of these men armed?'

'Yes, sir.'

'What with?'

'They had a great many pistols and guns, and some swords.'

'Thank you, Mr Anderson.' The Attorney-General briefly referred to some notes on his table before continuing, taking Anderson through events that occurred later in the night in question and when the riders had returned.

There was a brief easing of the tension in Anderson's neck and shoulders once Plunkett had concluded, but it quickly returned as he saw Richard Windeyer stand to begin the cross-examination.

Windeyer was in a hurry. Like a dog that has caught the scent of something on the breeze and frantically seeks its source, he immediately pursued a point which he believed would damage Anderson's credibility.

'Now, Mr Anderson, can you tell the jury why you asked the men to give you the gin that they left with you?'

'I didn't ask for that gin,' Anderson mumbled.

'You asked for a different gin, did you?'

'After they untied one for Davey, I asked them to leave one for me.'

'You still haven't answered the question, Mr Anderson. So they left one for Davey, but why did you ask them to leave a particular gin for yourself?'

'I wish they had left them all.'

Windeyer was not to be put off the scent. He persisted. 'Answer the question. You may have wished that but you asked for a particular gin. Why?'

'I wanted the gin that I had had before, not the one they left me,' Anderson conceded, glancing at Kilmeister, who he now knew must have told Windeyer about Ipeta. Kilmeister smirked as murmuring again rippled through the courtroom.

Sir James Dowling quickly cracked his gavel on the bench in front of him. 'Order, thank you.'

Silence was quickly restored and Windeyer pursued his quarry. 'If these men were supposedly rounding up all the blacks and taking them away, why didn't they take this Davey away with them?'

Anderson shrugged. 'I dunno.'

'Come on now, Mr Anderson, you're trying to tell the court these men supposedly tied up all the blacks and took them away, but they left these two gins and Davey behind? Why would they leave a gin with Davey? Why wouldn't they take Davey with them as well?'

'I dunno. The only thing I know is Davey is more naturalised.'

Windeyer paused in his pursuit, sniffled loudly, blew his nose, adjusted his wig and then continued. 'Can you tell the jury why you could remember so little when you were first examined by Mr Day? You said you didn't know the men, but then you suddenly remembered names and details when you were examined a second time.'

'I didn't know the others, but I always said I remembered Russell and Fleming, by name as well as by face.'

'But why did you have to be examined a second time?'

'Because I wanted to tell more which I'd recollected.'

Windeyer paused again before moving in for the kill. 'How long have you been in this colony, Anderson?'

'About five years.'

'And how long are you here for?'

'I'm here for life,' the hutkeeper muttered, rubbing the back of his neck.

'And you've boasted that this evidence would get you your liberty, haven't you?' speculated Windeyer.

Anderson was shocked by the accusation. 'No, I've never said my evidence would get me my liberty.'

'But you expect to get it after this case, don't you?'

'I'd take anything I could get.'

Windeyer continued to speculate. 'But you've asked for your liberty, haven't you?'

'No.' The convict stared at his tormentor. 'The only thing I've asked for is protection.'

Somewhat taken aback by his defeat on this point, Windeyer quickly changed tack. 'You're always in trouble with your master, aren't you, Anderson?'

'I've been punished twice, for neglect of duty and being absent from my station, but never at the Myall Creek station.'

'Your master, Mr Dangar, has had to take you to court to have you punished for your behaviour, hasn't he?'

'Once, when I was at New England, but I don't think that I deserved the punishment,' Anderson asserted firmly.

'Oh really?' Windeyer sneered, to the mirth of the public gallery.

That was enough for Anderson to fly to his own defence, still bitter as he was about both the punishment itself and the injustice with which Dangar had treated him. He was not about to sit there now and be ridiculed in public over the matter.

'I spoke the truth. I did not deserve the punishment; and if ya like, I'll tell ya about it and you can judge for yourselves.' Anderson did not give Windeyer a chance to respond. 'I was helping a man shift his cattle, and Mr Dangar charged me with failing to move me sheep folds and leaving the station. He marched me all the way to Patrick's Plains and back, eight days' hard walk, and I got two fifties – one hundred lashes,' Anderson explained, glaring down the courtroom at Henry Dangar.

Windeyer again quickly changed the subject. 'And what were you transported to this colony for?'

'For robbing my master, but I was ignorant and misled by others.'

'Ah, a thief,' remarked Windeyer.

Having put his life at risk by testifying, Anderson was not prepared to endure public taunts from anyone. 'I am no thief, sir,' he stated coldly.

Windeyer again changed tack and began a different line of questioning. 'Now, as to the identity of these blacks, we've only heard Daddy mentioned. Who were the others?'

'Old Joey —— '

'Who's he?' Windeyer interrupted.

'He was at the station with the others.'

'Who else?'

'King Sandy's wife and Joey – they were taken away.'

'Any others? Who was the gin you asked for?'

Anderson looked at the barrister, with his wig perched on his head and his flowing black robe. 'The gin I wanted was called Ipeta. She, Sandy, his wife, Martha, and their son, little Charley, was all taken away. There was another blackfella, called Tommy. I could name nearly all of them if they was before me. They was all tied and taken away.'

The illiterate convict hutkeeper was suddenly getting the better of the London-educated barrister whose line of questioning had led to names and identities being given to the 'anonymous black savages'. It was the last thing his case needed, as Windeyer's colleagues promptly reminded him, so he quickly resumed his seat.

John Plunkett rose to re-examine his most crucial witness, as they had the defence on the back foot. 'Mr Anderson, can you just clarify for the jury why these men did not take Davey away with the others?'

'Davey never belonged to that tribe.'

'Thank you. What tribe did he belong to?'

'The Peel River tribe.'

'And what was he doing on the station?' Plunkett asked gently.

'He brought some cattle down.'

'Good. So he worked on the station and he wasn't part of the tribe that were camped there?'

'That's right, sir.'

'Now, regarding you identifying these men, what did you mean when you said that at first you did not know them?'

'I meant I hadn't seen 'em before.'

'But when Mr Day had them in custody, did you recognise them then?'

'Yes, I knew 'em all by sight straight away when they was in custody, and I said at once there was two men there who did not come to the hut.'

'Thank you. Now, Mr Anderson, these men came back the next day, they stayed the night, and the following morning they went back up to the ridge. Is that correct?'

'Yes, sir.'

'Now, when they went back up to the ridge, did they leave their weapons behind?'

'Yes, sir.'

'What weapons were there?'

'There was muskets, pistols and swords.'

'How many?'

'I counted fifteen pistols but only two swords.'

The significance behind what George Anderson had just said did not appear to strike Plunkett, but his assistant, Roger Therry, suddenly looked ashen-faced.

Plunkett continued his questioning, apparently oblivious. 'Thank you, Mr Anderson. Now I just wish to clarify a matter regarding the identity of Sandy, the Aboriginal black. Were there two Sandys?'

'Yes, sir. One went with Mr Foster and the other was taken away. It was King Sandy who went with Mr Foster.'

'Thank you. No more questions for this witness, your Honour.'

George Anderson rose and stepped down from the witness box. At last it was all over. As he walked in front of the judge's bench, for a few paces he was heading directly toward the prisoners in the dock. He glanced at Kilmeister, who sneered at him. Anderson shook his head, looked away and followed his guard from the courtroom.

Plunkett resumed his seat beside the still distressed-looking Therry, who immediately whispered to him, 'Did you realise they only had two swords?'

'Three, actually,' came Plunkett's deadpan reply.

'Well, if they only fired two shots and they only had three swords, and they slaughtered and dismembered that many people, can you imagine how long that must have taken and the terror for those people, women and children, waiting their turn?'

Plunkett turned and faced Therry. 'I know. We must win this case.'

* * *

The trial continued as the afternoon wore on. Evidence was heard from John Bates, Andrew Burrowes, William Mace and Charles Reid, but they provided only limited benefit for the prosecution's case. Although Bates and Mace acknowledged that the stockmen had had breakfast at their station on the morning of the eleventh of June and had left a gin with them, they could identify only a few of the men. They both failed to identify or name either Fleming or Russell.

The case for the prosecution concluded with the calling of a dentist, Andrew Foss, as an expert witness to identify as human remains the jaw bone and teeth which Edward Denny Day had collected from the side of the ridge.

William a'Beckett consulted briefly with his colleagues and with Robert Scott, who leant forward in his seat to provide advice and direction. A'Beckett then rose to begin the case for the defence.

'Your Honour, having now heard the case the Attorney-General has put before this court, I submit, your Honour, that the case be dismissed, as there is nothing in the prosecution's case to go to the jury for their consideration. Your Honour, the whole of the charge is about Daddy, or a black native, name unknown, and the evidence is perfectly circumstantial. Mr Hobbs is the only one who speaks to the identity of Daddy, and he could not swear that the mass of putridity which he saw was a man or a woman.

'And as to the death of the black, name unknown, the charges relate respectively to that person losing his life from a shot from a pistol or assault with a sword. There has been no proof produced that this party lost their life in such a way.

'The point I would like to stress most strongly, your Honour, is that there has been no proof produced that the black known as Daddy is not still alive, or that a dead male black has been found. Finally, I respectfully remind your Honour of English Chief Justice Lord Hale's ruling that no conviction for murder should occur where no body has been found.'

Sir James Dowling looked down from his bench. 'Mr a'Beckett, it is clearly for the jury to decide whether the bulky remains found at the fire belonged to the man called Daddy. It is also for the jury to consider all the circumstances and decide on the manner of death of the Aboriginal black male and whether one of the bodies found was that of one of the other male Aborigines taken away by the accused. Your motion is therefore dismissed. Please proceed with the case for the defence.'

A'Beckett responded immediately. 'Well, if it pleases your Honour, we will not be seeking to disprove the Attorney-General's case by calling witnesses but instead will be relying upon the failure of the Crown to assume its onus of proof in establishing the guilt of the accused. We would, however, like to call several witnesses to attest to the good character of various members of the accused.'

'Very well, please proceed,' invited a slightly surprised Sir James Dowling.

John Plunkett and Roger Therry were stunned, and a ripple of murmuring again swept around the public gallery.

'What happened to their much publicised list of dozens of witnesses?' Therry muttered to Plunkett.

'I have no idea at all,' replied Plunkett as a'Beckett called his first witness, Henry Dangar, who looked very much the wealthy squatter in his fine, English-made charcoal grey suit with a highly starched white shirt and a black silk cravat. He entered the witness box and made his oath.

'Mr Dangar,' began a'Beckett, 'Charles Kilmeister is your servant, is that correct?'

'Yes, he has been in my service since 1834,' answered the squatter.

'And what sort of a servant is he?'

'He is a very good servant. He is trustworthy and obedient.'

'Thank you, Mr Dangar. And George Anderson is also your servant, is he not?'

'Yes, he is.'

'And what sort of a servant is he?'

'He is a very troublesome one. I would not believe him on his oath, as on the most trifling occasions he is addicted to lying.' Dangar looked down, brushed a tiny piece of fluff from the front of his immaculate white shirt, then looked back up at John Plunkett.

'Thank you, Mr Dangar. No more questions, your Honour.'

Plunkett rose to begin his cross-examination. 'Mr Dangar, how long has George Anderson been in your service?'

'Since 1833. For the first two years he was under my direct supervision, and for the last two years under Mr Hobbs'.'

'And why wouldn't you believe him at his oath?'

'Why, because he has been very troublesome and I've had to have him punished more than once. On a recent occasion I had to have him punished for leaving his station.'

'And what, sir, does his leaving his station have to do with you not believing him at his oath?'

Dangar hesitated, looked at Plunkett and repeated, 'I would not believe him at his oath.'

Plunkett changed the subject. 'Mr Dangar, I understand Mr Hobbs has earned your displeasure by reporting this matter?'

'Not at all, sir,' Dangar replied with mock indignation.

'Then why have you terminated his employment with you?'

'His term is up – it's as simple as that. It has nothing to do with this matter.'

'Very well, Mr Dangar. One last point, thank you. I understand you have subscribed to the defence fund for the prisoners. Is that correct?'

'Yes, it is,' Dangar conceded.

'And why, sir, would you contribute to the defence of men accused of such an horrific crime?'

'Because I have a servant amongst them who I believe to be honest and perfectly innocent.'

'How much did you subscribe to this defence fund, Mr Dangar?'

'I decline to answer that, sir.'

'Very well, I shall not press the point. No more questions, thank you, your Honour,' Plunkett concluded, resuming his seat.

A succession of squatters followed Henry Dangar into the witness box to attest to the quiet, peaceable characters of their convict servants who stood charged over the murder of Old Daddy and his people.

It was just after eight in the evening when Sir James Dowling began his summing up. 'We have now been engaged many hours in one of the most important cases which has ever come before the Supreme Court in New South Wales. The case has excited considerable interest, and you were warned at the outset to throw aside any impression which might have been made by hearing or reading descriptions of this affair. I recall to your minds that each of you invoked God to witness that he would be determined by the evidence and return a verdict according to the substance of that evidence.

'It is clear that a most grievous offence has been committed, that the lives of near thirty of our fellow creatures have been sacrificed, and in order to fulfil my duty I must tell you that the life of a black is as precious and valuable in the eye of the law as that of the highest noble in the land. The black is answerable for his crimes, and some short time before I had the honour of assuming my present seat on this bench, a native black was executed for the murder of a white man.

'Having made these observations for the benefit of the public as well as the prisoners, I will call your attention to the evidence. I leave you to discharge your duty by considering whether the prisoners at the bar were the parties who committed the crime which has been proved.

'I agree with the learned counsel for the defence that a man cannot be committed for murder before a body is found. Therefore the point you have to determine is whether Daddy was the unfortunate man who lost his life, as set forth in the indictment, or whether a man whose name is unknown came to his death by violent means from the prisoners' hands.'

The jury left the courtroom to consider their verdict as Sir James Dowling retired to his chambers.

Henry Dangar, Robert Scott and other prominent members of

the "squattocracy" stood in a large group, loudly discussing their opinions of the likely verdict. Those in the public gallery remained riveted to their chairs. They had waited throughout a very long day and were not going to leave the courtroom to stretch their legs, for fear of losing their seats.

John Plunkett and Roger Therry remained seated alone at the front of the room.

'What do you think, Mr Plunkett?'

'It is very hard to say. It could go either way. I think we have clearly established from the evidence that a large number of Aborigines were killed, and it is equally clear that the prisoners are the ones who committed the deed. However, if the jury wish, they can take the view that Daddy's body was not positively identified and that an Aboriginal male was not definitely found. Basically, Mr Therry, they can deliver a verdict in accordance with their predisposition; and knowing the prevailing sentiment in this colony, I fear that may be acquittal.'

'Yes, they're exactly my fears as well. The Governor will be most irate.'

'He most certainly will be; but perhaps we can avoid such a blatant injustice,' replied Plunkett.

'How could we do that, sir?'

Plunkett was about to explain, when the clerk of the court walked over and advised him the jury was ready to return.

'Already?' he said, stunned. He opened the fob watch sitting on the bench in front of him. 'Why, that's barely a quarter of an hour!'

The jury filed back in and resumed their seats on the two rows of timber benches as animated discussions swept across the public gallery. George Anderson stood at the back of the courtroom, between his guard and William Hobbs. Beads of sweat formed on his brow. It was hot and the room was crowded. He rubbed his neck and glanced sideways at Hobbs, looking for reassurance. Hobbs looked at him and shrugged.

'Why was they so quick, Mr 'obbs?'

'Don't know, George.'

Sir James Dowling entered and resumed his seat, immediately cracking his gavel on the bench. 'Order, thank you.'

Silence quickly descended upon the room. Sir James looked at Charles Holmes, the foreman of the jury. 'Gentlemen, have you reached a verdict?'

The foreman stood. 'We have, your Honour.'

'How say you?' asked Sir James.

'On all counts, we find the prisoners "Not Guilty".'

The words pierced Anderson like a cutlass. The public gallery erupted with cheering and clapping. Henry Dangar and Robert Scott leapt to their feet and shook hands vigorously, firstly with each other and then with the defence counsels Messrs a'Beckett, Foster and Windeyer. In the dock, Russell and Lamb embraced, while Kilmeister acknowledged smiles and mouthed congratulations from Dangar.

Hobbs looked at Anderson. The blood had drained from the convict's face. 'I can't believe it,' Hobbs murmured, shaking his head.

Sir James Dowling tolerated the cheering from the public gallery for only a few moments before attempting to restore order. 'Order!' His gavel cracked. 'Order! Order; or I'll have the Sheriff clear the court. Order!' His gavel cracked again and again.

Eventually the spontaneous joy of the mass was quelled and silence settled again in the courtroom. When it did, John Hubert Plunkett was immediately on his feet. 'Your Honour.'

'Yes, Mr Plunkett?'

'Your Honour, I would like to request that the prisoners be remanded in custody until Saturday next, at which time I will be ready with another indictment – different charges arising from this same incident.'

There was a stunned silence in the courtroom, followed by widespread mumbling, and then the sound of muffled booing and hissing emanated from the public gallery as they came to the realisation the prisoners were to face a second trial.

CHAPTER THIRTY SIX

Whatever the uproar that arose when the gang were first committed for trial, it was minor compared to the furore that erupted when the news swept through Sydney Town that they were to face another trial. A fierce debate broke out among the diversely owned press. The dominant newspaper, *The Sydney Herald*, claimed the evidence in the case was 'entirely circumstantial', and maintained its previous position, wondering 'how long are the white settlers to be left to the mercy of lawless savages'. It also opposed the fifty pound reward offered for the capture of John Fleming for 'the supposed murder of some marauding black'.

The Commercial Journal criticised Attorney-General John Plunkett for 'wasteful expenditure of public money on a case a lawyer's errand boy could see would not stand up'. *The Sydney Gazette*, though appalled by the massacre, accused Governor Gipps of causing the massacre by his 'culpable negligence' in failing to protect the white settlers.

The contrary view was taken by *The Australian*, which railed against the association of Hunter River squatters, including magistrates, formed for 'the extermination of the blacks'. *The Australian* was not entirely alone, however.

SYDNEY MONITOR.
Monday November 19 1838.
Editor - Edward Smith Hall.

The trial of eleven men for the slaughter of a company of Aborigines of both sexes and all ages, from sucking infants to old men, took place on the 15th of this month. We stated in our last edition that they were acquitted. Our readers will find a very full report of the trial in our Supplement of this day.

From the violent articles published by another newspaper during the last months against the black natives, we had been impressed with the belief, that not only had these slaughtered aborigines committed some wanton murders on our stockholders residing in the neighbourhood, but that their slaughter had been perpetrated in retaliation for such murders.

But in all the evidence given at the trial, our readers will perceive that the twenty-eight persons put to the sword by the eleven stock-keepers are not accused of committing any personal violence whatever, at any time, either on these men or on their neighbours.

A report which is gaining ground is that these men were set upon this deed of darkness by others; a deed for which we cannot find a parallel for cold blooded ferocity, even in the history of Cortez and the Mexicans, or of Pizarro and the Peruvians. The only monsters whose conduct will furnish us with a parallel is that of the Buccaneers of the West Indies.

It is not improper that these eleven men should have counsel hired for them. Three counsel, however, was a rather luxurious number. But while three gentlemen (the masters of these men, for instance,) might have hired one counsel each privately, it is not to the credit of New South Wales that a general subscription should have been raised among the magistrates and graziers of Hunter's River to an amount much larger than even three counsel could demand.

What was there in this murder of twenty eight poor helpless betrayed men, women and children, that should induce the magistrates and gentlemen of the Hunter's River to hire counsel for the murderers? Do they hire counsel for other men when tried for murder? How will this fact tell in England, in France, in Austria, in Prussia, and in America? For we doubt but there are men in the two Houses of Parliament who will now make the colony known all over the world - in kingdoms and cities where it was scarcely heard of before.

The verdict of acquittal was highly popular! It was with exertion that the Chief Justice could prevent the audience from cheering - such was their delight! The aristocracy of this Colony for once joined heart and hand with the prison population, in expressions of joy at the acquittal of these men.

We tremble to remain in a country where such feelings and principles prevail. For the verdict of Thursday shows, that only let a man or a family be sufficiently unpopular with the aristocracy and the prison population of this Colony conjoined (in this case) and their murder will pass unheeded; if not be a matter of rejoicing.

Money, lucre, profit - these are thy Gods, O Australia!'

CHAPTER THIRTY SEVEN

26 November 1838.

I t was late in the morning when the Governor's private secretary opened the door to Sir George Gipps' office and announced the arrival of the Attorney-General.

'Ah, Mr Plunkett, come in, come in. How are things going with the case this morning? Shouldn't you be in court?'

'Yes, well, that's where I've just come from, Excellency. We are in an adjournment and I just wanted to keep you informed of what was happening. There is also another matter I wanted to discuss with you.'

'Certainly. What is it?'

'Well, have you seen *The Herald* this morning, sir?'

'Yes, Mr Thomson showed me. The editorial was quite obviously a blatant attempt to prejudice the jury.'

'Yes, definitely, sir; however, it's not only the editorial but one of the articles and two of the letters they've published this morning that we are concerned about.'

'Yes, I saw the letters.'

'Well, I've raised the matter in court with Justice Burton, who, as you know, is hearing this new trial, and we have been preparing affidavits for an order forbidding the press from commenting on the case.'

'Good. Go on,' urged Gipps.

'Well, following our conversation yesterday, sir, we are also preparing an affidavit to pursue our friend, Mr Robert Scott, over his involvement in this whole affair – over his advice to the men in gaol and the formation of this illegal association to promote the destruction of the Aborigines. He is also quite obviously the correspondent who submitted this morning's letter to *The Herald* signed "Subscriber".'

'Yes, I thought that was obvious too, but … ' Gipps paused, sat back in his chair and stroked his brow before continuing. 'I've been thinking since yesterday, I don't really believe there is a great deal of benefit to be derived from pursuing Scott personally.'

'Oh,' was Plunkett's only response.

'Well, I just feel that we are alienating him and the other squatters enough by our stance on this whole Aboriginal issue. We have enough to fight about with them without going out of our way to deliberately antagonise them over matters that are not crucial. You know as well as I do that they are very powerful men, and if we are to achieve our aims regarding the protection of the Aborigines, as well as any of the numerous other issues which need to be resolved in this colony, we are going to need some sort of cooperation from them.'

'I realise that, sir, and I believe that is a reasonable view. It is certainly the politically intelligent thing to do,' acknowledged Plunkett.

'Thank you, Mr Plunkett. You are one of my very few genuine allies in this colony, and the last thing I am desirous to do is alienate you. I trust on this occasion, Mr Plunkett, in saying it is the "politically intelligent" thing to do, you also believe it is the "right thing" to do.'

'To be honest, Excellency, you may be the best judge of what is "right" in these particular circumstances.'

'Look, Mr Plunkett, you know I will not compromise on the whole Aboriginal issue. No arrogant, puffed up group of squatters will prevent me from doing everything within my power to protect them.'

'I know that, sir.'

'It's just that there are certain situations in which one must exercise a little discretion and judgement.'

'Certainly, Excellency. Well, we won't pursue this matter in regard to Mr Scott, then, sir.'

'Good. Thank you. Now, how is everything proceeding with the case itself? Is there still no sign of any of the four men we delayed proceeding against turning Queen's evidence, as we'd hoped?'

'No sign at all, sir, unfortunately. They are adhering to what we have been given to understand was Scott's original advice to them. They're all sticking together and saying nothing. However, sir, I have reason to believe that the defence may put some of the four on the stand to attempt to deny the others' involvement. If they do, I'm quite sure Mr Therry and I will be able to severely damage their defence in cross-examination.'

'Well, no matter what happens in that particular regard, it is obviously not going to be any easier to achieve a conviction this time. So do everything you can, Mr Plunkett.'

'You can be assured I will, sir. And no, it won't be easy but I am hopeful the way we have framed the charges this time should make our case easier to prove. Can I just say again, though, sir, how strongly I believe James Lamb should be included with the others in this case and not put off for the future. One only needs to speak to George Anderson for a few minutes to ascertain Lamb was one of the very worst of them – he, Fleming and Russell.'

'I appreciate what you're saying, Mr Plunkett, but you know my thinking on the matter. His close association with Major Nunn's campaign just makes it too difficult and sensitive. Imagine the furore in this town if Lamb came out and said that Nunn, in a government-sanctioned expedition, had killed ten times as many Aborigines as these men killed at Myall Creek. You know I am determined to pursue the investigation into Nunn's campaign, but I'll do it in my own way and in my own time. I'm not prepared to have the agenda set for me by some convict trying to protect his own neck. Anyway, we can proceed against Lamb and the others when the time is appropriate.'

'That's fine, sir; and I can understand the reasons for your decision. Excuse me observing, though, Excellency, it would seem a rather fortunate twist of fate for Lamb that he escapes prosecution for killing the native blacks by virtue of the fact that he has killed so many of them. It is a remarkable irony, sir.

Gipps paused for a moment before answering. 'Yes, well, I hadn't really thought of it in those particular terms; unfortunately, however, it cannot be helped in this particular instance.'

Plunkett further stressed the point. 'He and Fleming are obviously two of the very worst of them, and they have both escaped prosecution.'

'Only for the present, though, Mr Plunkett, only for the present. I certainly haven't given up hope of finding Fleming, and we will pursue the prosecution of Lamb when the time is appropriate. Anyway, if none of them are saying anything it may be all rather futile.'

'Yes, but unfortunately, Excellency, it may be that we have another problem with the case, and that is the absence of William Hobbs.'

'What? Where's he?'

'He went to Port Stephens, sir, and he was supposed to be back a couple of days ago, but apparently the Hunter's River steamers have been held up for days due to very strong winds in the area. I am led to believe, however, sir, that he should be back tomorrow.'

'Let's hope he is. But Justice Burton should grant you an adjournment, anyway, shouldn't he?'

'Yes, it should be fairly straightforward, sir. After we resolve some legal arguments over the charges and the prisoners' pleas, I will ask for a two day adjournment to await Hobbs' return.'

'Good, but what are the legal arguments about?'

'Well, as you know, sir, we have charged them with twenty counts:

five each for the murder of an Aboriginal black child, an Aboriginal male child, an Aboriginal female child and an Aboriginal child named Charley. The defence is arguing, sir, in relation to the Aboriginal black child, that the description is insufficiently certain; and in relation to the Aboriginal male child, that it is the same as one of the charges for which they were tried and acquitted at their first trial.'

'And what do you think, Mr Plunkett?'

'I'm quite confident, sir, that all the charges will stand.'

'Good. Let's hope they do. And by the way, Mr Plunkett, how is George Anderson bearing up? Ready to go through it all again, is he?'

'Yes, sir, he is. We have kept him in custody on Goat Island. He agreed to it without hesitation. He is, understandably, rather scared about the whole matter; but he doesn't say much, so it is hard to know what exactly is going on in that head of his.'

'Yes, well, I'll allow you to ponder the workings of the convict mind, Mr Plunkett.' Gipps smiled half-heartedly. 'Now, if there is nothing else ... '

'No, Excellency, nothing; and I should hurry back to court.'

CHAPTER THIRTY EIGHT

29 November 1838.

C harles Kilmeister shuffled into the courtroom and took his place in the dock beside his co-accused, John Russell, Edward Foley, John Johnstone, James Parry, James Oates and William Hawkins. He looked out into the body of the courtroom, which was full of the staring, pointing, whispering public. Then he saw Henry Dangar, once again seated with Robert Scott and the other squatters directly behind the defence counsels. Dangar nodded and smiled at him. Kilmeister nodded back, but a smile was more than he could manage. The legal arguments had been resolved and he knew his fate would be decided today.

The charges were read: twenty counts, for the murder of an Aboriginal black child, an Aboriginal male child, an Aboriginal female child and an Aboriginal child named Charley. A plea of "Not Guilty" was entered and Plunkett was immediately on his feet outlining the Crown's case. He explained that although the prisoners in the dock had recently been tried for a similar crime, it had already been legally established that the charges now were for a different crime.

After Thomas Foster had restated his evidence in terms very similar to those used in the first trial, William Hobbs took the stand. Plunkett took him through the details of his evidence, which were also similar to those outlined in the first trial; but this time, instead of focusing on the identity of Daddy, Plunkett focused on young Charley and the other children.

'And, Mr Hobbs, can you tell the court, was there a young boy named Charley with this party of Aborigines on your station?'

'Yes, there was. He was about six years old. His father was Sandy and his mother was Martha.'

'Can you tell us anything else about him?'

'Yes. He was a very friendly, forward, happy little chap. Quite a remarkable little fellow, really,' Hobbs answered.

'And was he at the station when you left?'

'Yes, he and his parents.'

'Now, Mr Hobbs, were there children's bodies at the place on the ridge where you found the bodies?'

'Yes, there were the remains of ten or twelve children.'

'Are you sure there were that many?'

'Yes, I can swear to that many because that's how many children's heads I counted.'

Justice Burton patiently let the murmuring from the public gallery subside before Plunkett continued. 'What ages would you say these children were?'

'Between about two and seven.'

'And were these the ages of the children that you left at the station?'

'Yes, they were, but there were more than ten or twelve children and babies at the station when I left.'

'Thank you, Mr Hobbs. Now, we have heard evidence from Mr Foster that when he attended the site with you the next morning he found only a few heads and bodies. Can you provide us with any explanation for the difference in your evidence?'

'Well, Mr Foster did not spend as long at the site as I had the previous evening; nor did he examine it as closely as I had.'

'Anything else?' Plunkett asked.

'Well, the remains had also been got at and dragged about the place by wild dogs.'

'Thank you, Mr Hobbs.' Plunkett paused for a moment before continuing. 'Would it also have been possible for someone to have removed remains, bodies and skulls from the site overnight without you knowing?'

Hobbs was a little surprised at the question. It was obvious who Plunkett thought that 'someone' might have been. Images of a desperate Kilmeister stumbling around in the dark, carrying the putrid rotting remains of the slaughtered Weraerai flashed into Hobbs' mind before he answered.

'Yes.'

'Thank you, Mr Hobbs. No more questions of this witness.'

While Hobbs was being questioned, George Anderson again sat in the anteroom outside the doors of the court. He was again accompanied by a single guard, but he was even more anxious this time than he had been two weeks earlier when sitting on the same seat. He rubbed his neck and shoulders as he tried to convince himself that it should be easier the second time. His problem was that, the first time, he had been quite sure the defendants would be found guilty. To him it had seemed a perfectly straightforward case. He had seen the defendants tie the blacks up and take them away. Davey had told him they had killed them, and Hobbs had found the bodies. He couldn't understand how there could be any doubt about the matter. They had, nevertheless, been found not guilty, and as he sat there, his mind racing, he feared they could be found not guilty again.

To make matters worse, this time only seven of them were standing trial – and Lamb was one of the four who weren't in the dock. He sat there, scratching at his beard and rubbing his back against the wall behind him, while inside the courtroom William Foster proceeded with the cross-examination of William Hobbs.

'Mr Hobbs, don't you know that there have been many depreda-tions committed by the blacks in this district?'

'I know that there had been depredations committed by the blacks some time before, but that was further down river and it certainly wasn't these blacks.'

'How can you be so sure of that?'

'Because these blacks had been living peacefully at McIntyre's for six or seven months before they came to our station.'

Foster changed tack. 'When you went up to the spot with Mr Foster, you didn't go over with him to where you say all these bodies were, did you?'

'No, I didn't. I had been overcome by the smell the evening before, so I remained a short distance away.'

'You have said in evidence that the bodies were in the same state as the evening before, and yet Mr Foster could only find a few skulls,' the defence counsel probed.

'I did not mean in reference to the number of bodies but to their state generally.'

'How could you know, if you were standing some distance away?'

'I was close enough to see them,' Hobbs retorted impatiently.

Foster persisted. 'But Mr Hobbs, why couldn't Mr Foster see all these skulls that you maintain were there the night before?'

'They were in the middle of where the fire had been, and unless a person went close up and stirred about the ashes, he could not see the skulls and bones that I had seen.' Hobbs glared at the defence counsel as he answered.

'But Mr Hobbs, how could you be sure that some of the skulls you say you found were children's skulls?'

'I examined them very minutely and I judged from their size whether they were children or adults.'

Foster again changed the subject completely, realising a discussion of children's skulls was not going to help his case. Seeking to finish on a positive note, he asked, 'Mr Hobbs, do you know what "myall" means?'

'I don't know exactly what it means, but I believe it is a type of tree or wood.'

'Did you know, Mr Hobbs, a "myall black" means a savage, ferocious black?'

'No, I didn't,' answered Hobbs, shaking his head.

'No more questions, thank you, your Honour,' said Foster, resuming his seat beside his colleagues.

John Plunkett was about to rise to re-examine Hobbs, but Justice Burton intervened. 'Mr Hobbs, when you examined the bodies, are you sure that they were the bodies of blacks?'

'Yes, your Honour, they were clearly the bodies of blacks, as the flesh in many parts remained on the bodies.'

As Hobbs answered, Roger Therry whispered to Plunkett in a frustrated tone. 'How can his Honour possibly have any doubt they were the bodies of blacks? What, does he think there may have been twenty-eight whites murdered out there and no one has noticed?'

Plunkett merely nodded before standing to re-examine Hobbs. 'Mr Hobbs, do you know why those particular blacks remained in the district around yours and McIntyre's stations?'

Hobbs' lengthy conversations around the campfire with the elders provided him with his answer. 'I believe those blacks belonged to that district and I do not believe the blacks would be allowed to go into another tribe's district.'

'Thank you, Mr Hobbs. No more questions, your Honour.'

Hobbs left the witness box and walked through the mumbling mass of the public gallery. He was a greatly relieved man when he finally exited the back of the courthouse. His relief, however, was short-lived.

'William Hobbs?'

Hobbs turned to be confronted by a bailiff. 'Yes,' he answered, slightly stunned.

'William Hobbs, you're under arrest,' said the bailiff coldly as he took hold of Hobbs.

'Under arrest?' Hobbs protested. 'What for?'

'For an outstanding debt,' the bailiff advised as he handcuffed an incredulous Hobbs.

'What debt?'

'You'll be given all the details later, Mr Hobbs. Now come with me.'

Edward Denny Day was in the witness box just finishing giving his evidence when Crown Solicitor Francis Fisher entered the back of the court and walked up to the Crown's table. John Plunkett was occupied questioning Day, so Fisher whispered to Roger Therry, Plunkett's assistant. 'Just thought you should know, William Hobbs has just been arrested.'

'What?' was Therry's stunned response.

'Something about an outstanding debt; but don't worry, I've sorted it out,' Fisher assured him.

'What have you done?'

'I've had the bailiff arrested for contempt of court and released Hobbs.'

Therry smiled. 'Good for you. Well done.'

A few moments later, when Plunkett had finished questioning Day, Therry immediately stood to address the court. 'Excuse me, your Honour, but a most disturbing matter has just been brought to my attention of which I must immediately inform the court.'

'What is it, Mr Therry?' asked Justice Burton.

'Your Honour, Mr William Hobbs, upon leaving the witness box just a short time ago, was arrested. Your Honour, this seems to be an example of a not uncommon practice of witnesses being arrested in an attempt to intimidate them, from a corrupt desire to hinder public justice.'

'It is certainly a matter for serious concern, Mr Therry. Has the matter been dealt with?'

'Yes, your Honour. The Crown Solicitor has charged the bailiff responsible with contempt of court.'

'Good. I will deal with it when we adjourn. Now, though, we

will proceed with the matter before us. Please call your next witness,' Burton instructed.

As George Anderson entered the courtroom he was again subjected to hateful glares from the prisoners in the dock and from various members of the public gallery. Anderson, however, refused to acknowledge those glares as he walked quickly to the witness box. He just wanted to get it all over with. After taking his oath he glanced toward Kilmeister in the dock. He could see the Myall Creek stockman was suffering from the ordeal. His weather-beaten skin was pale, his expression sullen and drawn, and his shoulders hunched forward.

Anderson then turned to focus on Plunkett as the Attorney-General began his questioning. Anderson's testimony was totally consistent with that he gave at the first trial, until near the conclusion when he mentioned the party of horsemen taking Billy with them to show them the way to McIntyre's. This was the first point Windeyer seized on as he began his cross-examination.

'Anderson, you've just told us about these men supposedly taking "Billy the Black" off with them to look for more blacks. If this is true, why didn't you tell the court about it at the first trial?'

'Because you interrupted me,' the hutkeeper responded, much to the mirth of the few sympathetic observers in the public gallery.

Windeyer quickly dropped the subject. 'How long have you been transported for?'

'For life.'

'And that's why you are giving this evidence for the Crown, is it not? You are merely seeking to get your term reduced.'

'I am perfectly willing to serve out my time; not in Mr Dangar's service, though. But don't you know I have no chance of getting a ticket-of-leave for some time?'

Windeyer ignored the question. 'Ah, so you did want to get out of Mr Dangar's service, then?'

Anderson looked straight at Dangar. 'I am glad to be away from Mr Dangar, but that has nothin' to do with me evidence.'

Windeyer was getting nowhere but pressed on nonetheless, trying different angles and tactics. He finally focused on the identity of 'Charley'.

'Did you know this "Charley"?'

'Yes.' Jackey-Jackey nodded, looking at Kilmeister. 'He was a very nice little boy.'

'How old was he?' Windeyer asked.

'About six or seven. He was up to about my waist.' He then added, 'Actually, there were two Charleys, with about two or three years between 'em.'

John Plunkett closed his eyes and gently shook his head in disbelief.

Windeyer couldn't believe his luck. 'Two Charleys?'

Anderson nodded. 'Yes. The young one was the son of Sandy and Martha, but I'm not sure about the older one.'

'So, Anderson, you are now telling the court that there were two young boys named "Charley" at your station?'

'Yes.'

Having succeeded in creating some confusion about the identity of the 'Charley' referred to in the charges, Windeyer began probing for further chinks in Anderson's evidence. Finding none, he finally pursued the convict on the matter of the gunshots he had heard.

'And you maintain you heard these gunshots plainly?'

Anderson paused, breathed deeply and then nodded. 'Yes, quite plainly. It was just after the sounds of the cryin' from the gins and the children had faded beyond me hearing.' He hated having to relive the horror of that night, particularly under the public glare of the courtroom, and he was relieved when Windeyer suddenly stopped his questioning and resumed his seat. The image of weeping women and children was not one the defence counsel wanted to conjure.

It was finally all over for George Anderson. He stepped down from the witness box and walked through the back door of the Supreme Court, with his guard trailing behind him. He looked down King Street toward the west. The sun was setting, leaving behind it the same fire-coloured evening sky that Ipeta had died beneath. The sound of the weeping women and children which he had just described in the courtroom seemed to drift on the breeze, bringing with it the image of his Weraerai friends being dragged away on that rope. He shut his eyes, trying to shut the image from his mind, but when he did it was immediately replaced by the image of Ipeta's face looking into his soul as they dragged her away. He opened his eyes again and stood staring at the horizon. His face quivered slightly as he whispered into the warm westerly wind, 'I've done what I can, my darlin' ... I'm so sorry.'

* * *

Henry Dangar entered the witness box as the case for the defence commenced. He once again testified that Kilmeister was an excellent servant but that he wouldn't believe Anderson on his oath as he was addicted to lying and was generally of bad character.

John Hubert Plunkett sprung to his feet and began the cross-examination with a deal more enthusiasm than in the first trial. 'Mr Dangar,' he began, 'have you ever seen George Anderson take an oath before this case?'

'No, I haven't, but I still wouldn't believe him, on account of his bad character,' Dangar retorted.

Plunkett ignored the comment and ploughed straight on. 'And when he was first assigned to you, he was under your immediate superintendence, was he not?'

'Yes, he was,' Dangar answered, at the same time adjusting the lace on his sleeve cuff.

'And during that time, did he receive religious instruction?'

'Yes,' conceded Dangar. 'Well, I had prayers every Sabbath at my house.'

'And did George Anderson attend these prayers?'

'Yes.'

'How often?' pursued Plunkett.

'Every Sabbath, when I was there,' Dangar conceded again.

'Now, Mr Dangar, you had reason to take George Anderson to court and have two fifties administered to him, did you not?'

Dangar nodded. 'Yes.'

'And what was that for?'

'For being absent from his station and not moving his hurdles.'

'So what you are telling the court, Mr Dangar, is that you would not believe a God-fearing, churchgoing man on his oath, simply because he neglects his duties occasionally?'

'No ... no, I don't mean to say that,' Dangar stumbled.

Plunkett had the squatter on the back foot and now set out to ambush him. 'Mr Dangar, were you not dismissed from a government position after grave allegations of impropriety were made against you?'

Dangar was stunned by the question. He hesitated, before attempting to brush it off. 'I was suspended, but I heard no more about it.'

'Were you not dismissed from your position?' Plunkett persisted.

'I was suspended,' Dangar snapped, now on the offensive.

'Were you not dismissed, I say, sir? You know what I mean.'

'I was *suspended*,' insisted the squatter.

'Answer me without equivocation, sir. Were you not dismissed, and not *suspended*, as you want us to believe?'

Dangar had nowhere to hide. He turned to Justice Burton. 'Do I have to answer that question, your Honour?'

'Yes, you do,' Burton replied coldly.

'I was a surveyor. I did not ask to be reinstated, so perhaps the Secretary of State might have given orders that I was not to be reinstated. It was ten or twelve years ago and I cannot recollect the contents of a letter of so remote a date. I was suspended,' he persisted defiantly.

Justice Burton intervened again. 'Mr Dangar, if you were not dismissed, say so without equivocation.'

The squatter was finally forced to concede. 'A suspension was tantamount to a dismissal. The Governor ordered my suspension and the Secretary of State ordered that I was not to be reinstated.'

'Thank you, Mr Dangar.' Plunkett allowed himself a half smile before continuing his pursuit of the squatter. 'Now, Mr Dangar, would you dismiss one of your servants for shooting a black man?'

'Most certainly, upon my oath, I would.'

'Then why did you dismiss William Hobbs?'

'He is not to continue in my service. His time has expired.'

Justice Burton had run out of patience. 'Mr Dangar, when you give an answer to a question, it is to be given fully, without reservation. Now, is that the only reason for his leaving your service?'

Dangar fidgeted with the highly starched collar of his shirt, which seemed to be getting tighter with every question. 'No, your Honour. I was going to add, he has not given me satisfaction in the care of my properties.'

Plunkett resumed his questioning. 'If that is true, sir, why did you tell Mr Day, in September, that you were well pleased with Hobbs, and then dismiss him in October?'

'I had already told my family that I intended to discharge him.'

'But you didn't tell Mr Hobbs that, did you?'

'No, but I hadn't had any contact with him.'

'If you hadn't had any contact with him, how could you be displeased with him? And why, when you've stated to this court that you didn't believe his evidence, did you say to Mr Day that Hobbs was an honest man?'

'I didn't say he was an honest man, I said he was a respectable young man and that I was pleased that Mr Day had found my station so well run.'

'So, if he's a respectable young man who is running your properties well, you can have no reason for dismissing him other than on account of his reporting these murders?'

A'Beckett, Foster and Windeyer looked at each other, shaking their heads in disbelief. Their case was evaporating before their very eyes, along with the sweat that now poured from the brow of the overdressed squatter.

'No, I made up my mind six months ago to discharge him,' Dangar protested feebly, but it was barely audible above the chatter from the public gallery.

Justice Burton cracked his gavel on the bench, demanding silence, which was immediately restored.

Plunkett continued, systematically trying to destroy every shred of Henry Dangar's credibility. 'You were about the court this morning, weren't you, Mr Dangar?'

'Yes, I was.'

'You know William Hobbs was arrested earlier today, don't you?'

'Yes.'

'And you knew he was going to be arrested, didn't you, Mr Dangar?'

'No, I didn't,' Dangar protested.

'And didn't you tell people to come in here to get on the jury?'

'No, I didn't.'

'Mr Dangar, you were heard questioning a man outside this court about why he had refused to sit on the jury.'

'I did not,' the squatter muttered.

'Mr Dangar, you were heard to question this man by Mr Fisher, the Crown Solicitor, and Mr Justice Willis.'

'I swear, I did not question anyone about sitting on the jury.'

'Mr Dangar, you are helping to defray the costs of the defence counsel, are you not?'

'I subscribed five pounds in August to defend my servant Kilmeister, who is a good and faithful one.'

'Mr Dangar, you have subscribed to the defence of men accused of a most horrific crime, the details of which we have heard described in this courtroom today. How can you justify that?'

'I subscribed before I heard the details of the matter,' Dangar explained feebly.

'You nonetheless knew they were charged with the murder of a large number of Aboriginal blacks, and yet you subscribed to their defence.'

Dangar did not reply.

Plunkett stood at his table in silence for a few moments, gathering himself, before launching his final assault on the squatter. 'Mr Dangar, when you were dismissed from your position as a government surveyor, one of the charges brought against you related to misappropriation of some land, did it not?'

'Yes,' the squatter murmured, almost inaudibly.

'And who had you misappropriated this land for, Mr Dangar?'

'My brother, William.'

'And did your brother have an assigned servant who was charged with the murder of a black five years ago?'

'Yes.'

Plunkett let the answer hang in the air before finally resuming his seat.

The stunned defence team called just one more witness, Thomas Hall; but after testifying to the quiet, peaceful nature of James Oates, Roger Therry had him quickly admitting that he only visited his properties twice a year. His knowledge of Oates' character was therefore deficient in the extreme. On that note the defence closed their case.

* * *

It was after ten in the evening when John Plunkett, for the Crown, and William Foster, for the defence, began their final addresses to the jury, but the courtroom was still packed. No-one had left. It was nearly eleven o'clock when Justice Burton finally began his summing up to the jury. After a very lengthy summation of all the evidence, he turned his attention to the credibility of the witnesses.

'The testimony of the man Anderson has been impeached from some frivolous cause by Mr Dangar; but if men charged with some trifling neglect of duty are to be incapacitated from giving evidence, then many crimes, including murder, would go unpunished. You have heard Mr Dangar's reasons for impeaching the credit of Anderson. It is for you to judge whether Anderson's testimony had been impeached, or whether Mr Dangar's testimony had not rather been impeached by himself. At all events, Mr Dangar had shown the bias of his mind. He has shown that his opinion had already been formed and that he came before the court prejudiced.

'It is clear from the evidence that a great number of human creatures have been slain, and in the whole of the evidence I can find no shadow of provocation for their slaughter. If the pecuniary interests of gentlemen requires that their servants go about armed, and this community has become so depraved that human life is considered to have no value, so that blacks can be indiscriminately killed wherever they are seen, then it is no wonder that this colony has been so afflicted of late by the displeasures and heavy visitations of God.

'The main question you have to decide upon, gentlemen of the jury, is whether Charley was taken with the others; and if so, had he perished with them. If you believe Anderson's evidence then you are bound to act according to that evidence; and I must press again that his evidence is corroborated at almost every point. Further, if you believe the evidence submitted by Anderson, there is no doubt the whole of the blacks taken away by these men were, according to the confession of Foley to Anderson, killed – with the exception of one woman. Therefore, if you are of the opinion that "Charley" was not killed, you could turn to the other counts and reach a verdict on the evidence you have heard.

'Gentlemen, I have stated what you must decide, now I leave the case to you.'

The large clock on the side wall of the Supreme Court struck one in the morning as the jury silently filed out to consider its verdict.

The public gallery remained abuzz with chatter throughout the jury's forty-five minute deliberation. George Anderson stood at the back of the court, watching in silence as the jury filed slowly back to its benches.

Justice Burton addressed the foreman of the jury. 'Gentlemen, have you reached a verdict?'

The foreman, George Sewell, stood and replied, 'We have, your Honour.'

'Prisoners in the dock, please stand.'

The clanking of chains was the only sound in the room as the prisoners stood. Anderson looked down the courtroom to Kilmeister, but he, like everyone else, was looking at the jury foreman.

'Gentlemen, how say you?'

Without pausing, Sewell responded, 'Not guilty.'

As it had upon hearing the verdict in the first trial, the public gallery erupted in cheers. The prisoners embraced, and Dangar, Scott and the defence team began shaking hands furiously. Kilmeister now looked to the back of the court to where George Anderson stood, but Anderson's head was hung in silent despair as his mind raced with fears of the reprisals he may now face. He rubbed the back of his neck.

At his bench, Justice Burton inscribed the words 'Not guilty' on the bottom of his notes, only to look up and notice one of the members of the jury on his feet. He was saying something but was not audible over the jubilation in the room. Justice Burton picked up his gavel and immediately cracked it several times on the bench. 'Order.'

A strange silence quickly befell the courtroom as its occupants focused on the lone juryman, William Knight, standing in the middle of the jury. 'Your Honour, your Honour.'

'Yes, what is it?' Justice Burton asked, a little concerned by the irregularity of the situation.

'Your Honour, the foreman has not correctly conveyed the jury's verdict. We found the defendants "Not Guilty" on the final fifteen counts, but on the first five counts, for the murder of an Aboriginal child, name unknown, we found the defendants "Guilty".'

CHAPTER THIRTY NINE

15 December 1838.

T he courtroom was packed yet again. It was a case that held no
end of fascination for the people of Sydney, and this, the sen-
tencing of the prisoners, was anticipated to be its penultimate scene.

Seven prisoners looking drained and distressed stood in the dock,
waiting for Justice Burton to enter the court and pronounce their fate.
In their gaol cell they had been managing to keep up the bravado of
the group, encouraged by the persistent rumours that the Governor
would ultimately buckle to the relentless pressure of the squatters.
Now, however, in the dock, each was isolated with his own thoughts
and fears.

Charles Kilmeister shifted nervously as Justice Burton entered and
took his seat behind the elevated bench upon which he slammed his
gavel. He looked down upon the accused and began. 'Prisoners at
the bar, you have been found guilty under an information charging
you with wilful murder. Whoever is convicted of murder is doomed
by the laws of England to suffer death. Death for murder is not only
a human law, it is also the law of God, promulgated when there

were but few men on earth; from whom all men are descended, of whatever colour, tongue or people, "Whoso sheddeth man's blood, by man shall his blood be shed". It may be doubted, and I myself doubt, whether the law should ever depart from a law so imperatively imposed by the Almighty. But there are circumstances in your case of such singular atrocity that you must long have suspected the result which now awaits you.

'It is not the murder of a single individual caused by provocation or drunken passion; nor is it a case where men's lives or properties were in danger which tempted you to the bloody deed. In your case the slaughter in cold blood, without provocation, of men, women and children, even to babes at their mothers' breasts. These defenceless blacks were peaceably residing in the vicinity of a hut inhabited by one of you, and under his protection. They were suddenly surrounded by an armed body of horsemen, among whom you seven prisoners at the bar were identified. The blacks, being so surrounded, fled for safety to the hut of one of you. This, however, proved to be a net for their destruction. In that hut their entreaties, groans and tears were of no avail. You tied them together and led them away to one common destruction. I am not recapitulating these points to aggravate your crime but to point out to persons standing by and to society of what kind of offence you have been found guilty. I cannot expect that any words of mine can reach your hearts, but I hope that the grace of God may reach them, for nothing else could reach those hardened hearts which could slay fathers, mothers and infants and surround the funeral pyre to consign their mangled bodies to the flames.

'There is striking proof of your guilt, for it pleased God in his providence the day before this crime was committed to send rain on the earth, through which your tracks to the fatal spot were easily traced. From the hut to the spot where the deed was committed there were the traces of horsemen on each side, and the naked feet of the blacks in the middle. This affords the strongest corroboration of the evidence provided by the man Anderson.

'I cannot think that men like you, educated in some principles of religion and speaking the English language, would have been guilty of a crime like this unless you thought you would be screened from public justice. You might have flattered yourselves that you would have been protected and screened – many did seek to conceal it, none endeavouring to bring it to light – but unhappy men, what you did was seen by God.

'I do my duty as a judge, but as a man I feel the awful situation in which you are placed. Whatever motive could have induced you to commit this crime, and I trust there were none other than mentioned in the indictment, but that you were moved and seduced by the devil. If they were not your only motives, if you did act at the instigation of others, I trust it will be brought to light and they will be equally answerable to the law as you have been.

'You were all transported to this colony, although some of you have since become free. Although so far removed as one hundred and fifty miles from the nearest police station and residing in a part of the colony where there was little protection either for yourselves or the unoffending blacks, that circumstance offer you no excuse. Although, I cannot but deplore that you should have been placed in such a situation, that such circumstances should have existed, and, above all, that you should have committed such a crime.'

Justice Burton paused for a moment and picked up the black cap from the bench in front of him. As he did so, Charles Kilmeister felt his entire inside burn as terror gripped his being. He had never felt so ill. He dropped his eyes, hung his head and clutched his stomach. He couldn't watch as Justice Burton placed the cap on his head and continued.

'But this commiseration must not interfere with the stern duty which, as a judge, the law enforces on me, which is to order that you, and each of you, be removed to the place from whence you came and thence to a place of public execution, and that at such time as His Excellency the Governor shall appoint, you be hanged by the neck until your bodies be dead, and may the Lord have mercy on your souls.'

CHAPTER FORTY

18 December 1838.

C harles Kilmeister was roused from a night's sleep full of screaming, tossing, falling, dreaming, turning and sweating by the sound of the guard's voice.

'Hey, you chaps, wake up! Mr Keck's been summoned by the Governor.'

Kilmeister gathered his frayed thoughts. It was barely light on this day he was due to hang.

'What?' he heard Russell snap at the guard.

'Mr Keck were just summoned by the Governor,' the guard repeated.

Russell and Foley were on their feet at the door of the cell.

'What are ya on about?' Russell inquired, rather irritated.

'Ya know yesterday I told ya the rumour that's been going around town in the last few days was that you'd get a reprieve, that the Governor would commute ya sentence?'

'Yair, that's what ya said. So?' Russell was, however, beginning to understand the significance of the guard's news.

Kilmeister was now at the cell door also.

'Well,' continued the guard, 'it looks like that must be right because the Governor just sent for the head gaoler, Mr Keck. He's just left a couple of minutes ago.'

Russell turned to Foley, a huge grin across his unshaven face. 'See, Ned, I told ya the squatters would look after us. I told ya Gipps wouldn't go through with it.'

'Do you think that's what it means, Jack?'

'Course it does. Why else would Gipps send for Keck at this hour of the mornin', just a few hours before we're supposed to hang?' assured Russell.

* * *

It was just on five thirty in the morning when Henry Keck was shown into the Governor's office. There with Gipps were the Attorney-General, John Plunkett; the Crown Solicitor, Francis Fischer; and the High Sheriff, Thomas Macquoid.

'Have a seat, please, Mr Keck,' invited a rather tired and slightly dishevelled looking Gipps.

'Thank you, Excellency,' answered Keck, somewhat overawed by his first visit to the Governor's office. It was an extraordinary visit at an extraordinary hour, and Keck wondered if the rumours he himself had heard might be true. He did not have to wait long to find out, as the exhausted Governor got straight to the point.

'Mr Keck, I have sent for you and Mr Macquoid this morning to check with you that all the necessary security precautions are in place for this morning's executions.'

'Oh! Yes, your Excellency, everything is ready,' answered Keck.

'Good. Mr Macquoid, do you think we will need any additional troops to prevent any possible outbreak of mob violence, if you think that is at all likely,' Gipps asked earnestly.

'No, Excellency, I believe the normal military guard which we use on such occasions will be quite adequate, sir. And we have also restricted entry to the area to those with passes, sir, so there will not be a large crowd inside. We distributed the passes yesterday, and people who didn't get one then will be unable to obtain entry.'

'Good. Fine. If you think everything will be all right, I will trust your judgement, gentlemen.'

There was silence for a moment, before Keck asked hesitantly, 'So, it is all to go ahead, sir?'

Gipps looked at him for a moment, before replying with an air of resigned determination. 'Yes, it is, Mr Keck. To be honest with you, though, Mr Plunkett, Mr Fisher and myself have spent the entire night going through the case to determine if there is any justification for granting clemency to these men, or to any individual amongst them, but there simply isn't any. We've looked through it all in great detail and there is no justification whatsoever.'

'None at all,' added Plunkett.

'Oh, I see, Excellency,' murmured Keck.

'Yes, most regrettable.' There was silence for a few moments before Gipps continued. 'Before you go to get on with your duties, though, gentlemen, can I just ask you, Mr Keck, if in the past few days the men have said anything. Have they confessed?' Gipps was seeking some kind of reassurance.

'Yes, your Excellency, they have. All of them have confessed; and Blake, Lamb and the others came in and prayed with them last night, sir.'

The tension eased from the Governor's brow. 'What precisely have they said?'

'Well, sir, they have said that they were only doing their masters' bidding and that they didn't know it was against the law to kill blacks, because it has happened so often throughout the colony.'

Gipps shook his head slowly. 'They didn't know it was against the law! How could they really believe that? And we shall see about their masters, too, shall we not, Mr Plunkett?' Gipps emitted something between a groan and a sigh, stood up and walked over to the window. He looked out across the magnificent gardens of Government House and onto the harbour. It was a beautiful scene on a warm, clear Sydney morning, but the observer was totally oblivious to it, his mind being focused on the darker side of the colony's establishment.

The others remained seated around the Governor's desk in awkward silence. Finally Gipps turned back to Keck and Macquoid. 'Thank you, gentlemen. Please go about your duties and prepare for the executions.'

The gaoler and the sheriff left. As the door closed behind them, Gipps turned to Plunkett. 'Has it really happened so often, Mr Plunkett, that men would be given to believe it was not against the law?'

'Sir, we both know it has been going on unabated since this colony started. As you have pointed out previously, in his report Day called it "a war of extermination against the Aborigines". Sir, the bitter truth is, we both know, much of it has been sanctioned or undertaken by the government, and the rest they have just turned a blind eye to. So perhaps it is understandable that some would believe it wasn't against the law.'

* * *

At ten minutes to nine, High Sheriff Macquoid led a guard of eighteen soldiers around the perimeter of the prison yard near the bottom of George Street at The Rocks. They halted in their positions facing the gallows.

At five minutes to nine the seven condemned men were led into the yard, accompanied by three clergymen. They all knelt and prayed earnestly with their ministers. After a few minutes Macquoid signalled for them to stand and ascend the scaffold. They stood and looked up the timber steps where seven empty nooses swung gently in a north easterly sea breeze.

Ned Foley turned to Macquoid. 'May I have permission to embrace the others, sir,' he asked as tears streamed down his face.

Macquoid nodded his consent, and all seven hugged each other desperately before shaking hands for the last time. Charles Kilmeister sobbed as he shook hands with John Russell, who could barely stand as the reality of his fate, which he had denied until now, finally hit him.

At exactly nine o'clock, in the company of the clergymen, the remnants of Death ascended the scaffold, where the executioner awaited. They commenced praying again as the executioner and his assistant placed a noose around each of their necks. The clergymen descended the stairs as each of the prisoners had a hood pulled over their face, shutting the world from their sight forever.

Charles Kilmeister was the last of them to see a fiery summer sun burning in a cloudless sky above the cool blue waters of Sydney Harbour. Then there was blackness. He instantly became acutely aware of the sound of his own breathing inside the hood. Panic-stricken, he clung desperately to each breath, hoping for just one more. He could hear nothing above the noise of his own frantic breathing but he could feel two things - the coarseness of the dreaded rope around his neck, and beneath his boots the feel of the precious timber which kept him alive. It felt so solid, so strong. For what seemed like an age to him but was actually only a moment, he stood there, breath, timber and rope his entire world ... Then there was only rope.

The crowd watched as the trap door crashed open and Charles, John, Edward, William, James, James and John hung, twitching and writhing as the life drained from their bodies.

* * *

That same morning, further along George Street, a large crowd had also turned out to see the first public appearance of the new Commander-in-Chief of the Armed Forces, Major General Sir Maurice O'Connell. He was to have a full review of the troops from the barracks. It was to be quite an event, and had been timed for 9 am to provide a veil of pomp and pageantry to distract the masses from the objectionable business of the hanging. It was thus hoped to minimise the crowd and avoid any risk of trouble at the controversial execution.

Leaning against a set of stone stairs a few yards from the back of the crowd was William Hobbs. Next to him, sitting on one of the lower steps, was George Anderson, still with a guard standing a few yards away.

'I believe you're going to be kept on Goat Island for a time, George, until they sort out the trials of the other men.'

'Yes, sir.'

'Well, you should be safe out there, and then you'll be assigned to a new master,' Hobbs said, placing a reassuring hand on Anderson's shoulder.

Anderson nodded. 'Yair, Mr 'obbs.'

There was a brief silence between the two men, which Hobbs broke. 'You've done a very brave thing, George; you know that, don't you?'

Anderson just shrugged; then, after a moment, he mumbled, 'I owed it to them, sir.'

'You owed it to them?' queried Hobbs.

'Yair, to the blacks, sir; to all of them, especially Ipeta.'

Hobbs' brow furrowed. 'Why her especially, George?'

Anderson hesitated, struggling to open up even to the trusted Hobbs.

'She were special, ya know, sir. Not just to me but to the blacks as well. Did ya ever notice, Mr 'obbs, that every one of the blacks had a white name, like Sandy, Daddy, Joey, Martha, Charley and all the rest?'

'Yes, I suppose they did.'

'Yair, sir, every one of them except her. Ipeta was Ipeta; she had no other name. You said I was brave, Mr 'obbs ... That night I weren't brave, sir. I was a coward, Mr 'obbs. I should have protected her and I didn't. I was scared, sir, especially with that squatter, Fleming, there. It was horrible ... Those poor people was screamin' and cryin' for help ... And the little ones ... They was all pleading for me to help them ... and I didn't ... '

'George, there was nothing you could do against all those armed men.'

'Maybe not, sir, but I could've at least tried and I didn't, sir. I should have tried to do something but I did nothin' … '

'What about Bobby's daughter? You saved her. And besides, if you had tried to stop them they would have killed you and you wouldn't have been around to give evidence, to see them brought to justice.'

Anderson continued as if he hadn't heard Hobbs. 'As they were draggin' Ipeta off, tied to that rope, I looked into those beautiful eyes of hers. You know what beautiful eyes she had, sir?' Hobbs nodded but Anderson didn't look up as he continued. 'That night, they was just full of terror, sir. The poor, beautiful thing was terrified, sir, and I did nothin'. And sir, she looked at me, Mr 'obbs; she looked right through me, sir, and … I wish I knew what she saw.' Anderson hesitated again. He could see her again now, as he did every night in his dreams and in his nightmares. She was there in front of him.

He composed himself enough to continue, his voice trembling. 'Maybe I shouldn't want to know, but I just don't know what she saw. Maybe my fear … As she looked into my eyes she shook her head, just a bit … but I don't know why, sir. I don't know if she were shaking her head because she knew I couldn't stop them and she didn't want me to get killed trying … or because she saw how scared I was and how weak I was, and after her people had come to us for protection, she was shaking her head at my fear and my weakness … because I hadn't even tried to stop them. Mr 'obbs, I owed it to Ipeta and her people because … '

Anderson looked up to Hobbs for the first time since he had started speaking. He was hoping to find understanding in the super-intendent's eyes. Having found it, he continued. 'I owed it to them because, sir, I'm a convict serving a life sentence. I hated it here – the loneliness, the torments, the floggings. If I get released it shan't be for many years. They treated me like I were somebody, somebody a little bit kind of special. You know, sir, they gave me my own name, Jackey-Jackey. I was the only one they gave a name to, sir … Mr 'obbs, I'd given up thinking I could ever be happy again before I met Ipeta and her people. She made me happy again and made me think my life could get better. When they killed her, sir, they took me happiness. But, sir, I realised a few weeks later that the feeling inside me somewhere, that believed things could get better, it were still there. That's when I decided to tell you and Mr Day all of what I saw. Sir, after knowing Ipeta, I just believe one day I might be happy again. It might take me a long time but I know now I can be … So I owed it to her, sir … even if they do kill me.'

William Hobbs said nothing, but again placed his hand on Jackey-Jackey's shoulder.

The crowd in front of them had continued to grow and was now only a couple of yards away. People were shuffling around, trying to get the best vantage point to view the proceedings. Two well-dressed gentlemen, one from the city and the other an associate from the country, came and stood in front of the two men from Myall Creek, who couldn't help overhearing the gentlemen's conversation. William Hobbs realised, the next day, that he and Anderson weren't the only ones who heard them, for the very conversation was reported in both *The Gazette* and the *Monitor*.

'Well, have they hung these men this morning?' asked the gentleman from the country.

'Yes, I understand they have,' his city friend replied.

'It is a damned shame; but we have fallen on a safer game in our part of the country.'

'Indeed? Pray, what is it?' the city gentleman asked.

'Oh, we poison them.'

'Good God! Poison them?'

'Yes, we have done so to a good many already, and serves them right, too.'

Anderson looked up at Hobbs, who was slowly shaking his bowed head.

'Perhaps it were all for nothing, Mr 'obbs.'

EPILOGUE

John Fleming - Was never brought to justice, despite the fifty pounds reward which George Gipps offered for his capture. How, exactly, he managed to escape is unknown, although given the very sparsely populated frontier regions it would have been a fairly straightforward matter for a free man. However, there were at the time, and have been since, a wide variety of explanations and theories offered. The one thing that the Fleming family legend and many other theories have in common is that he was sheltered from the law by family and friends. Where, exactly, is a matter of conjecture. How serious the authorities at the local level were about catching him is also questionable. They had certainly lost interest just two years later when, on 21 October 1840, in a very public wedding, he married Charlotte Dunstan at Wilberforce.

He went on to become a 'pillar of society', a church warden at Wilberforce and a magistrate. He died at the age of seventy-eight on 20 August 1894. He had no children.

He received a glowing obituary in *The Windsor Richmond Gazette*, which included the following line: *"The deceased used to tell some stirring stories of the early days of the colony and the troubles he had with the Blacks."*

Major James Nunn - Governor George Gipps finally had Edward Denny Day hold an inquiry into Nunn's campaign in April and May of 1839. Coming fifteen months after the event, the inquiry was basically a whitewash; and on 22 July 1839 the four man Executive Council of New South Wales (headed by Gipps) decided no action should be taken against Nunn over his campaign. A campaign in which he led thirty to forty mounted police and local stockmen in the slaughter of hundreds of Aborigines in the Big (Gwydir) River district throughout January of 1838, and which culminated in the Australia Day Massacre at Waterloo Creek. Nunn had, after all, been acting under the orders of Acting Governor Lt. Colonel Kenneth Snodgrass to "act according to your own judgement and use your utmost exertion to suppress" the outrages of the blacks in the Big River district.

James Lamb - Charges against him were dropped in February 1839, just two months after the others had been hanged. In August 1842 he was granted a ticket-of-leave, and in September 1846 he received a conditional pardon.

Charles Telluse - Charges against him were dropped in February 1839. In July 1842 he was granted a ticket-of-leave, and in March 1848 he received a conditional pardon.

John Blake - Charges against him were dropped in February 1839. In July 1842 he was granted a ticket-of-leave, and in July 1848 he received a conditional pardon. Several years later, after being crippled in a riding accident while sitting alone in an isolated stockmen's hut, he committed suicide by cutting his own throat.

George Palliser - After charges against him were dropped in February 1839, he continued working on Bell's station in the Big River district.

Robert Scott - Sold his interest in *The Herald* in 1839 and concentrated on his pastoral pursuits, including a horse stud in the Hunter Valley. He ran in to financial trouble in the recession of the 1840s and died, unmarried, in 1844, at the age of forty-five.

Henry Dangar - His humiliation at the hands of John Plunkett during the second Myall Creek trial did not provide even the slightest hiccup in his career. Neither did the fact that William Hobbs successfully sued him for nearly five months unpaid wages in March 1839. His wealth and landholdings continued to grow, and in the early 1840s his landholdings in northern NSW had expanded to 125,000 hectares. In 1845 he was elected to the NSW Legislative Council. He lived out his retirement in a harbourside mansion at Pott's Point, Sydney. He died at the age of sixty-four in 1861. Various streets in Sydney, Newcastle and Armidale, and an island in the Hawkesbury River, bear his family name.

Sir George Gipps - His battles to protect the lives of Australia's Aborigines continued, but with a little less passion than he displayed over the Myall Creek Massacre. His battles over this issue, and other land related issues, continued with the wealthy squatters throughout his term as Governor, and he was a sick and broken man when he was recalled to England in 1846, much to the joy of the "squattocracy" and the local press. He died on 28 February 1847, only a few months after he arrived back in England.

King Sandy - Nearly twenty years after the Myall Creek Massacre, a very old Aborigine is reported to have been the leader of a group of over thirty Aborigines who lived on what had been McIntyre's station (then owned by Allan MacPherson). He was known as "King Sandy".

Edward Denny Day - In 1840 he left Muswellbrook and became police magistrate at Maitland, where he gained further notoriety by capturing an infamous bushranger named Edward Davis in a dramatic shoot-out. In 1849 he was appointed police superintendent in Sydney. After spending time as stipendiary magistrate at Port Macquarie, in 1858 he returned to Maitland to serve as chief magistrate until he retired. He died there in 1876, a very popular figure in the town. He had lived seventy-five very colourful years.

William Hobbs - Received no thanks from anyone for his part in the conviction of the perpetrators of the Myall Creek Massacre. What had been a promising career in the young colony was simply shattered. He was victimised and physically threatened. The community at large ostracised him, and after being dismissed by Dangar he found it impossible to find employment. Even requests to Governor Gipps for a position as chief constable at Murrurundi fell on deaf ears, despite Hobbs having Day and Plunkett as referees. After Gipps returned to England, Hobbs petitioned the new governor, Fitzroy, for a similar position anywhere in New South Wales.

He finally had some luck, and in 1846, after eight years without regular employment, he was appointed chief constable at Wollombi. He transferred to Windsor and then Wollongong, where he served as a gaoler. Having married an ex-convict, Mary Anne Joyce, in 1842, he was survived by eleven children when he died in 1871 at the age of fifty-nine. After his death his wife asked the government for a small stipend, which she believed he was owed for his service with them and to assist with raising her eleven children. Her request was refused until one John Hubert Plunkett intervened to ensure it was paid to her. Hobbs' Gully, not far from Myall Creek, is named after him.

George Anderson - Received no special treatment from the Governor. He was given a ticket-of-leave in September 1841. His role in the conviction of the Myall Creek murderers had not been forgotten, however, and, to ensure he was protected from revenge attacks, his 'ticket' was conditional on him remaining in the service of a Mr Townsend, and he moved to Sydney. He was finally given a conditional pardon and regained his freedom in September 1846, the same month as James Lamb. It is not known what became of him after that date. It can only be hoped that he lived a long and happy life, because if any man in the history of this country deserved to, he did. No streets, suburbs or islands are named after him or his family. On the information signs at the memorial site, the contribution of Governor George Gipps and William Hobbs is correctly acknowledged, but George Anderson is not mentioned. He is remembered nowhere but in the history books as the only white man in Australia's history to witness the massacre of Aborigines, not participate, and have the courage to give evidence in court against the perpetrators.

HISTORICAL SIGNIFICANCE

The Myall Creek Massacre was the first in Australia's history in which men were convicted and hung for the massacre of Aborigines. It was in fact the only time in the entire nineteenth-century, despite the countless massacres that went on throughout the whole country. It is therefore of enormous historical significance; and because of Day's investigation and the two trials, it is extremely well documented, with many primary source documents still available providing irrefutable proof of the atrocities inflicted on the Aboriginal people of Australia.

At 9 am on 18 December 1838, when seven brutalised outcasts from the British Empire fell to their deaths through the gallow's trap doors, they died in the service of the insatiable expansion of that Empire. In their deaths, they joined their Weraerai victims as expendable pawns in the game of greed and economic expediency which the Empire fostered.

On 10 June 2000, a group of Australians, both Aboriginal and non-Aboriginal, met on the western ridge overlooking the Myall Creek station to open a memorial erected to the memory of the twenty-eight Weraerai who had been slain there. It is a memorial that had been thirty-five years in the making, having first been proposed by a local resident, Len Payne, in 1965. All attempts to see it built had been frustrated by everything from apathy to outright hostility. Finally, a grass roots movement led by Kamilaroi/Weraerai people and Aboriginal leaders Lyall Munro and Sue Blacklock and the Reverend John Brown, with the cooperation of local Councils, constructed the long overdue memorial.

Among those attending the opening of the memorial were Des Blake, the great-great grandson of John Blake, and Beaulah Adams, the great-great niece of Edward Foley. In an unprecedented act of reconciliation, they stood with and were embraced by Lyall Munro and Sue Blacklock, a descendant of one of the Weraerai boys who had escaped the massacre by hiding in Myall Creek.

There is a rainbow.

AUTHOR'S NOTE

Perhaps the most commonly asked question about *Demons at Dusk* will be: 'How much of it is true?' As stated in the introduction to the List of Characters at the start of the book, all the significant events and characters are true. The benefit of writing a book about the Myall Creek Massacre is the fact that there is a huge amount of information available on the historic record. This is because the case was so thoroughly investigated at the time and because of the evidence in the two trials. Some of the actual conversations I have used in *Demons* are as recorded at the time. The evidence given at all three trials mentioned – George Anderson's in the Prologue and the two Myall Creek trials – are taken from the transcripts of those trials, with only very minor additions to illustrate how someone may have been feeling or to highlight the importance of a particular piece of evidence. Therefore, reference to the trial scenes is a good way to check the truth of various parts of the book.

In some cases, what would appear to be the most incredible minor details of the story are in fact true. For example, William Hobbs was arrested after giving evidence, and the jury foremen at the second trial did give the wrong verdict and was corrected by juryman William Knight.

My approach to writing this book has been that the power of the story lies in its truth, not in anything that I can invent. The parts that are invented have been invented with a view to illustrating the known facts. For example, we know that Anderson and Kilmeister did not get on, they argued regularly and Kilmeister picked on Anderson. I have therefore invented some scenes and dialogue to illustrate these facts. I have also tried to get into the hearts and minds of the characters, and therefore I have also speculated on how various characters may have thought or felt at different times.

In regard to the relationship between Anderson and Ipeta, what is known is that they did have a sexual relationship and that he did try to save her on the evening of the massacre by asking Russell to spare her. Whether he loved her in the way I have portrayed in this book is anyone's guess, but Roger Milliss does speculate in *Waterloo Creek* that he may have loved her, and that is good enough for me, because what Anderson did was absolutely extraordinary. What motivated him to do it? Well, we can all draw our own conclusions. I have invented the scenes showing the development of their relationship.

The massacre itself is of course true. Anderson saw them led away and heard just the two shots, while Hobbs discovered the mutilated remains. Actual details of who killed whom, what was said, etc., are of course unknown. The reference to babies being bashed against trees and rocks cannot necessarily be attributed to this massacre but, as it was reportedly done in other massacres, it has been included here to illustrate the atrocities to which the Aborigines were subjected. Whether Davey actually witnessed the massacre itself is the subject of some conflicting evidence.

The attack on the remainder of the group who were with King Sandy at McIntyre's a couple days later, and the subsequent massacre at Keera Creek, are also true; but full details are not available as these attacks are not as well documented as the massacre at Myall Creek.

For those interested in discovering the plain facts of the Myall Creek Massacre and the others which occurred in this area around this time, I highly recommend Roger Milliss's *Waterloo Creek*. For information on some of the various other massacres of Aborigines which took place across the country, I recommend Bruce Elder's *Blood on the Wattle*. Richard Trudgen's *Why Warriors Lie Down and Die*, and Henry Reynolds' *Why Weren't We Told* are excellent for providing an overview of the destructive impact on Australia's indigenous people of both British colonisation and Government policies based on ignorance and arrogance.

Finally, Reynolds' *The Other Side of the Frontier* provides information about Aboriginal resistance to British settlement/invasion of their land. Reynolds provides extensive evidence of the battle (the undeclared war) on the frontier, and for his contention that there were 20,000 Aborigines and 2,000 Europeans killed in that war.

* * *

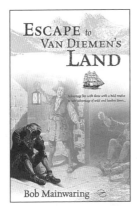

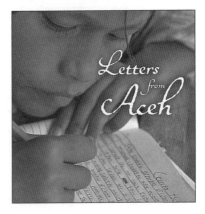

New Releases… also from Sid Harta Publishers

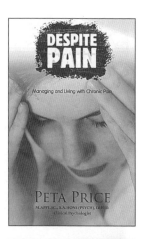

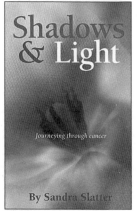

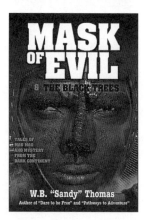

OTHER BEST SELLING SID HARTA TITLES CAN BE FOUND AT

http://www.sidharta.com.au   http://Anzac.sidharta.com

***

HAVE YOU WRITTEN A STORY?

http://www.publisher-guidelines.com

Best-selling titles by Kerry B. Collison

Readers are invited to visit our publishing websites at:
http://www.sidharta.com.au
http://www.publisher-guidelines.com/
http://temple-house.com/

Kerry B. Collison's home pages:
http://www.authorsden.com/visit/author.asp?AuthorID=2239
http://www.expat.or.id/sponsors/collison.html
http://clubs.yahoo.com/clubs/asianintelligencesresources
email: author@sidharta.com.au

Purchase Sid Harta titles online at
http://www.sidharta.com.au